SPEAKING TO POWER
27 Voice Tools

Studies in Rural Participation Series-7

1. Participation Rural Appraisal: Methodology and Applications/*Neela Mukherjee*
2. Participatory Rural Appraisal and Questionnaire Survey (Comparative Field Experience and Methodological Innovations)/*Neela Mukherjee*
3. Participatory Rural Appraisal of Natural Resources/*Neela Mukherjee*
4. Participatory Learning and Action: With 100 Field Methods/*Neela Mukherjee*
5. Participatory Rural Appraisal: Methods and Applications in Rural Planning (Second Revised Edition)/*Amitava Mukherjee*
6. Participatory Learning & Action: Monitoring & Evaluation and Participatory Monitoring & Evaluation (Second Revised Edition)/*Amitava Mukherjee*
7. Speaking to Power: 27 Voice Tools Building Bridges for Participatory Learning, Action and Policy Making/*Neela Mukherjee*

ABOUT THE AUTHOR

Dr. Neela Mukherjee is currently engaged as a development practitioner, researcher, teacher and a resource person to multiple development organizations, both within India and abroad. Formerly, a Professor of Economics at the LBS National Academy of Administration Mussoorie and an alumna of the London School of Economics and Political Science, her major areas of current research include participatory and sustainable developmental practices, design and methodologies, PRA micro planning, participatory monitoring & impact assessment, gender issues and livelihoods sustainability. Her books include "Participatory Rural Appraisal, Methodology and Applications" (1993), "Questionnaire Survey & Participatory Rural Appraisal" (1995), "Participatory Appraisal of Natural Resources" (1997) and "Learning to Share" volumes 1, 2 and 3 (1997, 2000 & 2004) published by Concept Publishing Co., Delhi and "Alternative Perspectives on Livelihoods, Agriculture And Air Pollution, Agriculture in urban and peri-urban areas in a developing country" (2001) published by Ashgate publishers, UK and Concept Publishing Co., Delhi.

Studies in Rural Participation Series–7

SPEAKING TO POWER

27 VOICE TOOLS

Building Bridges for Participatory Learning, Action and Policy-making

NEELA MUKHERJEE

Foreword by
Robert Chambers

CONCEPT PUBLISHING COMPANY, NEW DELHI-110059

ISBN 13: 978-81-8069-588-9 (HB) **ISBN 10: 81-8069-588-3 (HB)**

First Published 2009

Published and Printed by

Concept Publishing Company
Regd. Office:
A/15-16, Commercial Block, Mohan Garden
New Delhi-110059 (India)
Phones : 25351460, 25351794, *Fax* : 091-11-25357109
Email : publishing@conceptpub.com,
website: www.conceptpub.com

Editorial Office:
H-13, Bali Nagar, New Delhi-110 015, India.

Cataloging in Publication Data--*Courtesy:* D.K. Agencies (P) Ltd. <docinfo@dkagencies.com>

Mukherjee, Neela.
Speaking to power : 27 voice tools : building bridges for participatory learning, action and policy-making / Neela Mukherjee ; foreword by Robert Chambers.
p. cm. -- (Studies in rural participation series ; 7)
Includes bibliographical references and index.
ISBN 13: 9788180695889 (hb) ISBN 10: 8180695883 (hb)
ISBN 13: 9788180696060 (pb) ISBN 10 8180696065 (pb)

1. Rural development--India. 2. Rural development. 3. Political participation--India. 4. Political participation. I. Title. II. Series: Studies in rural participation ;7.

DDC 307.141 209 54 22s

To the Memory of

Mitali Sen-Gavai

Foreword

Enabling people who live in poverty to analyse their realities, articulate their priorities, and have effective voice to influence policies, is one of the most pressing and most neglected issues of our time. The conditions that poor people experience, and their awareness, aspirations and priorities, are changing faster than perhaps ever before. At the same time many of those in positions of policy making power are isolated in capital cities and other large urban centres, meeting one another and hearing one another's voices but not those of the poor whom they are meant to be serving. Thus out of touch, their mindsets, views and actions are liable to be informed not by grounded realities but by their own professional training, official data with all their limitations, and the latest fashions of development discourse. Where they have personal experience of the lives and conditions of poor people, it is likely to have been earlier in their careers, and now with accelerating change at the grassroots, to be seriously out of date. Decisions and policies are then, more than ever, in danger of being a bad fit with real needs and at worst even harmful.

At the same time, the explosion of participatory methodologies of the past two decades provides unprecedented means for bringing policy-makers into touch and up-to-date. The tragedy is that so many of them are unaware of the methods we now have to hand, and that those methods are not more used.

Neela Mukherjee's book is thus located in a critical gap, as she puts it "building bridges for participatory learning, action and policy making". She shows that there is an extraordinarily rich repertoire of approaches and methods that can facilitate and amplify the voices of poor people. The range of personal practical field experience on which she draws is impressive, indeed awesome. Many of the methods described in this book are the result of the methodological creativity she has herself shown in her professional life in an extraordinary variety of field situations. No one who has seen this book can doubt that there are indeed many ways of bridging the participatory learning, action and policy-making gap.

Many issues are faced and many ways of tackling them are presented here. Among those that repeatedly surface in practice are finding and empowering those who are weaker and more marginalised in communities to analyse and express their views and priorities. To influence those in power, data must be authentic and credible. As Dr. Mukherjee shows, there are ways in which their realities as poor people express them can be quantified from dispersed participatory processes, gaining the credibility and influence of numbers and statistics. The authentic and insightful findings that result from these varied participatory methods and approaches have a record of being persuasive when they are relevant to the decision-making of those in power. And Dr. Mukherjee's recommendation of experiential field learning for economists and technical experts is yet another way forward, with the advantage of their seeing the methods in action, meeting poor people, and hearing their voices directly, face-to-face.

By bringing together so many of the threads of participatory development practice, Neela Mukherjee has done poor people and the development community a signal service. For even a quick scan of the contents of the book will tell the reader that there is here a wealth of different approaches and methods on which to draw. May this book have the impact it should and that poor people deserve. May it lead to changes in official thinking and practice. May it inspire creativity among others who likewise pioneer participatory approaches and methods. May it inform and inspire many and lead to more widespread, sensitive and effective measures to enable those who are poor and excluded to speak to power. May its wide repertoire of ways to give voice to those who are normally unheard be used intelligently and sensitively so that policy-makers are more in touch and up-to-date with the diverse and changing realities, needs and priorities of those who live in poverty. And in these ways, through more grounded policies and practice, may it, as it should, mean again and again, a better life for many of those who are most deprived.

10 December 2008 **Robert Chambers**

Preface

The present book is mainly concerned with practical means to enable ordinary people to 'speak to power'. It is indeed difficult for ordinary people to communicate with those in 'power'. It is also naïve to assume that 'power' listens to ordinary people. On the contrary, it rarely does so. Those whose voices are most often silenced include the women, minority groups, indigenous peoples and the poor (Maiese: 2005). 'Power' has little or no space to listen to ordinary people and the problem of making people's voice heard in policy-making remains a chronic issue. In this context, it becomes necessary to challenge the conventional idea that 'public policy-making lies in the realm of policy-making experts' and also to seek mechanisms towards constructing 'larger picture' of community voice.

The book is based on the presumption that if 'power' does not listen to ordinary people then the latter can at least use their own power of united voice to try and influence the top power-holders. It is in this context, the book provides evolving mechanisms to organize people's voices for transmission to power-holders. It presents ways to construct larger pictures of people's voice from learning exercises at the grassroots. In short, it attempts to connect the 'micro' community voice at the local level with public policy-making and decision-taking at higher levels of 'power'.

In specific terms, the objectives of the book are as follows:

- To focus on practical means to enable ordinary people to 'speak to power'.
- To provide a menu of voice tools as to how ordinary people can actually do it.
- To evolve tools and mechanisms for arriving at larger pictures of community voice for public policy-making.

Though field experience across the world indicates that local communities are immensely capable of expressing their views, flagging their own problems and preferences, and suggesting appropriate actions, it has not been easy to navigate mechanisms for effective portraying of their voice to public policy-makers. There also exists no automatic route for transmission of such voices into the realms of public-policy making. The voice of local communities still remains blurred and marginalized with many obstacles and hindrances. Though there have been projects and programmes which have helped bring forth such community voices to public platforms with advocacy strategies built around them, systematic inclusion of such voices for public policy-making still lags far behind. Despite numerous attempts to make such voice traverse public institutions, there has been little or no effort at institutionalizing it in any serious manner.

Today, the ideas and propositions of the top public policy makers are being increasingly challenged, especially by local communities and civil societies in many countries of the world. A range of participatory exercises are being locally facilitated across the world (with or without donor-support) to seek local community perspectives on policies and programmes. However, such invaluable community perspectives remain mostly deprived of their due share of recognition or legitimacy by those concerned with public policy-making. On the contrary, many learning opportunities from local knowledge and experience are getting lost in the labyrinths of complex and sophisticated policy-making exercises. Essentially, there is lack of policy space for community voice.

In practice, several attempts have been made to link local level community voice with domain of public policy-making. One main objective of many grassroots-oriented exercises such as Participatory Poverty Assessments (PPAs) has been to enable the voice of the poor to reach the corridors of public policy-making whether by institutions/ CBOs engaged in advocacy work; and/or directly by poor groups of women and men making their own presentations to the policy-makers; or through sharing of reports and documents from the field. However, one main challenge in this regard lies in finding suitable mechanisms for sharing community perspectives with higher echelons of public policy-making, especially when such voice covers large chunks of population and/or large area/s. It has often been a case where lack of appropriate tools has posed a limit to the 'reach' of people's voices. The issue not only relates to construction of larger pictures of community voice for large sized population but also that of finding user-friendly (implying user-friendly in terms of public policy-makers) ways to share and transmit such community voice from the grassroots to the domain of macro/meso-level policy-making. Again, it is not only important to make community voice appropriately accessible to policy-makers but it is also crucial to have mechanisms and space for helping institutionalize them as integral part of policy-making exercises.

Often PPAs have been shelved by policy-making bodies and policy advisers since they find it difficult to have any classic 'handle' on them. They often term them as 'qualitative', 'not representative' and 'not based on rigorous sampling and data collection and collation procedures'. It has been mentioned by many experts that such PPAs are not only not representative enough but also not amenable to the usual statistical treatment. They also have major problems in convergence with the conventional statistical data system or information base or planning systems, which many countries have. They are generally overlooked and shelved by experts because they are not considered user-friendly and not acceptable for integration into standard classical formats for policy-making.

Drawing from field research, the book emphasizes the importance of finding ways to capture community voice and also explores tools for micro-meso-macro linkages for gaining the larger picture and institutional space. It is important to recognize that field tools are still evolving for connecting 'micro'-level community voice to macro-level policy-making. The book describes 27 voice tools to listen to community voice and for construction of larger pictures. Such mechanisms for portraying people's voice in analytical framework/s help provide crucial support towards ongoing learning processes and action for bettering of governance at different levels—local, regional and higher levels.

While trying to construct bridge/s between community voice at local level and public policy-making at higher levels, the book tries to provide answers to Professor Uphoff's (quoted in Kanbur: 2005) 3 basic questions:

"(1) How can we know how representative are the persons who speak as members of 'the set of poor people'?

(2) How can the different aspects of being poor be summarized to gain some idea of the severity of magnitude of personal poverty?

(3) And how can we know trends among the poor, whether their numbers are increasing or decreasing, and whether their poverty is getting 'deeper' or more bearable over time?"

The book tries to bridge some methodological gaps in projecting local voice at higher levels. It focuses upon construction of two main types of 'larger pictures' from the 'bottom':

- One type is that of participatory situational assessment, and
- Other type is that of social accountability assessment by people.

The significance of the book lies in the following aspects:

(i) The book presents 27 voice tools from practice, which is important for the policy-makers and practitioners to read and find out for themselves what can work and how and how much.
(ii) It also provides a menu of choice to practitioners, policy-makers, planners and civil society on community voice tools for linking 'micro' with 'macro' policy-making.
(iii) It meets a long term need for documentation on emerging voice tools from practice. There is lack of much published material for bringing together such tools in a comparative framework.

"Speaking to Power" is a research frontier which is one main contribution of this book. The findings indicate existing research gaps which professionals working in this area can further investigate.

The distribution of the book chapters is as follows:

Chapter 1 states the objectives of the book and explains 'voice' in policy-making and whose 'voice' counts. It also evolves a rationale for listening to the 'voice'. It discusses the barriers to 'voice' in public policy-making; the 'elitist' domain of public policy-making; and the effect of not considering people's voice and choice. It also outlines the approaches to community voice, standardization aspects and issues related to underestimating power of people's voice. This is followed by a discussion on what factors influence community voice and the crucial aspects of unheard community voice.

Chapter 2 contains a discussion on the key principles of listening to community voice such as 'listening and learning', 'offsetting biases', 'utilization of precious community time', 'seeking diversity', 'cross-checking process and outputs', 'optimal ignorance and appropriate imprecision'. A discussion on the foundation pillars for listening to community voice such as 'attitude and behaviour', 'process', 'methods' and 'sharing' is also included in this chapter.

Chapter 3 describes the types of community voice tools/ mechanisms, the key stakeholders involved in such tools and related institutional mechanisms. For mapping community voice, it brings together 27 voice tools, many of which are described with illustrations from the field. It contains two sets of tools—one is for participatory assessments, while the other is for social accountability. As given below, the following tools are included in the Chapter:

Tools for Participatory Assessments

(i) Participatory Poverty Assessment
(ii) Participatory Priority/Need Assessment & Problem Analysis
(iii) Participatory Planning and Action
(iv) Sustainable Livelihoods Assessment
(v) Participatory Empowerment Assessment
(vi) Participatory Assessment of Social Capital
(vii) Holistic Participatory Assessment
(viii) Participatory Process Assessment
(ix) Participatory Impact/Outcome Assessment
(x) Integrated Impact Assessment
(xi) Participatory Monitoring and Evaluation
(xii) Participatory Public Policy-Making
(xiii) Constructing Picture/Word Picture
(xiv) Most Significant Change Tool

Tools for Social Accountability

(i) Citizens' Report Card
(ii) Citizens' Voice Card
(iii) Citizens' Participation in Public Policy-Making
(iv) Participatory Budgeting

(v) Public Expenditure Tracking/Monitoring
(vi) Family Satisfaction Survey
(vii) Citizen Monitoring of Public Service Delivery
(viii) Citizens' Advisory Boards
(ix) Social Audit
(x) Special Accountability Institutions, e.g. Human Rights Commission
(xi) Lobbying and Advocacy Campaigns
(xii) Pro-Poor Public Interest Litigation
(xiii) People's Court/s

Chapter 4 explains and illustrates Participatory Poverty Assessment (PPA) and the related learning process. It provides practical illustration from the field at a micro level.

Chapter 5 has a description of the components of Sustainable Livelihoods' Assessment (SLA) Framework, its background, its application in the field, an SLA-type micro picture and an SLA-type 'larger picture' of community voices at a sub-national level.

Chapter 6 discusses in detail Integrated Participatory Poverty Assessment (IPPA), where different dimensions of human poverty and their proximate causes and solutions are captured through IPPA. It explains how IPPA is a tool to map poverty assessment and changes at a local level and their integration at higher levels to produce a synthesis picture of poverty as mapped by local stakeholders. It includes discussion on the components of IPPA as follows:

Component A – Social Group/Well-Being Assessment
Component B – Asset/Resource Assessment
Component C – Vulnerability and Risk Assessment
Component D – Livelihoods Assessment
Component E – Problem-Opportunity Assessment
Component F – Gender Assessment
Component G – Institutional Assessment
Component H – Social Opportunity Assessment

Chapter 7 describes a voice tool for assessment of governance for social accountability purposes, for which, the communities/ citizens/groups provide their views, opinions, scores on selected aspects, e.g. performance of government related to quality, coverage, efficiency, cost, responsiveness of public/private services, such as in areas related to child care, drinking water, primary schooling and others. The tool described in this chapter is mainly based on qualitative responses though validated by semi-structured questionnaire and a mechanism for up-scaling it.

Chapter 8 contains selected aspects of institutionalizing community voice including major gaps and weaknesses of the conventional policy framework, aspects of institutional mechanism and limitations of 'voice' mechanism.

The purpose of Annexes 'A' and 'B' is to discuss a suitable methodological design, objectives, and scope for issue-based poverty assessment from the perspective of the poor.

The author is grateful to a number of local communities from many developing countries for providing their valuable time and knowledge towards evolving of such tools in practice as part of their engagement with a host of development initiatives and innovative practices. Special thanks are due to the national governments of Nepal, Moldova, Maldives, Bangladesh, provincial governments of China and state government of West Bengal (India) and their donor community who were considerably open to exploration of tools and mechanisms in participatory situational assessments and participatory social accountability mechanisms. Thanks are also due to Robert Chambers who kindly agreed to write the foreword to this book.

The book is meant for policy-makers, policy experts, planners, development practitioners, action researchers, civil societies, advocacy groups, students and teachers in development, donor community and other organizations, and individuals engaged in community development, poverty reduction and social development. It is essentially an intermediate product since field exploration in voice tools is an ongoing process, which is continuously evolving. I will consider writing of this book as fruitful if more practitioners and action researchers can work and evolve innovative ways to bridge existing methodological gaps in voice tools and find more 'connects' between 'micro' voices and 'macro' level policy-making.

New Delhi **Neela Mukherjee**
11 July 2008

REFERENCES

Maiese, Michelle (2005). Source: http://www.beyondintractability.org/essay/voice/,June

Petesch in Kanbur (2005). Q-Squared—Qualitative and Quantitative Poverty Appraisal: Complementarities, Tensions and the Way Forward, Q-Squared Working Paper No. 1, October.

Acknowledgements

LOCAL COMMUNITIES

India

Haryana

Faridabad villages—Kadhaoli, Sagarpur, Uncha Gaon, Baroli, Pali Kasba, Chandawali, Jajru, Pyala, Sahupura, Sahapur Kalan, Sumper, Sohtai and Malema.

Kerala

Kodakara Gram Panchayat, Thrissur

Rajasthan

Kheda Rasulpur village, Shakarpura village, Dadwara, Kota

Uttarakhand

Siriyo, Babbani, Kodsi, Kol and Pali Majhola villages, Rishikesh, Uttarakhand Koti village, Bhagwanpur village

Uttar Pradesh

Varanasi villages—Chandpur, Navampura Kala, Seer Govardhanpur, Sarai Dongre, Lohta, Chitaipur, Nathupur, Tikri, Maraon, Maheshpur, Adityanagar, Karamanbir, Nuaon and Tarapur

West Bengal

Purulia District—Kula Bahal village, Jabora GP, Hurra block, Jamtoria village, Manbazar -2 blocks, Makarkanti village, Manbazar-1 block, Bargeriya village, Manbazar -2 blocks, Gopalpur village, Bagda GP, Puncha block, Cheka, Simlapara village, Jhalda-2 blocks, Balarampur village, Balarampur block, Herbona village, Barobazar block, Kanchanpur village, Belma GP, Purulia – 2 blocks, Fatepur village, Para block, Hariharpur village, Jhara Jabarrah-1 GP, Para block, Dhaboni village, Bandowan block, Chirudi village, Bandowan block, Raghunath pur village, Raghunath pur block, Digha village, Neturia block, Murradih village, Murradih GP, Santuri block, Paharpur village, Kashipur block, Madandih village, Jonardandi GP, Neturia block, Puara village block Arsha.

Bankura District—Kama village, Rudra GP, Ranibandh block, Kadmagarh village, Raipur block, Chunamasia village, Bishnupur block, Kuchidih village, Sonamukhi block, Agariband village, Onda block, Beldangra village, Bonkathi GP, Bankura -1 block, Susunia Pahar village, Chatna GP, Bankura - 2 blocks, Lohadi village, Togheri GP, Chatna block, Shirpur nama village, Bamantore GP, Saltora block, Dubrajpur village, Dubrajpur GP, Simplipal block, Chandkuri village Taldengra GP, Taldengra block, Jharia kucha village, Hirbundh block, Pachmura village, Pachmura GP, Taldengra block. Urban area Baisnabpara, Bishnupur block, Maukhali village, Maukhali GP, Bishnupur—II Block.

Malda District—Dakshin Maldanga village, Karkochi GP, Gazal block, Santoshpur village, Motiharpur GP, Chanchai -1 block, Hariharpur village, Shantii GP, Harishchandrapur -2 blocks, Kalpiche village, Habibpur GP, Habibpur block, Jaiton village Pokhar hat GP, Bamongola block, Kagachira village, Pukuria GP, Ratua - 2 blocks, Samabalpur village, Maharajpur GP, Ratua - 2 blocks, Maharajpur village, Maharajpur GP, Ratua - 2 blocks, Mihir das colony village, Kotwali GP, English Bazar block, Gopalpur village, Kaliachak -2 blocks, Bangal village, Enaitpur GP, Manikchak block, Narayanpur village, Manikchak GP, Manikchak block.

Murshidabad District—Ramnagar village, Lalgola GP, Lalgola block, Nabagram village, Bahadpur GP, Jianganj block, Balarampur village, Haridas Moti GP, Berhampore block, Angarpura village, Alugram GP, Bharatpur-1 block, Durgapur village, Nimtita GP, Dhuliajan block, Pyarapur village, Basantipara, Jyotkamal GP, Jangipur block.

Birbhum District—Mohula village, Mayurer Sara—1 GP, Kanachi block, Gaganpur village, Mararai block, Lohat village, Sainthia block, Haranandpur village, Lapur GP, Jajan block.

Uttar Dinajpur District—Tepur village, Manai GP, Itahar block, Tenohari village, Manaikura GP, Raiganj block, Belbari village, Surjapur GP, Goalpukur, Chainnagar village, Chainnagar GP, Hemtabad.

Paschim Medinipur District—Panchkhuri village, Bagghora village, Pathra village, Charka village, Khetua village, Domahani village, Lakhanpur village, Dhanyagori village, Krishna Rakshit Chak village, Bhuruchati village, Nakrakhudi village, Lohameliya village, Gobindopur village, Bankathi village, Berapal village, Kalsigeriya village, Mulbandh village, Benagariya village, Tungadhua village, Geriashuli village, Susnigeriya village

Barddhaman District—Phatikgram village, Babia village, Ukta village, Kherobar village, Jhantiba village, Baishnab village, Tamaghata village, Bhaiki village.

Bangladesh

Charbhuai village, district Shariatpur, Gossairhat Upozela, Union Nalmuri, Mahiskandi village, district Shariatpur, Upozela Gossairhat, Union Idilpur, Musurgaon village, district Barisal, Upozela Hizia, Union Kuchoiputti, Telikandi village, district Madaripur, Upozela Rajouri, Union Amgram, Madhyakandi village, district Gopalganj, Upozela Kotalipara, Union Kalahari, Bandergaon village, district Moulavibazar, Upozela Kamalganj, Union Adampur, Subidpur village, district Hobiganj, Upozela Baniyachong, Union Subidpur, Gayasi, district Sylhet, Upozela Fenchuganj Union Fenchuganj, Bhimkhil village, district Barisal, Upozela Hizia, Union Kuchoiputti, Rajapur Village, district Gopalganj, Upozela Kotalipara, Union Ramsheel, Lawachora village, Srimongal, district Moulavibazar, Upozela Sreemangal, Union No. 3, Isia Punjee village, district Moulavibazar, Upozela Kulaura, Union Baramchand, Majhergaon village, district Moulavibazar, Upozela Kamalganj, Union Madhavpur.

Siranganj—Pumimagati Union Parishad (UP), Ullapara Upozilia, Jhaboil UP, Kamarkhand Upozilla, Daulatpur UP, Belkuchi Upozilia, Dhangora UP, Raiganj Upozilia, Barohar UP, Ullapara Upozilia, Brahmogachha UP, Raiganj Upozilia and Pangashi UP, Raiganj Upozilia.

Cambodia

Chantrea village, Chantrea vommune, Chantrea district, Svay Rieng province; Tuol Ampil, Dambok Chuor, Both Sloeuk, Samaki, Kompout Sear and Batsleut villages, Chrok Moteas commune, Svay Tiep district, Svay Rieng province; Trapaeng Bunteay and Baus villages, Tros commune, Romeas Haik district, Svay Rieng prvince.

Thkov village, Prasat commune,Kampong Trabek district; Prey Veng province;

Chmar Lot village, Smoune Teone Commune, Kamchay Mear district, Prey Veng province;

Chone Toul village, Svay Chrun commune, Mesang district, Prey Veng province

China

Shengqi, Hongshe and Gao Yuan villages in Longxi-Hongkou National Nature Reserve, Sichuan province; Honghe National Nature Reserve and Sanjiang National Nature Reserve, Heilongjiang province, Pingzhai and Yangmai hamlets Guangxi province.

Kazakhstan

Shimkent

Lao PDR

Attepeu province—Vangyang and Huaykeo villages, Phouvong district; Donngeua and Kengmekhua villages, Saysetta district and Vonxai and Mai villages Sanxai district;

Sayabouri province—Sante and Pakthio villages, Sayabouri district, Laosano and Namkhom villages, Xienghone district, Napoung and Namayom villages, Hongsa district, Huay nguen and Huamuang villages, Khorp district and Nanyang and Thong villages, Nguen district.

Maldives

Community islands in *Shaviyani Atoll*—Komandoo, Feydhoo, Kanditheem, Narudhoo, Funadhoo and Lhaimagu; *Noonu Atoll*—Kudafari, Manadhoo and Miladhoo; and *Laviyani Atoll*—Naifuru and Olhuvelifushi.

Moldova

Zubresti and Galesti villages, Straseni rayon.

Nepal

Baniyatar village, Ghansikuan VDC, Tanahu District, Damartole Hamlet, Harnamadi VDC, Makwanpur District, Chaukitole Hamlet, Manahari VDC, Makwanpur District, Ramanthali village, Padampokhari VDC, Makwanpur District, Phurkechour village, Harnamadi VDC, Makwanpur District, Lamidanda village, Darechowk VDC, Chitwan District, Dahophokhari village, Haibung VDC, Sindhupalchowk District, Thulosirubari village, Thulosirubari VDC, Sindhupalchowk District, Mathio Mugi Khola village, Bhatauli VDC, Ramechhap District, Raigaun village, Pakarbas VDC, Ramechhap District.

Vietnam

Thon Trung and Tien Phong villages, Vo Ninh Commune, Quang Ninh District, Quang Binh province and villages in Ha Giang.

INDIVIDUALS

India

Delhi

Simon Croxton, Sujatha Viswanthan, Raghabendra Rao, Catherine Amold, V.S. Tomar, V.K. Singh, Ashok Mittal, Nitin Mittal, Vinita Kumar, Amitava Mukherjee

Madhya Pradesh

Anil Gulati, Veena Bandyopadhayay, Ranu Srivastava, Sambhav, Pradeep Singh Tomar, Sambhav, Ghuman Singh, Rachna, Manoj Singh Bhadoriya, Sambhav, Mukesh Moj, Sambhav, Arun Singh Bhadoriya, Parhit, Sivaram Kushiwal, CID.

Uttarakhand

Jyostna Sitling, STS Lepcha, Mahendra Singh Yadav, Shahista Khan, Sudha Thakur, Sunita Rawat, Pathak, Umesh Chandra Thapliyal, Geeta Mamgain, Surekha Dhasmana, Balbir Singh Bharti.

Uttar Pradesh

Pradeep Bhargava, Sunit Singh, U. Kalpagam.

Kerala

KILA, Thrissur, Kerala—PP Balan, P. Lakhsmanan, Santosh Kumar, K.M. Vijayanand, Secretary, Kodakara GP, Members GP, Pamchayat Vice President, Kodakara GP.

West Bengal

M.N. Roy, Dilıp Ghosh, Dilip Pal, Subrataa Chakravarty, Nivedita Roy, SRD Team, Meera Jayaswal, Manab Sen, Sumita Roy, Madhumita Parihari Kalindi Kumari, K. K. Singh, Prabhat Pathak, Shanti Mardi, Rupa Addhya, Bibekananda Satpathy, Bindubasini Singh, Madhusree Mazumdar, A. Mohan, Roshm Sahu, Biman Mtsnra, Sadanando Soren, Kuddus Ansari, Shakya Singha Mahato, Nitya Gopal Mahato, Sourav Roy, Dr. K. K. Datta, Arunima Mukherjee, Baisakhi Bannerjee, Rajashri Narayan, Atui Rahim,

Jayanta Upadhyaya, Bandita Sen Gupta.

Bangladesh

Dr. Nasreen Jahan, Makshuda Nupur Akhter.

Cambodia

Cate Turton, Catherine Arnold, Somony Thay, Soun Seng, Prak Sereyvath, National Consultant.

China

Se, Liu Hongyu.

IFAD, Rome

Nigel Brett, Edward Mallorie, Youqiong Wang, Shyam Khadka, Imelda Posadas, Martina Spisiakova, Julian Hamilton-Peach (DFID).

Kazakhstan

Vladimir Mikhalev, Alma Raissova, Alma Buirakulova, Massimiliano Riva, Malin Berggren, Maral Sheshemvekova, Alma Karavasova.

Laos

Zhou Shengkun, Soulichanh, Chanthaly, Changpheng, Khamvai, Kouthong, Phouvang, Saythoung, Sien, Singthong, Bokeo, Sisouk, Sayfoan, Vongphet.

Maldives

A. Bari, Shaheem Razee, Mohamed Zahid, Subash C. Wadhwa, Ahmed Mujthaba, Ibrahim Naeem Ismail, Ibrahim Naseem, Mariyam Waheeda, Saeeda Umar.

Moldova

Mihail Peleah, Igor Grosu, Adrian Cojocaru, Jigau Ion, Diana D.Cheianu.

Norway

John Y. Jones, Helen Wangusa, Aud Oppedal, Eau Lahn Eunden, Bente Mathsen Leper, Solvey Sandalones, Aguete Strom.

Nepal

Bikash Sharma, Sharad Neupane, Binod Kumar Bhattarai, Bishwa Nath Tiwari, Hari Pradhan, Balananda Paudel, Teertha Dhakal, Yam

Nath Sharma Mahendra Bhattarai, Sascha Mueller, Deepak Timsina, Sarita Lama.

Sri Lanka

Anathaie, Nirmala, Sridevi, Jayalalitha, Valliamma, Vellamma, Sivapackyam, Elisabeth, Parashakthy, Kavitha, Rohon, Harini, Samuel, Smjaya, Susmtha, Padmaroni, Wasanthi, Vasanthi Perva, Kanthi Costa, Malkanthi Wanigasooriya, Gilthea da Silva, Maalini Gunawardne.

UK

Jules Pretty, Yvonne Rydin, Robert Chambers, Richard Bond, Keith Virgo, Steve Jones, Zoe Stephenson, Johanna Pennarz, Julian Brar, Nicole Kenton, IIED, Angela Milligan, Holly Ashley, Janet Gardener.

USA

Norman Uphoff

Vietnam

Nguyen Thi Mai Huong, Le Van Hong, Lam.

INSTITUTIONS

Atoll & Planning Ministry, Government of Maldives
Asian Development Bank, Manila
Asian Development Bank, Delhi
BRAC, Dhaka and Field Offices, Bangladesh
CARE, Kolkata
DFID, China
DFID, Delhi
DFID, London
FAO, Regional office, Bangkok
FOKUS Secretariat, Oslo, Norway
Government of India
Government of West Bengal
Government of Kerala
Government of Haryana
Government of Bangladesh
Government of Cambodia
Government of China
Government of Laos

Government of Kazakhstan
Government of Maldives
Government of Moldova
Government of Nepal
Gramin Vikas Trust, Delhi
Gramin Bank, Bangladesh
Gramin Motshyo Foundation, Bangladesh
Group of 14 Women, Bergin, Norway
Health Systems Development Initiative (HSDI), Government of West Bengal, Kolkata
IFFDC, Delhi and Rajasthan
Indigenous People's Foundation, Kathmandu, Nepal
International Fund for Agriculture Development, Rome
International Institute for Environment & Development, London
London School of Economics, London
NEST—Kare House, Colombo, National YWCA, Colombo, Sri Lanka
Participation Council, Chisinau, Moldova
Planning Commission, Kathmandu, Nepal
PWG, Hatton, Sri Lanka
RECOFTC, Bangkok
Sambhav, Shivpuri, Madhya Pradesh, India
United Nations Development Programme, Bangladesh
United Nations Development Programme, Almaty, Kazakhstan
United Nations Development Programme, Chisinau, Moldova
United Nations Development Programme, Male, Maldives
United Nations Development Programme, Kathmandu, Nepal
United Nations Development Programme, Hanoi, Vietnam
United Nations Development Programme, Regional Centre, Colombo, Sri Lanka
UNCDF/UNDP, Bangladesh
UNCDF, New York
UNCDF, Kathmandu, Nepal
UNICEF, Bhopal, Madhya Pradesh
University of Essex, UK
University of Manchester, UK
World Bank, Washington D.C.
ITC/World Export Development Forum, Geneva

Contents

List of Tables, Boxes and Charts

TABLES

BOXES

CHARTS

Glossary of Local Terms

Boro	—	a variety of paddy crop
Bidi	—	Rolled tobacco leaf for smoking
Gram panchayat	—	Local government at village level
Gram sanshad	—	village assembly
Mahajan	—	money lender
Panchayat	—	Local Government
Para	—	hamlet
Patta land	—	land provided by Government under land reforms

Abbreviations

BPL	—	Below Poverty Line
CBO	—	Community-Based Organization
DRDA/C	—	District Rural Development Agency/Cell
HYV	—	High Yielding Variety
IAY	—	Indira Awas Yojana
ICDS	—	Integrated Child Development Scheme
IGA	—	Income Generating Activities
IRDP	—	Integrated Rural Development Scheme
INR	—	Indian Rupees
NGO	—	Non-Government Organization
NTFP	—	Non-Timber Forest Produce, e.g. sal leaf, *and* others
PLA	—	Participatory Learning and Action
PRA	—	Participatory Rural Appraisal
PRRA	—	Participatory Rapid Rural Appraisal
SGSY	—	Swarnajayanti Gram Swarojgar Yojana
SHG	—	Self-Help Group
SLA	—	Sustainable Livelihoods Analysis
SSK	—	Shishu Shiksha Kendra (Learning Centre for Children)

Measurement and Conversion

20 Katha	=	1 Bigha
1 Bigha	=	1/3 Acre (0.1338 Hectare or 0.3306 Acre)
7.5 Bigha	=	1 Hectare
100 Decimal	=	1 Acre

Indian Months to English Calendar

Baishak	—	Mid-April to mid-May
Jaiyshtha	—	Mid-May to mid-June
Ashar	—	Mid-June to mid-July
Sraban	—	Mid-July to mid-August
Bhadra	—	Mid-August to mid-September
Ashwin	—	Mid-September to mid-October
Kartik	—	Mid-October to mid-November
Agrahyan	—	Mid-November to mid-December
Poush	—	Mid-December to mid-January
Magh	—	Mid-January to mid-February
Falgun	—	Mid-February to mid-March
Chaitra	—	Mid-March to mid-April

1

Community Voice and Participatory Assessments

The present book is mainly concerned with practical means to enable ordinary people to 'speak to power'. Since 'power' does not listen to the ordinary people, at least people can use their own power, their united voice—to try to influence the top power-holder/s. In this context, this Chapter states the objectives of the book and explains 'voice' in 'policy' making and whose 'voice' should count and why it does not count. It attempts to evolve a rationale for listening to the ordinary people's 'voice', especially the poor and the marginalized. It discusses the barriers to 'voice' in public policy-making; its 'elitist' domain, standardization aspects and issues related to underestimating power of people's 'voice'. It also contains factors affecting community 'voice', aspects of unheard community 'voice' and some existing approaches to community 'voice' and participation.

Such local community participation is generally based on participatory action research or alternatively, on application of participatory tools to research or both. The term 'participation' has a range of meanings where the embodied degree of participation, its usage and its intensity vary from one situation to another. One can draw a primary distinction between participatory action research and research based on application of participatory methods. Whereas the first type is concerned with participation to facilitate local action, the second one is to construct better and realistic picture for outsiders and is considered extractive to that extent. There is also the possibility of combining the two primary approaches as above for initiating local action and also for generating data for.external sources (Brock and Pettit: 2007; Ozanne and Saatcioglu: 2007). The book explores ways and mechanisms to construct larger pictures of community 'voice' whether through participatory action research, application of participatory methods or combination of both the approaches.

For many developing countries, participatory situational assessments, whether at the national, regional and/or at local levels are being recognized as important elements to be fed into public-policy-making processes. However, there exists, among others, factors such as lack of political will and considerable methodological gaps between accepting and institutionalizing such findings from participatory situational assessments and translating them into practice for public policy-making.

1.1 SPECIFIC OBJECTIVES

As mentioned above, the main aim of this book is an attempt to evolve ways to construct larger pictures from participatory learning and action sessions at the grassroots based on people's voice. In specific terms the objectives of the book are as follows:

- To focus on practical means to enable ordinary people to use the power they have—their united voice to 'speak to power',
- To provide a menu of voice tools as to how ordinary people can influence policy-making, and
- To evolve tools and mechanisms for arriving at larger pictures of community voice for public policy-making.

The book attempts to link the 'micro' or people's voice at the local level with the 'macro' or the public policy-making and decision-taking at higher levels. It describes 27 voice tools to listen to community voice and towards construction of larger pictures.

1.2 WHAT IS 'VOICE' IN 'POLICY-MAKING'?

'Voice' in policy-making could be explained as people's engagement to express their own views, their united voice so as to influence or assess a policy, which is a deliberate plan of action or practical action to guide decisions and achieve desirable outcomes. Policy refers to the process of making important organizational decisions and choosing amongst them on the basis of expected impact/s that they could have. 'Voice' in policy-making refers to the ability to engage (or even attempting to engage) in meaningful ways, and (attempting) to make a difference and (attempting) to have a say in key decisions and strategies to reach key goals.

A policy generally takes the form of a governing principle, plan, or course of action. Legislative bodies make public policy decisions while others perform the administrative task of implementing those policies[1]. The voice that needs to be heard and recognized is connected to people's sense of justice and their desire for validation (Maiese: 2005). Effective public policy must include meaningful inputs from the people who are affected by those policies. Grassroots community groups can play a very important role in correcting related shortcomings and, in the process, can be more effective in working on behalf of the policies they advocate (Mitchell: 2002).

1.3 WHOSE VOICE?

Often there is no "right" choice or correct technical answer to the issue/s at hand. Policy-making can be an adversarial process, characterized by the clash of competing and conflicting interests and viewpoints rather than an impartial, disinterested, or "objective" search for "correct" solutions for policy issues. The larger and more diverse the constituency, the more difficult policy-making becomes particularly when addressing regional issues. Therefore, the issue is whose voice is generally considered for improving upon public policies and programmes, especially with diverse interest groups. Those whose voices are most often silenced include the women, minority groups, indigenous peoples and the poor (Maiese: 2005). Voice centres on inclusive conversations (interactions) that are grounded in "mutuality, understanding and accessibility" (Lederach: 2005). There are increasingly new spaces and opportunities emerging for citizen engagement in policy processes from local to global levels. One related issue in this context is whether it does really open up avenues for real influence and whether such citizen engagement will really change anything (Gaventa: 2005). Hence, doubts have been raised by civil societies as to whether the emerging realities related to such assessments actually get considered seriously for improving upon public policies and programmes. Or are they more in the nature of 'lip service' paid by policy-makers to keep people contented that, at least, their voice gets heard (though not acted upon)?

There are both intended and unintended effects of policies. The community can, and should, play a significant role in setting public policy goals and in advocating for them. But it will be most effective if there is some structure—even if it's informal—to define lines of communication and responsibility. Community people (*i.e.*, the grassroots) must tell the organization's public policy cosntacts about their experiences, observations and ideas regarding what works—and what *doesn't* work[2]. Box 1.1 on Naga City governance shows how the government has adopted participatory processes to interact with its citizens and communities.

Box 1.1: Naga City Governance

Naga, a city of more than 150,000 in central Philippines, is noted for its participatory government processes and mechanisms which have led to empowering processes of communities and individuals. Its continuous evolvement has also found new ways to engage ordinary residents in governance. At the operational level, it covered the following phases: (i) confidence building; (ii) institution building; (iii) continuous improvement; and (iv) insights. Some strategies adopted in this regard are: community organizing, tripartism, policy making....

Source: Robredo (2007).

1.4 RATIONALE OF LISTENING TO THE 'VOICE'

In general, listening to community voice help de-construct poverty from people's perspective and contribute towards the following:

- To learn about people's perspectives,
- To learn about people's knowledge and ideas,
- To touch base on social justice,
- To motivate people to think/act on their problems/solutions,
- To consult and be in touch with people's reality, and
- To improve service delivery.

Rationale for public participation (and providing space for their voice) as an inherent component of sustainable development abound in theories related to community and social development, local development, good governance, vibrant citizenship and effective resource management. Such rationale is also propounded for an active civil society towards management of rapid changes, societal uncertainties and adaptations (Devine: 2003; Kapoor: 2001; Walter: 1995; Dryzek: 1990; Gujit and Shah: 1998; and Kothari: 2001). People's engagement is mutually beneficial to both the policy-makers and the citizens (OECD: 2007) in the following ways:

- It improves transparency/accountability,
- It improves responsiveness, and
- It improves effectiveness.

In addition, community voice is important for public policy-making for other proximate reasons as given below:

- Community voice can provide direct support in progressing towards poverty reduction policy and strategy in terms of mainstreaming voice of the socially excluded and the disadvantaged groups;
- Community voice can help provide people's feedback on the quality and availability of the socio-economic services and infrastructure at the grassroots;
- Community voice can help improve governance in terms of better standards of service delivery, efficiency, accountability, transparency and reduction of corruption;
- Community voice can help arrive at field findings for meaningful policy support for different sectors and sub-sectors as required. A "larger picture" of community voice at the national level can add real value in terms of tracking macro poverty indicators whether in terms of implementation, planning, budgeting, process and outcomes. The core pillars of poverty reduction strategies and different yardsticks in terms of assessing them could provide a substantive basis for comparison of progress and achievements in terms of poverty reduction; and
- There are many excluded communities, whose voice can help undertake a series of programme/project proposals, which then become demand-led.

Community voice can throw up innovative and practical ways based on people's perspectives and create scope for people's engagement and contribution. The communities have considerable past experience and local knowledge. A consultation process with local communities based on two-way communication can help take stock on the poverty front. Existing participatory approaches adopted in different sites/locations/programmes/projects in developing countries include:

- Evolving strategies for approaching local communities,
- Making resource allocation effective according to local needs,
- Prioritizing investment according to local priorities,
- Offsetting sector and regional imbalances and inequities, and
- Eventually achieving higher levels of growth and development.

The benefits reaped by communities from providing their voice are also considerable such as:

- Increased citizens' scrutiny of government,
- Increased awareness, knowledge or skills, and
- Increased trust in government.

There are also some risks involved (OECD: 2007) in such a process, as listed below:

- Conflicts may emerge with politicians/representatives since under such a process the politicians would need to give up their absolute powers of decision-making and may need to consider people's perspectives.
- There could be delays in decision-making and implementation, especially where many groups would have to be consulted to arrive at decisions and consensus-building can take time.
- Hijacking of the process by special interest groups is also a possibility, especially where those groups at the margin are a minority voice and are not empowered enough to counter such hijackings.
- Increase of administrative burdens is also a possibility since approaching different groups for listening to their voice and processing of such data imply additional administrative workload not in line with the usual mechanisms of decision-making.

Some existing constraints and the state-of-the-art in this regard are as follows:

- There is lack of space for people's response with no institutional space or mechanism for feedback to both higher institutions and those at the local level.
- There are not many ways to know whether participants and beneficiaries are benefiting from existing policies and programmes and what kind of impact they have. Community voice helps in cross-verification of conventional indicators.
- Many countries/institutions/programmes/projects have some kind of umbrella assessment and monitoring system from the 'top', which is useful for reporting on the physical targets though not for non-physical targets. Such system works better for areas which are easily accessible and also for those groups which are relatively vocal.
- There is seemingly low awareness level of top leaders in comparison to rising expectations of the people. There are also limited ways to capture differential social impacts and lack of understanding as to why despite well designed policies and programmes some people still remain poor.

In this context, one challenge lies in bringing the marginalized groups to raise their issues and have their voice in policy-making. Such challenge can be easily met provided such groups bring new and useful information and diverse perspectives without undermining state's responsibilities for sustainable policy-making, legitimacy and representation (Perkins: 2005). However, depending on how the voice of the marginalized group is brought into the process, matters can get complicated as mentioned by Kothari (2001) on how public participation can support dominant groups to reassert control and power if people are brought into the process in a disempowering manner. Kothari (2001) also points out that participation allows participants to subvert the process by resisting inclusion and choosing when not to participate. So participation *per se* is not either bad or good, much depends on how it is done (Perkins: 2005).

1.5 SOME BARRIERS TO 'VOICE' IN PUBLIC POLICY-MAKING

Some barriers to inclusion of people's voice in public policy-making are described below:

- Is public policy-making an 'elitist' domain?
- Is the inability to consider people's voice and choice inherent?
- Is there paucity of tools?
- Do aspects of standardization stand in the way?
- Whether environment is not conducive enough?
- Are experts overlooking people's perspectives?
- Is there underestimation of power of people's voice?

1.5.1 Is Public Policy-Making—An 'Elitist' Domain?

In most countries, domains of public policy-making are mostly dominated by elite groups including policy advisers/Cosmopolitan Development Experts (CDEs) at different levels and tiers of such policy-making and it is they who tend to exercise control over public-policy instruments, their usage and related policy frameworks. With such dominance, the elite groups and CDEs tend to easily influence and lend shape to public policies and programmes, while the non-elite groups—the poor, the marginalized and the disadvantaged groups—have little or no space to make their voice felt or heard.

Some of the characteristic attributes of such elitist public policy-making bodies include:

(i) Having pre-defined framework and agenda.
(ii) Making straight-jacket analysis and thinking.
(iii) Having limited vision and exposure (especially those who are relatively young) and of all attributes—having much naïvety and linear thinking in understanding of development processes.
(iv) Prescribing standardized solutions for development.
(v) Producing mystified policies/outputs with a set of academic jargons.
(vi) Exerting dominance over policy-making as 'know all' types.
(vii) Having low accountability.
(viii) Having tacit collusion with other domestic/international groups.

(ix) Being 'politically' correct and having thoughts/ideas 'within the box'.

1.5.2 Is the Inability to Consider People's Voice and Choice Inherent?

Even when different channels are explored for mainstreaming people's voice, *e.g.* through public advocacy, they are often perceived to be less important by the policy-makers. In some cases, they are treated with contempt by the elite policy-making bodies for different reasons such as 'unrepresentative data', 'qualitative overviews not fitting with sleek planning models', 'noisy and biased data', etc. One such oft-cited reason to overlook/exclude people's plans made at a local/sub-national levels is the view that such people's plans are mostly naïve, simplistic and 'micro' and are not consistent/convergent with planning ministry's/planning organizatation's sophisticated data system and indicators. In addition, there could also be a tendency for the policy-influencing elite groups to find excuses to exclude people's plans for obvious reasons such as conflicting claims on resources with those of elite/dominant groups in face of existing resource crunch. See Box 1.2 for illustration.

Box 1.2: Influential Groups in Planning Outcomes: No Space for the Poor

Even at a meso level, such elite dominance could hold strong influence over decision making. For examples, a meso level village panchayat leader from India explained how investment patterns at the meso level were influenced by local elite groups. A five year plan was being made involving villagers in 40 villages covering 2800 households in 9 election booths. With 3-day training of Panchayat members, the local planning process got engaged in consultations with women and men groups in different hamlets over 15-20 days.

In such a planning process, apart from the Panchayat members, the service holders, teachers, local women representatives and members of other political parties were also included. The Panchayat aimed to utilize the local planning process to involve people in constructing local assets since it was of the view that such efforts generally yielded better dividends in terms of ownership

(*contd.*)

(*contd.*)

> and maintenance. In addition to this view, it was almost becoming obligatory since most development schemes required beneficiary/user-group formation as a prerequisite for further action.
>
> However, one major issue was that of problem prioritization of the local groups. It raised questions such as—For whom was the planned development meant for? Was it for the development of poor households or that of the area/locality concerned? The local well-off groups wanted to prioritize social assets/infrastructure in the locality, while the poor and the marginalized groups in the locality were in favour of having personal/household assets to meet their asset gaps. There was no specific space for the priorities of the poor groups to be a part of decision-making.
>
> The local decision makers were in a problematic situation since there was not only acute shortage of development funds but it was also difficult to compress demand from local elite groups, where most demand was for infrastructure, especially for irrigation. It was argued by the elite groups that in case of investment in irrigation structure some poor and landless households could also get engaged in shared-cultivation of second crop and benefit thereby. The local decision makers found that such argument had some logic and finalized their plans in favour of the local elite groups.

Source: Field Notes, Neela Mukherjee and Madhumita Parihari, Development Tracks, 2005.

In few countries, where such marginal voice are being engaged in participatory assessments, it needs to be validated whether such exercises are more of a ritualistic exercises of 'power' in terms of mere consultation with poor groups or are such consultations powerful enough to extend the frontiers of people's voice in terms of getting mainstreamed into policy-making. It is a matter of public concern when such 'voice' actually gets heard but does not get assimilated into policy and decision-making. See Box 1.3 for some related observations on Nepal.

1.5.3 Is there a Paucity of Tools?

One often hears from policy-makers, government officials, civil societies, CDEs and local development practitioners that there are not enough tools, mechanisms and channels to capture the realities of the poor and convert people's voice into vectors.and elements of policy-making and practice.

Box 1.3: Seven and More PPAs

At least seven Participatory Poverty Assessment (PPA) exercises were conducted between 1995 and 2002 in 40 districts of Nepal covering about 52 per cent of the country. Some new PPA exercises were also being initiated. The main objective of such PPA exercises was to mainstream the voice of the poor in the development process and to enable the poor groups to assess their poverty situation in their own way. A combination of qualitative and quantitative methods such as focus group discussion, structured interview and household surveys were used in some of the PPA exercises. However, one main issue identified was the lack of institutional mechanism for monitoring outcome and impact and/or updating PPA-related data (Samuhik Abhiyan: 2002). As a related point, it was also observed (Samuhik Abhiyan: 2002) that much was required in terms of capacity building of PPA facilitators for widening their understanding of development issues, PPA methodologies and facilitation skills.

Source: Samuhik Abhiyan (2002): Participatory Poverty Assessment: An Emerging Trend, A synthesis of PPA exercises undertaken in Nepal. Report prepared by Basu Dev Neupane and Niranjan Dhungel, submitted to DFID, Nepal.

Though much of what the people express at local levels is often easy to appreciate and understand; such essence gets almost lost at higher levels, for example, at meso, regional and macro levels. The 'larger pictures' of people's voice are often not easy to construct from the base and such 'larger pictures' often lack clarity, get blurred and fade away and even recede into oblivion. This is partly borne out by the World Bank's Project on "Consultations with the Poor", which was undertaken with poor people in 23 countries to feed into the World Development Report 2000-01 on Poverty and Development. The Project aimed at understanding poor people's perspectives on four key themes:

- Ill-being and well-being,
- Problems and priorities,

- Institutional relationships, and
- Gender issues.

Apart from the 23 countries, the Bank also examined similar work on ill-being and well-being carried out by different researchers. However, in terms of incorporating people's views into policy-making, such PPAs were useful only in a few countries. For instance, in case of Vietnam, 1999 proved to be an important year for poverty-related research and policy development with 4 PPAs, both rural and urban, by the collaborative efforts of the government agencies, donors and NGOs (Turk: 2000). However, its policy impact in terms of institutionalizing PPAs still remains to be captured in many countries of the world including Vietnam. The challenge lies in institutionalizing participatory methods. There is not much dispute that PPAs bring value to poverty diagnosis, the question is about longer term role for participatory information in future planning and policy work. Though some government agencies in Vietnam expressed interest to integrate participatory methods into their work for targeting poor households; informing their programme; and monitoring the impacts, they did not proceed much further. The two main institutional challenges remained—one, to generate equitable and sustainable poverty reduction, and the other, to ensure that the overall plans and poverty reduction strategies are rooted in the realities of the poor households (Turk: 2000).

1.5.4 Do Aspects of Standardization Stand in the Way?

In participatory research and data generation, one issue relates to that of standardization of methods, sequencing and data types. Such need for standardization could stem from externally driven information requirement such as measurement of impacts and outcomes and/or to inform policy and theory. The very process of adaptation and standardization of participatory approaches and scaling up can result in loss of certain elements of a methodology such as its flexibility, retaining diversity, innovativeness, etc., which are considered essential to ensure its participatory nature. Hence, standardization of methods and indicators for use with larger population groups need not be quite participatory. However, from a data gathering standpoint, researchers see that a degree of standardization is necessary (Levy, Barahona, Noponen and

Remenyi: 2007). Such standardization allows data to be aggregated and compared usually by outside investigators to inform policy and practice. The present study agrees that though standardization may become necessary for the ease of syndicating the data, there are problems related to unevenness of data generated through participation and much depends on how they are treated for reducing their unevenness. There are obvious risks in standardization where indicators may not be updated against time or adjusted to context (Brock and Pettit: 2007) and may become too aggregated. One main challenge is how to maintain diversity of people's perspectives and yet arrive at larger picture/s.

Box 1.4: Elements of Diversity in a Standardization Process

The main problem domain is generic but the dimensions indicate different qualifying features to reckon with. For example, lack of drinking water could mean that (a) the public tube-well had broken down and so water was not available and the poor women brought water from other's homes and/or distant places; or (b) alternatively, it may mean that the existing tube-well was not working since there were stones/rocks underground; or (c) it may also imply that the ground water level had fallen and/or got depleted, especially during the lean seasons.

In one of the participatory exercises, after problem-analysis, the local participants were facilitated to apply scoring/ranking methods to prioritize their list of problems. The results of the discussions on the problems from different sessions were collated for inter-community comparisons. Different communities/groups felt comfortable using different tools for analyzing and prioritizing their problems. Some used fixed scoring (*i.e.* apportioning a fixed score to the set of problems and then a fixed number of stones/ seeds to each problem), others used free scoring (*i.e.* using any number of scores with stones/seeds thus reflecting weight of each problem), while others only ranked their problems without scoring. Some others merely listed their problems and neither scored nor ranked them. This led to considerable heterogeneity in group outputs. For comparison across communities and in order to retain diversity and maximum information, the scores, ranks and frequencies of problem listing were indexed to arrive at a set of

(*contd.*)

(*contd.*)

Prioritised Problem Indices of Poor Communities (PPIPs) (UNDP:1996). This index was constructed for different groups/ communities in the study areas. The most common priority problems from all the study locations were compiled. There were a total of 45 problems listed by local poor communities, which were grouped into three sets of problems in terms of their levels of coverage: (i) About 18 most common problems running across many areas/districts; (ii) About six less common problems applicable to a few areas/districts; and (iii) About 21 problems, which were locality-specific.

Source: Development Tracks (2005).

Though there have been many efforts to reduce the gap between local and external information needs, there remain some outstanding issues to resolve. The tension is about over-extractive use of methods by outsiders termed as 'policing and measuring' [*see* Mayoux in Brock and Pettit (ed.) 2007]. It has been pointed out that while a balance between local needs and external needs could be struck, the two needs are quite different and require different inquiry processes [Barahona in Brock and Pettit (ed.): 2007]. In this context, it has been argued that while collecting information allows policy-makers to take reality-based decisions, it can also enable local communities to improve decision-making processes and to support development at the local level [*see* Levy in Brock and Pettit (ed.): 2007].

1.5.5 Whether Environment is not Conducive?

Drawing from Vietnam's case study (Turk: 2000), it is important that participatory research requires certain conducive forces to be present for its use in policy-making. There were a number of factors which profoundly influenced the potential to use this participatory research for both programme development and policy formulation (Turk: 2000). Such factors were:

(i) Leadership and significant commitment of resources;

(ii) Excellent technical capacity and strong relationship with local communities and local authorities in the PPA agencies combined with eagerness to engage at the national policy level;

(iii) Emphasis on ensuring government ownership of PPA. One other factor was that of ownership and access to poverty research. The government agencies which were responsible for drafting key parts of the plan were linked to the implementation of PPAs and analysis of findings through the mechanism of the Poverty Working Group;

(iv) Availability of high quality household survey data to corroborate;

(v) Appropriate timing: It appears that the *timing* of the PPAs in 1999 was quite appropriate from the point of view of influencing policy as during 2000 the government was drafting its new five-year plan, a new socio-economic strategy from 2001-2010, and its longer term vision to 2020; and

(vi) Acceptance of findings: Another factor was the widespread acceptance of findings within donor-NGO community and their joint advocacy and collaborative work both prior to PPA and after, to translate poverty diagnostic work into actionable strategies.

1.5.6 Are Experts Overlooking People's Perspectives?

One plausible reason for lack of clarity in people's voice as projected by elitist experts and consultants (who are often responsible for construction of such larger pictures of community voice) could lie with their linear thinking, ignorance and lack of adequate field exposure. Appropriate appreciation of people's perspectives is often constrained by their elitist training and education which tend to block the understanding, and interpreting and integrating people's realities with policy making. Many elitist experts not only tend to falter in construction of such larger pictures but also often end up blaming people's ignorance and lack of knowledge. There is obviously an underlying attitudinal problem. There are many experts in the public policy domain who strongly opine that the ordinary people, the poor and the marginalized are too ignorant and simplistic to have enough knowledge and understanding for providing effective assessments towards improving policies or providing inputs for policy-making. Policy-making is considered to be a sophisticated and elegant preserve of experts and intellectuals where less educated/uneducated, illiterate and ignorant people are not relevant for they can rarely understand the complexities or play any effective role. In most countries, it is this type of a myth surrounding policy-making that needs to be challenged and changed through better tools, better mechanisms and channels and, last but not the least, better and improved 'mindsets' of policy-makers and experts.

1.5.7 Is there an Underestimation of the Power of People's Voice?

To those elites, who (also) put the blame of such construction of 'larger picture' of people's voice on lack of methods and tools, it may be pointed out that there are participatory mechanisms/tools evolving in different countries. Such evolving mechanisms help provide opportunities for the government and political leaders to learn from their key stakeholders about people's realities and feedback. In most cases, there is a big question as to whether there is enough political will to recognize such opportunities. However, over time, political leaders and policy-makers in some countries are also beginning to realize that not listening to voice from the grassroots can prove to be politically risky and could make their functioning difficult and costly. They are gradually becoming aware that ignoring people's voice also has parallel implications in terms of not being responsive, transparent and accountable. Also, a handful of them would tend to agree that it is a missed opportunity when they are not appreciating and utilizing the vast repertoire of people's knowledge and information available for learning and decision-making. And, many leaders are sometimes forced to realize that a narrow base for development and growth process by means of excluding space for people's participation often turns out to be counter-productive and results in destabilizing any meaningful change, human development and other laudable national goals.

1.6 WHAT FACTORS INFLUENCE COMMUNITY VOICE?

As mentioned by Gloppen *et al.*: 2003, there are at least three main factors influencing community voice:

(a) Ability of the poor/their advocates to articulate their concerns,
(b) Legal basis of poverty reduction, and
(c) Institutional channels for effecting voicing.

For the ability of the poor groups and those marginalized to articulate their concerns, it is important to have tools and mechanisms and organizational set-ups, whether formal or informal, to voice their perspectives. It is possible to gain greater voice in policy decision through coalition formation and organization. This helps express their group needs in a way that alters power relations. In this way, disempowered parties can have a say in key decisions and advance their interests. Trade unions have used collective bargaining to influence labour policies. Similarly, networking amongst groups can help form power base and influence decisions. There could also be constituency groups, the powerful, traditionally disempowered, the politically active and the bystanders. Listening plays a key role in fostering parties' sense of voice (Maiese: 2005).

As we shall see in this study that there exists a range of tools and mechanisms, which can help articulate community voice to be listened by different sets of policy-makers and decision-takers with different objectives. There could be some laws to act as legal basis for poverty reduction, which is important in terms of a legal framework to support the poor and gradually could become more effective over time in terms of legal backing and legal aid to the poor. For those poor residing in countries without a legal framework for support towards pro-poor issues, lack of legal backing constitutes a major weakness to that extent.

For determining the power of voice through institutional channels, the type and quality of governance could become an important factor. As far as the institutional channels are concerned, accountability as a criterion is also important (Gloppen *et al.*: 2003). By 'accountability' is meant relationship between bearer of a right or legitimate claim and the agents or agencies responsible for fulfilling that right or legitimate claim. It involves transparency to take decisions and actions openly; answerability to justify their decisions publicly; and controllability or checks and balances. Another important characteristic in this regard is the responsiveness of the governance. By responsiveness is meant the way in which a decision-maker—public or private—perceives the needs and responds to the demand of particular groups—say the poor groups. This is largely influenced by the political and organizational culture, emerging priorities of the poor, weight of poor relative to other interest groups, ability of decision makers to appreciate the concerns of the poor and other related factors.

1.7 UNHEARD COMMUNITY VOICE

Some voice is difficult to hear and there are many unheard voices of the poor, the marginalized and the disadvantaged. This is because of different reasons, some characteristic features of such unheard voice are:

(a) Are disempowered
(b) Are powerless: have little or no power
(c) Are discriminated upon
(d) Suffer from others' prejudice
(e) Have social stigma attached
(f) Are socially excluded
(g) Are vulnerable
(h) Are marginalized
(i) Are denied access
(j) Are ill-treated
(k) Have lack of assets/capital
(l) Are deprived
(m) Suffer from ill-being and stress

Such voice is indeed not easy to hear though can be heard when such community members are able to mobilize themselves, gather enough confidence and courage to express their views in their own ways. The unheard voice of the community members has characteristic features which need to be cared for while making space for listening to their views. The related concepts and their ramifications have been referred and analysed in the development literature by various authors[3]. Some of the related concepts are explained below:

- Disempowerment
- Power relations
- Powerlessness
- Discrimination
- Prejudice
- Social stigma

- Social Exclusion
- Vulnerability
- Marginalization
- Denial of access
- Ill-treatment
- Lack of assets/capital
- Deprivation
- Ill-being and stress

1.7.1 Disempowerment, Power Relations and Powerlessness

Drawing from the definitions of empowerment, the idea of 'power' and 'power relations' is at the root of the term empowerment. Power can be understood in at least four different ways: "power over" (relationship of dominance and subordination), "power to" (having decision-making authority and power to solve problems), "power with" (people organizing with a common purpose to achieve collective goals) and "power within" (to gain self-confidence, self-awareness and be assertive) (Oxal and Braden: 1997). For example, for bonded labourers, it is "power over" them by others in a disempowering relationship of subordination to others' will and domination forcing them to act without freedom of choice; most often resulting in threats of violence and intimidation. The powerless and hapless bonded labourers have little or no means of resistance or means of access to redress their grievances. Such powerlessness would tend to vary with factors such as gender, age-group, type of activity and location, and could have different implications under different circumstances. The societal power relation is iniquitous and there is stark powerlessness as far as some community groups may be concerned. The challenge is how negative use of power can be converted to reduce power imbalances or how it can be tilted in favour of the powerless groups and for constructive purposes.

1.7.2 Discrimination, Prejudice, Stigma and Power

Feelings of prejudice have an underlying attitude of aversion and hostility towards those individuals or groups, which are presumed to have objectionable qualities ascribed to them due to culture and social norms, stigma and practices. This may result in discrimination or differential treatment. 'Power' is one concept underlying discrimination[4]. Goulden and Glyde[5] write that questions of injustice and inequality lie underneath the question of power. Our task lies in identifying the negative uses and the dynamics of power and transforming them to constructive ends. The process of understanding power may begin as a personal one. Chambers (2004) writes: "The primacy of personal actions and non-actions in development points to the need for pedagogy for the non-oppressed. This includes self-critical awareness, thinking through the effects of actions, and enabling those with power and wealth to experience being better off with less." Responsible well-being of the richer and the more powerful imply their obligations to ensure rights of the poorer and the weakest, to recognize power as a central issue, to integrate institutional and personal change and to take responsibility (Chambers: 2004) and to act and count on the realities of the poor and the disadvantaged.

1.7.3 Social Exclusion

Social exclusion involves systematic denial of access of services to specific social group/s or individuals. Social exclusion involves four factors—the excluded; the institutions from which they are excluded; the agents whose actions result in exclusion; and the process through which such exclusion occurs. Different forms of disadvantage give rise to different kinds of disadvantaged groups. Disadvantage results in social exclusion (Kabeer: 2000). The concept of social exclusion focuses on the multi-dimensionality of deprivation, in the economic, social and the political spheres, where people are often deprived of different things at the same time (de Haan, Arjan: 1999). The real value of the concept of "social exclusion" lies at the meso level in the analysis of institutions. With regard to accessibility, the excluded people such as the disadvantaged groups have limited access to different resources as well as institutions.

Main mechanisms for social exclusion, in order of increasing severity, are: (i) geography, (ii) entry barriers, (iii) corruption, (iv) intimidation, and (v) physical violence (Bradley: 1994). Those socially excluded tend to be more exploited by the powerful because of their social condition/s. Exclusion and exploitation both enhance inequality within the society, which tend to increase the vulnerability of the poor and the disadvantaged.

1.7.4 Vulnerability

Vulnerability connotes particular sensitivity to an event or occurrence that poses an immediate threat to one's socio-economic well-being and the inability to cope with shock or misfortune. As defined by Chambers, "Vulnerability has two sides: an external side of risk, and stress to which an individual or household is subject and an internal side which is defencelessness, meaning a lack of ability to cope without damaging loss" (Chambers: 1989). The vulnerability 'context' in which different assets exist are in terms of trends, shocks, seasonality and local cultural practices, which affect livelihoods of the poor[6]. It is the result of many factors including impact of policies and institutions and lack of assets. Vulnerability is a 'silent emergency' that is intimately linked to weak local governance. Poor need to be less vulnerable to external shocks[7]. Social vulnerability comes from insecurities related to social status caused by exclusion, discrimination and lack of protection, so apt in the case of the poor groups and the disadvantaged.

1.8 COMMUNITY VOICE AND APPROACHES

Based on the three factors influencing community voice, we may cluster different approaches to poverty reduction and decision-making under three types of criteria:

(i) Ability of poor to articulate their concerns:

- Participatory Approaches (PA)
- Sustainable Livelihoods Approaches (SLA)
- Empowerment Approaches (EA)
- Entitlement and Capabilities Approach (ECA)

(ii) Legal framework

- Rights-Based Approaches (RBA)

(iii) Institutional framework and channels

- It is possible to draw upon elements of Empowerment Approaches (EA) and Entitlement and Capabilities Approach (ECA) to fit the criteria related to institutional channels.

Different approaches to poverty reduction and basis of decision-making are explained below:

1.8.1 Participatory Approaches

Voice and choices of the poor and the disadvantaged—Complete understanding of poverty requires the inclusion of not only the social factors and issues related to power, rights, empowerment and well-being but also the perspectives of the poor in their own voice, having their own space and in their own way. Participatory Assessment (PA), based on interactive sessions held *in situ,* helps understand the complexities of poverty from people's perspective, their problems and priorities, and their ideas and suggestions. Participatory assessments are interactive exercises in which, poor communities/groups and others as stakeholders do their own assessment of poverty based on their experience and knowledge. It is a demand-driven approach and empowers the poor and the disadvantaged to assess their own situation, causal forces and make suggestions on ways to improve their own lives. It is a kind of feedback mechanism from poor people and if conducted with regularity can provide a system for built-in accountability for the "top" decision-makers. World Bank's *World Development Report 2000-01*, while adopting a multi-dimensional concept of poverty emphasized that the ambit of poverty is wider than mere inadequacy of income or human poverty—poverty is vulnerability, lack of voice, power and representation[8].

1.8.2 Sustainable Livelihoods Approaches

A sustainable livelihoods (SL) framework encompasses the factors that contribute to poverty and vulnerability. It is aimed to improve upon the lives of the poor and to strengthen their livelihoods. As defined in the sustainable livelihoods (SL) framework, "a livelihood comprises the capabilities, assets (stores, resources, claims and access) and activities required for a means of living. A livelihood is sustainable which can cope with and recover from stresses and shocks; maintain or enhance its capabilities and assets; provide sustainable livelihoods-related opportunities for the next generation; and which contributes net benefits to other livelihoods at the local and global level and in the long and the short-term" (Chambers and Conway: 1992). The poor lack some or all of the five livelihood assets of human, social, financial, physical and natural capital. The sustainable livelihoods framework helps understand the factors, which influence the vulnerability of the poor, the exclusion processes within the policies, institutions and processes, which determine the lack of livelihoods assets and the consequent livelihoods strategies adopted by the poor and the outcomes thereby. These are based on people's own interpretation and priorities for their livelihoods. Some core aspects of sustainable livelihoods (SL) approaches include: (a) people-centred aspects; (b) holistic; (c) dynamic—thus learning from change; (d) building on people's strengths rather than their needs; and (e) establishing macro-micro linkages. Such approaches also emphasize the need for higher-level policy development and planning to be informed by the lessons learnt and insights gained at the local level[9,10].

1.8.3 Empowerment Approaches

Empowerment implies increasing the relative power and ability of people, particularly the disadvantaged groups in terms of socio-economic and political environment. In a broader sense, empowerment is about the expansion of assets and capabilities of people to participate fully in decisions and processes that shape their lives and negotiate with, influence, control, and hold accountable institutions that affect their lives (World Bank: 2002). Empowerment implies transformation of existing power relations in favour of women, disadvantaged groups and, more generally, the poor (Oxal and Baden: 1997). The rural poor, especially the women, rarely choose or control the conditions under which they earn their livelihoods. Hence efforts are required to address gender inequalities. Poor including the women need to have influence over major decisions affecting their well-being[11]. Participation and inclusion, access to information, power, voice, accountability, organizational capacity building, human rights and access to service/assets are crucial elements of empowerment[12]. It is not just individuals but organizations which also constitute focus of the empowerment process. Core activities to bring about the change are political mobilization, legal changes, consciousness raising and popular education. Empowerment is essentially a bottom-up process with appropriate external support as required. On the indicators of empowerment—the Human Development Report (UNDP: 1995) states 'empowerment' as one of the four essential components of the human development paradigm, the others being 'productivity', 'equity' and 'sustainability'. Empowerment is described as fully participating in the decision-making and processes that shape their (poor people's) lives.

1.8.4 Rights-Based Approaches

Poverty is a denial of human rights. A rights-based approach (RBA) is based on empowerment, equality of entitlement, inclusion, dignity, justice and respect for all people. It encourages poor people to demand services actively, according to their own priorities, and thereby raises self-esteem and promotes autonomy. Human rights are fundamental moral and legal entitlements related to basic well-being and dignity. They are "social and political guarantees necessary to protect individuals from the standard threats to human dignity posed by the modern state and the modern markets" (Donnelly: 1989). It implies obligations by society to enable people to claim their rights and have access to redress mechanisms, as and when required. Rights-based approaches focus on individuals as citizens and highlight the importance of accountability and governance. Rights can be understood as claims that have been legitimized by social structure and norms. Claims can relate to the definition, interpretation or implementation of rights (Moser and Norton: 2001). Usually there are five types of rights identified—social, economic, cultural, political and civil rights. Social and economic rights are particularly problematic because they are hard to define, costly to supply and difficult to enforce. Most work in the rights-based areas focuses on empowering people to claim their rights and less attention is paid to obligations and responsibilities on the part of individuals, groups, states, etc.

Human rights law recognizes three groups of agents (i) rights-holders, (ii) duty-bearers, and (iii) "other actors". All human beings belong to the first group. A human rights approach has many elements in common with other development approaches. However, there are three basic distinctions between the former and the latter approaches. These are (i) the legal basis, (ii) the normative framework, and (iii) the process of realizing the overall goal of ensuring human rights. The normative framework has six key principles derived from the human rights instruments, which are (a) universalism, (b) equality and non-discrimination, (c) indivisibility and interdependence of human rights, (d) participation and inclusion, (e) accountability, and (f) the rule of law. These six principals are the integral constituents of rights-based approach (Ljungman: 2005).

1.8.5 Entitlements and Capabilities Approaches

Entitlement approach provides a framework for analysing the relationship between rights, interpersonal obligations and individual entitlements to things. A person's entitlement is a way of characterising his or her 'overall' command over things including relevant rights and obligations. Entitlement has two dimensions: endowment and exchange. An individual or a household is endowed with a set of resources (material, human and social), which helps create the availability of the economic options for the individual or the household. Both institutional and economic factors add to or diminish entitlement including customs, tradition, laws and welfare transfers (Sen: 1981). Closely related is the *capability* approach, in which the number of options that people have, and their freedom to choose among those options, contribute to human well-being. 'Capabilities' is described as the alternative combinations of functioning that are feasible for a person to achieve. In this context, poverty may be best characterised in terms of absence or deprivation of certain basic capabilities to do this or to be that (Sen: 1999). The main theme is to develop human freedom, which includes five instruments—political freedom, economic facilities, social opportunity, transparency guarantee and protective security. The Human Development Index based on entitlements and capabilities' approach is considered in terms of the expansion of three valuable human capabilities—having a long life, acquiring knowledge and achieving a decent standard of living (UNDP: 1997, 2000). Similarly, the Gender-related Development Index of UNDP captures gender-based inequities in the achievement of these capabilities based on the multi-dimensionality of poverty.

We see above that there are diverse approaches and conceptual basis for factors influencing community voice, especially towards organizing such voice, providing legal backing and validity and institutional channels. Though the approaches are not altogether mutually exclusive and do overlap to some extent, they provide a meaningful basis for appreciating different frameworks and methods for approaching community voice.

After a discussion on selected concepts, rationale of listening to people's voice and related approaches, the next chapter lays down some core principles and foundation for eliciting such voice.

NOTES

1. "Policy-Making Introduction, MRSC", September 2000" http://www.ci.hunts-point.wa.us/Subjects/Governance/legislative/intro.aspx.
2. *Ibid*
3. Also see Chambers: 2004, UNDP: 1995, Sen: 1997; Narayan: 1999; Goulden and Glyde: www.careinternation.org.uk; Zoe *et al.*: 1999; Bond and Mukherjee: 2001, Williams: 1994, Scott-Villiers: 2004.
4. Drawn from Goulden and Glyde: Care International.
5. Quoting Just Associates in their *Tools for Analyzing Power, Inclusion and Exclusion.*
6. See www.livelihoods.org
7. See IFAD: www.ifad.org
8. For further discussion and case studies on PPA see "Voice of the Poor" at http://www.worldbank.org/poverty/voice/reports/canany/ch1.pdf and "Hearing the Voice of the Poor", Human Development Report, 2002, UNDP.
9. Livelihoods-based approaches have been adopted by many development agencies including DFID, Oxfam, CARE and UNDP. For a comparison of the approaches see Carney *et al.*: 1999.
10. UNDP's Sustainable Human Development policy embodies the essential components of equity, empowerment and sustainability (www.sdnp.undp.org/gender/). UNDP's community empowerment for sustainable development creates and supports partnerships to fight poverty and provides advice and resources to empower the poor (www.undp.org.za/projects/community_empowerment/).
11. IFAD: Strategic Framework www.ifad.org
12. UNDP in 1998 adopted its policy of *Integrating Human Rights with Sustainable Human Development towards* strengthening its policy programming and capacity development support with emphasis on participation, empowerment and non-discrimination as integral parts of a human rights-based approach to poverty reduction. For a framework on human rights integration in poverty reduction see UNDP's: *Human Development Report, 2000*: Human Rights and Human Development, New York, OUP and UNDP Practice Notes on *Poverty Reduction and Human Rights.*

REFERENCES

Barahona, Carlos (2007). "Navigating the trade-offs in the use of participatory approaches for research" in Brock, Karen and Jethro Pettit (ed.) (2007), *Springs of Participation: Creating and Evolving Methods for Participatory Development*, Practical Action Publishing, Institute of Development Studies at Sussex, Intermediate Technology Limited., Warwickshire.

Bradley, Christine (1994). Why Male Violence against Women is a Development Issue: Reflections from Papua New Guinea in Miranda Davies ed. *Women and Violence: Realities and Responses, Worldwide*, London, Zed Books.

Brock, Karen and Jethro Pettit (ed.) (2007). *Springs of Participation: Creating and Evolving Methods for Participatory Development*, Practical Action Publishing, Institute of Development Studies at Sussex, Intermediate Technology Limited, Warwickshire.

Carney, Diana with Michael Drinkwater, Tamara Rusinow, Koos Neefjes, Samir Wanmali and Naresh Singh (1999). *Livelihoods Approaches Compared*, DFID, November; www.livelihoods.org

Chambers, Robert (2004). *Ideas for Development: Reflecting Forwards*, IDS Working Paper 238, Institute of Development Studies, November, Brighton.

——(1991). 'Shortcut and Participatory Methods for Gaining Social Information for Projects, in Cernea, Michael M. (ed.), *Putting People First, Sociological Variables in Rural Development*, published for the World Bank, Oxford University Press.

——(1993). *Challenging the Professions: Frontiers for rural development*, Intermediate Technology Publications, London.

——(1994). 'Participatory Rural Appraisal (PRA): Analysis of Experience', *World Development*, Vol.22, No.9, pp.1253-1268.

——(1997). *Whose Reality Counts? Putting the First Last*, IT Publications, London.

——(2005). *Ideas for Development*, Earthscan Publications, London DFID UK website

Chambers, R. and G. Conway: (1992). *Sustainable Rural Livelihoods: Practical Concepts for the 21st Century*, IDS Discussion Paper 296. Brighton: IDS.

Chambers, Robert (1989) Editorial Introduction: Vulnerability, Coping, and Policy *IDS Bulletin*, 20(2): 1-7.

Development Tracks, RTC (2002). *Livelihoods Scoping Study*, West Bengal, Draft Report submitted to DFID, India, November.

——RTC (2005). *Participatory Poverty Assessment*, West Bengal, Draft Report submitted to Asian Development Bank, Manila, June.

De Haan, Arjan (1999) *Social Exclusion: Towards an Holistic Understanding of Deprivation*.

Devine, Pat (2003). *Industrial Policy, Ecological Economics and Deliberative Democracy*. European Society for Ecological Economics. FRONTIERS2: European Application of Ecological Economics, Tenerife, Canary Islands, February 11-16.

Donelly, Jack (1989). *Universal Human Rights in Theory and Practice*, Cornell University Press, Ithaca, N.Y.

Dryzek, John S. (1996). Strategies of Ecological Democratization. In *Democracy and the Environment*. ed. William M. Lafferty and James Meadowcraft. Cheltenham, UK: Edward Elgar, pp. 108-123.

Freire, Paulo (1970). *Pedagogy of the Oppressed*, The Seabury Press, New York.

Gaventa, John (2005). Reflections on the Users of the 'Power Cube' Approach for Analyzing the Spaces, Places and Dynamics of Civil Society Participation and Engagement, CFP Evaluation Series 2003-2006: No.4, Institute of Development Studies, University of Sussex, UK., October.

Gloppen, Siri L. Rakner, A. Tostensen (2003). "Responsiveness to the Concerns of the Poor and Accountability to the Commitment to Poverty Reduction" (WP 2003 : 9, Chr. Michelsen Institute, Development Studies and Human Rights, Bergen, Norway).

Guijt, Irene and Meera Kaul Shah (eds.) (1998). *The Myth of Community: Gender Issues in Participatory Development*. Intermediate Technology Publications, London.

Goulden, Jay and Sarah Glyde, *Development of a Rights-Based Monitoring Tool for CARE Malawi*, www.careinternational.org.uk/resource_centre/human rights/

IFAD, Strategic Framework, www.ifad.org

ITAD (2004). PPA Manual, PRCD Project Guangxi, ITAD/DFID/The World Bank, Guangxi Province, China.

Just Associate, *Tools for Analyzing Power, Inclusion and Exclusion*.

Kabeer, Naila, (2000). Social Exclusion, Poverty and Discrimination, Towards an Analytical Framework, *IDS Bulletin*, Volume 31, No.4.

Kanbur, Ravi (ed), (2005). *Q-Squared-Qualitative and Quantitative Poverty Appraisal: Complementarities, Tensions and the Way Forward*, Q-Squared Working Paper No.1, October.

Kapoor, Ilan (2001). Towards participatory environmental management? *Journal of Environmental Management* 63: 269-279.

Kothari, Uma (2001). Power, Knowledge and Social Control in Participatory Development. In: Cooke, Bill and Uma Kothari. *Participation: The New Tyranny?* Zed Books, London.

Lederach, John Paul (2005). *The Moral Imagination: The Art and Soul of Building Peace*, Oxford University Press, New York.

Levy, Sarah (2007). "Using numerical data from participatory research to support the Millennium Development Goals: the case for locally owned information systems" in Brock, Karen and Jethro Pettit (ed.) (2007), *Springs of Participation: Creating and Evolving Methods for Participatory Development*, Practical Action Publishing, Institute of Development Studies at Sussex, Intermediate Technology Limited, Warwickshire.

Ljungman, Cecilia M. (2004). *Applying a Rights-Based Approach to Development: Concepts and Principles*, Conference Paper: The Winners and Losers from Rights-Based Approaches to Development, COWI, November, based on a chapter in Britha Mikkelsen's *Methods for Development Work and Research—A New Guide for Practitioners* (2005). 2e, Sage Publications, New Delhi, February.

Maiese, Michelle (2005). Source: http://www.beyondintractability.org/essay/voice/, June.

Max-Neef, A. Manfred, Antonio, Elizalde and Martin, Hopenhayn, (1991). *Human Scale Development, Conception, Application and Further Reflections*, The Apex Press, New York.

Mitchell, Laura Remson (2002). On "Public Policy Making and the Grssroots" http://www.geocities.com/dhcpolwnk/grassroots.html

Moser, C. and A. Norton: (2001). *To claim our rights: livelihood security, human rights and sustainable development*, ODI, London.

MRDP (1999). "Lao Cai Province: A Participatory Poverty Assessment", Hanoi, Vietnam-Sweden Mountain Rural Development Programme and the Vietnam-Sweden Health Cooperation Programme.

Mukherjee, Amitava, (ed.) (2004). *Participatory Rural Appraisal, Methods & Applications in Rural Planning*, Concept Publishing Company, New Delhi.

Mukherjee, Amitava, (ed.) (2004). *Participatory Monitoring*, Concept Publishing Company, New Delhi.

Mukherjee, Neela, (1993). *Participatory Rural Appraisal, Methodology & Applications*, Concept Publishing Co., New Delhi

—— (1995). *Participatory Rural Appraisal & Questionnaire Survey: Comparative field experience and methodological innovations*, Concept Publishing Co., New Delhi.

—— (2002). *Participatory Learning and Action with 100 Field Methods*, Concept Publishing Co., New Delhi.

Narayan, Deepa (1999). *Bonds and Bridges: Social Capital and Poverty*, Poverty Research Working Paper No. 2167, The World Bank D.C., July.

Narayan, Deepa with Raj Patel, Kai Schafft, Anne Rademacher and Sarah Koch-Schulte (2000). *Voice of the Poor, Can Anyone Hear Us?* Published by Oxford University Press for the World Bank, Washington D.C.

Naponen, Helzi (2007). "It's not just about the picture, it's also about principles, process and power tensions in the development of the internal learning system", in Brock, Karen and Jethro Pettit (ed.) (2007), *Springs of Participation: Creating and Evolving Methods for Participatory Development*, Practical Action Publishing, Institute of Development Studies at Sussex, Intermediate Technology Limited, Warwickshire.

OECD, (2007). Inclusive Civic Engagement: citizens' voice in policy making, 7th Global Forum Building Trust in Government, Workshop V, Civic Engagement, 28th June 2007, Tanja Timmermans, OECD.

Oxfam, GB (1999). "Tra Vinh Province: A Participatory Poverty Assessment", Hanoi.

Ozanne, Julie L. and Saatcioglu, Bige (2007). "Understanding Subsistence Marketplaces: Exploring the Contributions of Participatory Action Research" in Rosa, Jose Antonio and Madhubala Viswanathan (ed). *Product and Market Development for Subsistence Marketplaces*, Advances in International Management, Volume 20, Elsevier, Oxford.

Perkins, Patricia E. (2005). Public Participation and Ecological Valuation: Inclusive Radical, Presented at the Capitalism Nature Socialism Conference, July 22-24, Faculty of Environmental Studies, York University.

"Policy-Making Introduction, MRSC", September 2000, http://www.ci.hunts-point.wa.us/Subjects/Governance/legislative/intro.aspx

Poverty Working Group, (1999). "Vietnam: Attacking Poverty", Joint Report of the Government of Vietnam-Donor-NGO Poverty Working Group, Hanoi.

Remenyi, Joe (2007). "Participatory village poverty reduction planning and index-based poverty mapping in China" in Brock, Karen and Jethro Pettit (ed.) (2007). *Springs of Participation: Creating and Evolving Methods for Participatory Development*, Practical Action Publishing, Institute of Development Studies at Sussex, Intermediate Technology Limited, Warwickshire.

Robredo, J. M. (2007). "Engaging People in Local Development: The Experience of Naga City, Philippines", Paper presented at Conference on Active Citizenship and Social Accountability sponsored by Australian Council for International Development (Mayor of Naga City), Monash University, Victoria, Australia, July 3rd.

Sainath, P. (1996). *Everybody Loves a Good Drought, Stories from India's Poorest Districts*, Penguin Books, New Delhi.

Save the Children UK (1999). "Ho Chi Minh City: A Participatory Poverty Assessment", Hanoi.

Schwandt, Thomas R. (1990). 'Paths to Inquiry in the Social Disciplines—Scientific, Constructivist and Critical Theory Methodologies', in Guba Egon G. (ed.) The *Paradigm Dialog,* Sage, California.

Sen, A.K. (1981). *Poverty and Famine: An Essay on Entitlement and Deprivation,* Oxford: Clarendon.

—— (1999) *Development as Freedom,* New York: Knopf Press.

The World Bank, http://www.worldbank.org/poverty/voice/reports/canany/ch1.pdf

Turk, Carrier (2000). *Linking Participatory Poverty Assessments to Policy and Policy Making: Experience from Vietnam*, The World Bank, Vietnam.

UNDP, (1996). *UNDP's 1996 Report on Human Development in Bangladesh—A Pro-Poor Agenda*, United Nations Development Programme, Dhaka.

UNDP, (1995, 1997 and 2000). *Human Development Reports,* United Nations Development Programme, New York.

Walter, Tom (1995). Knowledge, Power, and Environmental Policy: Expertise, the Lay Public, and Water Management in the Western United States. *The Environmental Professional*, Vol. 17: 153-166.

Williams, Suzanne, Seed, Janet and Mwau Adelina (1994). *Oxfam Gender Training Manual*, Oxfam, Oxford.

World Bank (2002). "Empowerment: A Framework for Policy and Practice" http://poverty.worldbank.org/library/topic/10143/)

World Bank (2000-01). *World Development Report 2000*.

World Bank, *Voice of the Poor:* http://www.worldbank.org/poverty/voice/reports

www.livelihoods.org

www.Wikipedia.com

Oxal, Zoe with Sally. Baden (1997) Gender and Empowerment Definitions, Approaches and Implications for Policy, Report No. 40, www.ids.ac.uk/bridge/Reports.

2

Community Voice and Principles

This chapter deals the underlying principles of listening to community voices such as 'listening and learning', 'offsetting biases', 'utilization of precious community time', 'seeking diversity', 'cross-checking process and outputs', 'optimal ignorance and appropriate imprecision'. A discussion on the foundation pillars for listening to community voice—attitude and behaviour, process, methods and sharing is also included in the chapter.

THE PRINCIPLES UNDERLYING 'VOICE' IN POLICY MAKING

Some key principles for 'voice' in policy making are discussed below:

2.1 Listening and Learning

'Voice'-based policy making is based on the principle of listening and learning through participatory interactions and learning progressively. Common people have their knowledge, their experience, their history and culture, their views and ideas and their priorities and preferences. Listening to people helps portray their 'worldview', which otherwise remains latent and not revealed. Such learning can increase progressively and it is important to be mentally prepared to listen, learn and to show respect towards those from whom such learning can take place.

2.2 Offsetting Biases

This principle aims at offsetting biases, which generally accompany a 'rushed' appraisal for achieving quick results. Our biases often lead us to:

- meet and consult people at convenient locations, such as road side locations (not interior locations);
- meet at convenient times (not in times of say difficult seasons) when the season/weather is favourable;
- meet and consult people (mostly men) who are generally educated and better off.

In order to offset such biases, it is important to be in a learning mode; be relaxed and be able to listen to others; seek participation from people who are relatively worse off; visit remote and interior locations; and interact with local communities at their convenience.

2.3 Utilization of Precious Community Time

One other principle for learning from local people is related to utilisation of precious community time in the best possible manner. Local community members are busy in pursuing local livelihoods and it is important to keep track of their time and learn from them as their time permits. It also implies that community members may be requested to spare their valuable time so as to interact at their convenience. The learning needs to be focused so as to make proper utilisation of such time.

2.4 Seeking Diversity

Public participation also involves learning from diverse conditions and different actors. In the complex maze of learning there are different events, processes and forces, which help understand issues from different perspectives. For any analysis, the greater the diversity of people's reality and their inter-connections, the better becomes the understanding and ability to appreciate complex realities.

2.5 Cross Checking

The process of crosschecking and validation is an important principle related to people's participation for minimising errors in learning and undertaking mid-way corrections. Since there are different sources from which information flows, it is important to crosscheck the reliability and validity of such information by putting it to different tests. There are different ways to check the validity of the people's data such as by changing tools and methods, by changing locations, by changing timing, by changing participant groups and by changing facilitators.

2.6 Optimal Ignorance and Appropriate Imprecision

In order to minimize cost and time, the principle of optimal ignorance is a handy principle to keep in mind. It means knowing what is worth knowing and knowing enough to serve the purpose and not knowing the rest or not trying to find out more. Associated with this is seeking appropriate imprecision or avoiding precision of information that is not necessary.

The principles described above help to:

(i) make learning iterative;
(ii) support better facilitation of participatory sessions;
(iii) make such processes interactive, innovative and informal;
(iv) make effective use of time; and
(v) lower costs.

2.7 Foundation of Community Voice

There are four pillars of community voice, where each has a crucial role to play while influencing the other (Mukherjee: 1993 and 2002). The four pillars are as follows:

- Attitude, Belief and Behaviour,
- Process,
- Sharing, and
- Voice Tools.

Each of the pillars is incomplete without the other as explained below:

2.7.1 Attitude, Belief and Behaviour

Such process of learning from the people is hardly an automatic process, so also is that of changing oneself towards attitude and belief that it is important to learn from ordinary people's experience and views. This is not an easy task and it is for this reason that many institutions often find it difficult to gear up in terms of their mental make up for soliciting people's participation. One probable reason could be in terms of their closed mindsets, often lacking a window to embrace such paradigmatic shift.

2.7.1.1 The Paradigmatic Shift

Development paradigms are in a transition phase, evolving from 'top-down' to 'bottom-up' approaches. The following illustrates some of the dimensions of such changes taking place, both in theory and practice:

- From 'command and control' system towards more decentralized approaches;
- From 'positivist' framework to 'constructivist' approaches;
- From 'closed' mindsets to more 'open' mindsets;
- From 'lecturing' mode to 'listening' and 'learning' mode;
- From theoretical approaches to more practical and field-based approaches;
- From narrow approaches to more holistic approaches;
- From pursuing 'targets' towards enabling participatory processes; and
- From considering people as 'objects' to viewing people as 'participants'.

Over the past years, there have such paradigmatic shifts in the field of development where people's participation, people's voice and people's knowledge have gained momentum, whether through field research or lessons learnt from civil society, government, development agencies and donors. The essence of the new paradigm, though still evolving, is:

- To learn from the field,
- To learn to respect and recognize field knowledge and experience,
- To listen to alternate perspectives,
- To appreciate other people's reality, and
- To learn *in situ* through 'hands on' practice.

One stimulus to such a change has come from field-related experience of what works in practice and what does not work and what make things work better, especially the role of people's wisdom, their engagement, their views and priorities. Field results have amply demonstrated that conventional 'top-down' solutions to development issues are increasingly becoming less effective and are seldom yielding the desired results.

One core message from such paradigmatic shift is that we learn best from the field, from practice, from listening to other's views and experience and also learning from our own reflections and mistakes. As an iterative process, the quality of such learning is relatively rich since it is based on practical and field-based information and can accommodate mistakes and errors in decision-making. This is especially important in the field of development when there are no tailor-made solutions to choose from. Such paradigmatic shift is taking place across civil societies, state institutions, donor agencies, programme/project management, research bodies, technology-development institutions and other sectors related to social development. The winds of change are on and there is a gradual realization emerging in many quarters that the challenge of development lies in its relevance to the people as participants; and development initiatives are best sorted out in the realm of people-centred development. However, the pace of change has varied considerably across institutions with the paradigmatic shift in the field of development catching up faster with the civil societies and programme/project management at the field level as compared to those actors at higher levels of policy making. This has led to an opportunity for field practitioners, managers and researchers to work in open-ended field conditions, work with people as partners, have seamless learning experience and have ability to critically reflect upon. Many people as participants (though many are yet to be included) have also got an opportunity to be engaged with their own local development process in their terms and in their own ways with their voices getting heard (though not that responded).

2.7.1.2 Factors Influencing Paradigmatic Shift

What factors are contributing towards shifts in development paradigm/s? We can attribute such paradigmatic shift to five important factors, as listed below:

- Realization that there is a whole gamut of indigenous knowledge systems lying in the people's domain;
- There are multiple perspectives of stakeholders in the process of development and they are often at variance with perspective/s from the 'top';
- There are not enough answers to what type of development is appropriate and ways of coping with uncertainty of 'changes';
- Exploring answers about who 'owns' this development process and how sustainable is the process; and
- Specific issues raised by groups excluded from the conventional mainstream development about human rights and fulfilment of basic needs.

2.7.1.3 Whose Knowledge Counts?

The conventional world of social development has been slow in recognizing the significance of indigenous knowledge. Experts have been considerably reluctant in appreciating the vast storehouse of indigenous knowledge systems. Local knowledge retrieval and management has been a major omission in our conventional pursuit of development goals and activities. This has often resulted in local communities appearing as a bundle of problems, rather than as a basket of opportunities. The outsiders have often perceived that they have solutions to the local problems. Max-Neef *et al.* (1991) wrote, "We live and work within models of society that overlook the growing complexity of the real society in which we are immersed. Therefore, we watch the feverish and obsessive doings of the technocrats who design solutions before having identified where the real problems lie."

In the process of adopting external solutions, local knowledge, local initiative and local experience have been discouraged. A common example of imposing external solutions from the 'top' is that of providing exotic breeds of livestock to local communities. One such experience is described in Box 2.1. These and other sophisticated solutions as illustrated in Box 2.1 through project intervention of exotic breed of livestock have been rampantly experimented by experts in many parts of the world and have caused irreparable damages, considerable loss to poor communities and failure stories in terms of unsustainable development. With exogenous solutions creating chaos rather than resolving problems, it is being gradually realised that such solutions are mostly not workable technologically and they do not fit with the context of the problem, local ethos and are not 'owned' by the people concerned. Development experience from different areas shows that many of such external solutions have been abandoned, found risky and have achieved little success.

Box 2.1: Imposing Exotic Bulls

Sainath (1996) writes about the Orissa experience where the hi-breed bull scheme was introduced and how it failed miserably and led to considerable damage to local lives and livelihoods. The scheme was to create a new breed of cattle for which the livestock inspector relentlessly castrated all bulls in the area. Then the cows were done artificial insemination for hi-breed. As a consequence of mass castrations the indigenous Khariar bulls were completely wiped out while the exotic variety of livestock, with low immunity, vanished before long. The indigenous Khariar breed, which was made extinct, was capable of yielding 4 to 5 litres of milk per day. Prior to such extinction, the earlier practice for cattle breeders from other areas was to visit this area to buy Khariar bulls. They were popular as studs and helped improve breeds elsewhere. With Khariar breed getting wiped out, cattle population in the area declined rapidly which increased the vulnerability of the poor. This was more pronounced in the lean years when they had no cattle to sell as source of livelihood. With loss of cattle, there was local disaster all around and migration to 'better off' areas increased. Such disaster arose because people were never consulted, rather they were allured to raise exotic livestock through gift of land, which later turned into a farce. Eventually, some NGOs started a project to revive the Khariar bull but reversal of the process, slow in itself, meant hard work and money.

Source: Adapted from Sainath, P., (1996), *Everybody Loves a Good Drought, Stories from India's Poorest Districts*, Penguin Books, New Delhi.

In today's world, it is being increasingly recognised that the local communities have vast reservoir of indigenous technical knowledge (ITK) and most often they are maintained through oral traditions. It is possible to find samples of such knowledge in books and reports, however, most of it flows through 'word of mouth', both at intra- and inter-generation levels. This has helped preserve, conserve and augment such knowledge. Such indigenous knowledge has evolved over time based on years of experience, ethnic practices, culture and intuition. Many of such knowledge items have been processed and organised through couplets, songs, poems, practice, prejudices, anecdotes and other handy forms.

2.7.1.4 Types of Knowledge

Knowledge can be broadly grouped into two, explicit and tacit. Explicit knowledge is that kind of knowledge that one gathers directly from reports, books, computers, etc. Such knowledge is available easily and can be replicated, if necessary. Tacit knowledge is that kind of knowledge which one can learn only by means of direct interaction with individuals/groups/communities, by creating opportunities for individuals to reveal that knowledge. Indigenous knowledge system is tacit knowledge and for accessing tacit knowledge appropriate 'mindsets' and communication skills are important. It implies a learner's attitude and behaviour as one congenial factor in establishing rapport with a person who has this knowledge. Such knowledge varies across people, communities and areas and is often specific to locality, age, gender, class, caste, etc. Such ITK is important because such knowledge is contextual; includes answers to many questions; helps augment problem-solving abilities of both local communities and external agencies; and helps probe relational linkages between factors and issues from different dimensions.

2.7.1.5 Why Change 'Our' Mindsets?

Are we missing something beyond the smokescreen of our limited knowledge and experience, our training and bias? Why are we unable to see beyond the narrow confines of the 'predictable' world? With our conventional mindsets, we miss out on new outcomes, new experience and knowledge, new vision and new ways of looking at ourselves[1]. One plain and simple reason for changing our mindsets is that it blocks many opportunities to augment our knowledge frontier and hinders learning of new lessons, new practices and new ways of doing things. Many of us are also unaware that such structured mindsets often lead to a typical syndrome of 'I know it all' where it may become difficult to undertake real learning. The following points provide some logic of unshackling our mindsets and the importance of learning from others:

- It helps increase our learning about other people's reality. It helps us realize that for any outcome there are multiple stakeholders and multiple views to reckon with.
- With fixed mindsets we tend to offer no better than stereotyped solutions to ever-increasing problems. Today's problems are complex and contextual and many of them are unprecedented and not easily predictable. Any simplistic exposition of such problems runs the risk of ignoring their determinant forces, often beyond the comprehension, competency and control of 'limited mindsets'.
- Our stereotyped mindsets cannot gauge appropriate solutions. Imposing stereotyped solutions can only lead to future complications. With flexible mindsets we are able to create space for people's knowledge and initiatives as alternate resource base. Flexible mindsets often help find triangulated ways of overcoming problems by involving other stakeholders.

2.7.1.6 De-constructing 'Our' Mindsets

On the positive side, there are abundant examples to show that many stereotyped mindsets have been de-constructed both at the organizational and individual levels and a process of change has been triggered off. Such changes in mindsets have been brought about in different ways such as 'hands on' training, self-learning, reflecting, persistent practising, mentoring, counselling, role modelling, role reversing, exposure visits, peer group pressures, etc. There are different methods for broadening and changing mindsets, which may vary in their effectiveness depending on the situation and the person concerned. It is important to mention that mechanisms for deconstruction of mindsets have no 'blueprint'; are context-specific; and are better geared when based on the principle of "learning-by-doing".

For learning to take place, our 'mindset' as a learner is the most crucial factor. There are different levels of such learning process and different kinds of learners, some more eager than others, some fast to learn, some recalcitrant and others slow. The main issue in the context of participatory approaches is "are we ready to learn"? Can we adapt to have the 'mindset' of a learner? Even when a learner has a 'mindset', what about the accompanying social skills? These questions are directly relevant in today's context because it helps us appreciate the fact that despite a window of opportunity created in the world of social development, many of us are still in our old syndrome and are considerably handicapped to that extent.

2.7.1.7 'Our' Attitude and Behaviour

As already mentioned above, one essential prerequisite for listening to people's voice is about our attitude and behaviour—whether they are conducive enough. Chambers (1993, 1997) writes about "we"-"they" syndrome where "we" as outsiders think that "they" (local communities) are problems to which "we" have solutions. Our normal professionalism is handicapped by conditioning through education, training and socialization and internalization of normal professional concepts, values, beliefs, methods and behaviour. Our dominance is reflected in our speech and behaviour and we distance ourselves from the lower in normal hierarchy and also blame them. Chamber (1993) writes that new development professionalism needs to keep pace with the new development paradigm and lists the changes required as listed in Box 2.2, which though radical are practicable.

Box 2.2: Personal and Professional Changes Required

- To question our values
- To be self-critically aware
- To look beyond simple often as optimal
- To offset our spatial and seasonal biases
- To help local communities do their own analysis
- To stay in locality and learn from and with people
- To test and use participatory approaches
- To change methods and procedures
- To encourage decentralization and diversity
- To put people before things
- To put poor people first of all

Source: Chambers (1993, 1997).

Chambers (1993, 1997) states that such new professionalism tends to threaten the citadels of learning, their traditional textbooks, treadmill teaching, conservative curricula and assurance of timeless knowledge. New professionalism reverses power relations by putting the last first in choice of clients (poor, more deprived), professional values (readiness to learn), research methods (more field-oriented holistic approach) and role (with people as teachers). Such reversals are already happening though gradually and slowly and not enough is happening.

New development professionalism calls for appropriate behaviour. Without appropriate behaviour of an 'outsider', local participants can feel left out, remain withdrawn and not wish to express themselves. In such a case, an opportunity for communication can be lost. Generally, an outsider's entry in any locality could raise questions and curiosity in the minds of local community members. Hence the behaviour of that 'outsider' is essential to remove doubts and to build rapport with the residents of that locality. Not only is the attribute of listening important but learning from others and showing respect is equally important. In such cases, social analysts have pointed out the importance of body language showing respect, concern and a serious intention to learn from others. Non-verbal behaviour is important and one needs to be aware that body language can be quite different in different cultures. For soliciting people's voices, it is important to be a good listener and at the same time ask probing questions. Respectful behaviour can have several advantages. It can help the outsider gain entry or acceptance in a local community. However, distorted behaviour can make for distortion of impressions in the minds of local community members, discourage them from expressing their opinions or can even distort the information required.

2.7.1.8 Improving Individual Skills and Performance

The issue is about improving individual skills and performance. In this context, it is important to appreciate that there are different levels of learning and what a learner can do at those levels. Though each learner needs to be self-aware about individual limitations of faculties and disposition, it is important to strive hard for improving one's learning abilities by moving from one learning level to another. In 1956, a group of education psychologists developed a classification of behaviour important for learning. Commonly known as "Blooms

Taxonomy", it provides us a basis for classifying different types of human behaviour starting from simple to complex. The "Blooms Taxonomy" is shown in Box 2.3 and there are at least 4 levels of learning and what a learner can do at different levels.

Box 2.3: "Blooms Taxonomy"

- *Knowledge level*—identify, name, list, repeat, recognize, state, match and define;
- *Comprehension level*—explain, discuss, interpret, classify, categorize, cite evidence for, compare, contrast, illustrate, give examples of, differentiate and distinguish between;
- *Application level*—demonstrate, calculate, operate, implement, compute, construct, measure, prepare and produce; and
- *Problem-solving level*—troubleshoot, analysis, create, develop, devise, evaluate, formulate, generalize, infer, integrate, invent, plan, predict, re-organize, solve and synthesize.

Note: The verbs described in each category of learning provide an idea of what a learner is able to do at different levels.

2.7.1.9 Learning by Organization

It is not only individuals who need to learn but also organizational learning is important for approaching community voice. In today's dynamic environment, a development organization's ability to learn is critical to its performance. The issue is what are the characteristics and processes of an organization, which wants to learn. In this context, we can draw upon a study done in the corporate sector in May 1993 sponsored by the International Consortium for Executive Development Research in Lexington and the University of Michigan at Ann Arbor, USA. Some findings of the study are as follows: Organizations have different styles of learning. Using three methods of research-literature review, in-depth case studies and survey of 1359 managers from companies around the world—the researchers identified four basic types of organizational learning as shown in Box 2.4.

The study, as above, while drawing general lessons for organizational learning, concludes that process-oriented 'changes' go through a series of phases that, as a whole usually require considerable length of time. Skipping steps create only the illusion of speed and seldom produces a satisfying result. Critical mistakes in any of the learning phases can have a devastating impact, slowing momentum and negating hard won gains. Hence, it is important to take stock of the learning process, monitor it and identify the shortcomings from time to time and ways of overcoming them. In this context, another study by Garvin *et al.* (2008) mentions three broad factors as building blocks for organizational learning and adaptability: a supportive learning environment; concrete learning processes and practices; and leadership behaviour that provides reinforcements.

Box 2.4: Types of Organizational Learning

- *Competence acquisition*—For acquiring competence, organizations cultivate new capabilities in either teams or individuals. They continuously seek new learning to work and promote learning as a fundamental part of their business strategy.
- *Experimentation*—Some organizations experiment with new ideas. They attempt to be first to market with new processes or products.
- *Continuous improvement*—Organizations aiming at continuous improvement strive to master each step in a process before moving on to the next. Their goal is to become the recognized technical leader for a particular process or product.
- *Boundary spanning*—Organizations in this case continuously scan other organizations' efforts, by benchmarking their progress against competitors' and by pursuing information from sources outside their organization.

Source: International Consortium for Executive Development Research in Lexington and the University of Michigan at Ann Arbor, USA, 1993.

2.7.1.10 Ways of Learning

Here the will and the attitude to learn are important for any learning to take place. Our readiness to learn helps us be good listeners. It helps us accept weak, deprived and marginal people as teachers, to learn from their voices about their skills, professions, ways of life, livelihoods, coping strategies, their problems, priorities and preferences. Appropriate probing, body language, patient listening and a positive approach help enrich such learning process by "breaking the ice" and building rapport and trust with local communities. Respectful behaviour of outsiders for local communities tends to create positive vibes in terms of soliciting participation of the latter. In a learning session, provoking or sensitive comments are generally avoided and transparency is maintained with minimum interruptions.

Improving upon personal attitude and behaviour through training programmes is one major way of raising awareness about one's personal qualities and limitations and for acquiring new skills. Good training sessions have proved to be effective in the past for some but not for all since the mode of training has its own limitations, especially when training is a one-off exercise. Even when training is done in a sequence, it is important to create space for other ways of capacity building by other means. Some tested ways to influence attitude and behaviour of any team in an organization are listed in Box 2.5.

Box 2.5: Some Ways to Influence Attitude and Behaviour

- Training,
- Building teams of motivated individuals,
- Periodic performance assessment by peer-group/s,
- Forming informal learning groups,
- Informal discussions with other stakeholders on a periodic basis,
- Holding workshops with local communities/other institutions,
- Holding participatory 'clinics' for resolving field issues,
- Mentoring[2] by seniors,
- Counselling by team members,
- Competing/collaborating[3] in small groups,
- Imitating role models,
- Self-learning from field, and
- Providing incentives/reward for good and creative work.

Any learning to be strong requires opportunities for self-critical reflection. It is important to mention that activities based on participatory approaches require continuous need assessment by the participants. Though most of the generic needs are easy to identify, others crop up at different stages of work. Hence, a first round of capacity building would at best be a starting point and the process can be built upon through a sequence of inputs coupled with self-awareness and self-critical sessions.

2.7.1.11 Role Reversal in the Field

For listening to community voices, it is important to develop keen observation power and the ability to interpret and assess different situations and to appreciate one's role as an outsider. The role of an outsider soliciting community voice is complex, can be chaotic and normally keeps evolving depending on the context and situation. The role of an outsider is not limited to that of a facilitator. Kaplan (1996) writes that pure facilitative fieldwork is not appropriate where there is no activity on the ground to facilitate. In such situations, an outsider soliciting community voice needs to work more as an animator, as activist providing leadership, which is lacking, providing 'voice' in the midst of Freire's oppressed 'culture of silence'. Kaplan (1996) further writes that the same attitude of an activist will appear 'paternalistic and patronising' when the local groups/organizations attain a certain degree of capacity and some confidence to speak their minds. The same attitude becomes detrimental and tends to block mindsets as and when local development makes progress. It is important to recognise that there need to take place shifts in strategies and attitude and ways of interacting with local communities. There are alternative roles of an outsider soliciting community voice as welfare worker, animator, activist and fieldworker facilitating and supporting communities towards self-reliance, consulting and assisting. All these roles call for different strategies and activities as situation demands and often call for differential approaches. Often the practitioner and development agency fails to differentiate between different roles and approaches in development practice. This reflects the underlying tensions in sharing of power. It is important to perceive one's role in community participation as constituting different phases of more dependence, less dependence, little dependence and no dependence. In the ultimate analysis, the local communities' need to voice their views and need to take charge of their own development process and accordingly it is desirable that the dependence on outsiders and outside agencies reduce over time.

2.7.2 Process of Participation

The process of participation in soliciting community voices implies way or ways in which participation occurs or takes place. The process of participation is important for it answers important questions such as who participates in the discussions/activities, how such participation happens, with whom it happens, why and where it happens, how many times it happens, etc. Answers to such questions would indicate the nature, quality, breadth and depth of participation. For instance, the process and quality of participation as reflected in the following aspects leaves much to be desired:

(a) If local community members are forced to participate by order from government;
(b) Only men are asked to participate in a programme and not women;
(c) Poor households participate in meetings in which they have little or no say; and
(d) Such meetings are held in locations situated in well-off areas where poor households feel inhibited to speak openly.

In (a) it is a process of forced participation; in (b) the process of participation discriminates against women and is gender-insensitive; in (c) it is a process of passive participation of poor people and in (d) there is a locational bias in the process in favour of well off areas/ groups. It is important to be aware of such pitfalls in a participatory process and to search for opportunities for mid-way correction so as to make the process more equitable and enabling for the poor, the weak and the deprived to participate.

2.7.2.1 Process of Rapport-Building

A participatory process is involved in the act of establishing communication links with local people. Such a process has its own pace depending on the circumstances. The process of rapport building is neither quick nor a short-term event. Establishing communication links can often be a slow process or it may even fail to happen. Considering that the process of rapport building is a stepping stone to effective participation, conscious efforts are required to build proper rapport with local people. It is a kind of capital investment in participation for obtaining positive results for the present as well as the future. For many governmental and non-governmental agencies, which have demonstrated weak performance in field-situations, the process of 'rapport building' with local communities has been a major gap.

Proper rapport building with local communities is often time-consuming for a variety of reasons. For participatory sessions, people need to be relaxed and also require a reasonable level of trust and faith in the outsiders/external agencies, which are visiting them. To start with, many of them may not appreciate or show interest in participatory sessions/activities and hence, may not be willing to join. Again, some local communities/groups may not be willing to participate beyond a point due to reasons such as lack of time or tiredness and fatigue. If stretched beyond a point, participatory sessions can become unproductive. The community may also lack time for interaction. There are those social characters, *e.g.* gate keepers and musclemen that are skeptical of any outsider approaching their locality. They tend to have strong hold over the community and can influence public opinion, so as not to let an outsider have easy entry into that community. One such experience during the fieldwork on Human Development Report of UNDP Bangladesh (1996) is given in Box 2.6. The experience indicates that we need to be prepared for odd incidents during our interactive field sessions and also try our wit in handling dominant people who tend to obstruct and disturb participatory processes.

Some individuals/groups may casually join for some time and then drop out or not join at all. Sometimes, rapport can be built with local people only when they know that such intervention is going to be of some use to them. In case expectations of local communities from outsiders/external agencies are on the higher side, management of such expectations also becomes important. In case of suspicion by local people of outside agencies, the process of rapport building requires greater effort for clarification of doubts and creation of congenial atmosphere. In any case, it is important for outsiders/external agencies to clarify their objectives right from the beginning. This also helps in not raising expectations of local community members unnecessarily.

Box 2.6: With the Help of a Muscleman

> ...We went to Madhya Bagra again on the second day of our field visit. While entering the village, we were confronted by a young man, who rudely told us that we could not enter the village because we should not disturb the women as it was their day for paying installments to the local Grameen Bank. We suggested that some women had asked us to visit them and we would make sure not to talk to those women who had to pay their installments. We were firmly told by the young man that this was not possible. We saw Farook standing close-by, whom we had met the previous day. We immediately asked him to help us interact with those women who were not paying installments on that day. Farook had observed our work the earlier day and was favourably disposed towards us. He told the others that they should cooperate with us. We were surprised since Farook was exceedingly rude to us the previous day and had disturbed our interactive sessions. His attitude had changed after he had observed what we were doing and he was convinced that our intentions were genuine. The young man that we had met also stopped harassing us once Farook intervened. We later discovered that Farook was a local muscleman, but he was very helpful to us.

Source: From the field notes of Neela Mukherjee on village Madhya Bagra, Bangladesh, January 1996.

2.7.2.2 Pace of Interactive Process

The process of direct participation with people is basically a learning process and has its own pace which varies with time, communities, groups, facilitators of participation, issues at hand, ways, motivation, location, expectations, etc. Participation is relatively easy in communities, which are more equitable, relatively cohesive and smaller in size. In case a local community is not a homogenous entity, participatory processes with community members as a whole and with different groups provide clue to subsequent ways of improving upon such participation.

2.7.3 Process of 'Sharing'

'Sharing' is dissemination of learning arising from participatory sessions and activities. Learning from local communities helps create a joint pool of voice-based data, knowledge/information, which also needs to be shared with others for further learning to take place. Such learning from individuals, groups and communities at a local level when shared with others enrich the learning process and help in emphasizing local perspectives. Sharing is an integral part in soliciting community voices. Without sharing participation becomes a limited engagement. Unless the local people are willing to share their views and time, the outsiders cannot learn from them. Sharing is also important for cross-checking of things learnt and their validation. The process of sharing leads to new points, provides new insights, provides opportunities to those left out from stating their views, generates additional information and helps in analysis and validation of data.

2.7.3.1 How 'Sharing' Helps?

The significance of the process of sharing as the fourth pillar for community voice is listed below:

- Sharing process reinforces learning from, with and by local communities.
- Sharing process increases transparency and understanding. Sharing enriches analysis, provides opportunities to clarify issues, fill gaps, highlight different perspectives of any problem, and helps revise, add, alter and make changes.
- Sharing process helps overcoming hidden barriers in communication. It provides opportunities to those who are not self-starters to come forward and to express their opinions and ideas. Some people come forward only when they listen to the ideas which others have offered.
- It throws up opportunities for exchange of ideas, discussions and follow-ups.
- It helps in intra- and inter-group resolution of conflicts amongst local groups/communities and outsiders. Sharing helps in clarifying doubts and resolving issues.
- It helps in cross-checking of errors and omissions.
- It helps identify areas of co-ordination and co-operation between community members and others such as outsiders/ relevant agencies.
- It helps identify resource persons.

2.7.4 Diverse Voice Tools

Though attitude and behaviour conducive to participation are essential prerequisites for outsiders to listen to community voice, they are not sufficient. Skills in tools and methods are also important, so are the skills as facilitators and also their role. Such tools for soliciting community voice needs to be appreciated in a setting which is flexible, unstructured, broad, innovative and continuously evolving. A range of voice tools has been discussed in Chapter 3 of this book. In the following chapters of this book we shall see the inventory of voice tools, and also the fact that use of different voice tools depends on the kind of inquiry, objectives at hand, local situation and processes data requirements, the resource/topic/issue in question and facilitator's capabilities.

NOTES

1. Also see Chambers (1991, 1993 and 1994).
2. In mentoring, a close relationship with a senior staff in that organization with proven behaviour and skill is likely to keep a young staff open and yearning for growth. Organizations can nurture such relationship by assigning mentors to junior staff members. The mentor has to create effective channels of communication, inspire and instil values in the junior, encourage positive attitude, and discourage cynicism and negative attitude in the junior. This would increase the confidence of junior staff mentored upon, open channels of communication and influence way of thinking and thereby create opportunities for attitudinal change.
3. Some people change their behaviour after observing others at work. Teams of junior and senior members of an organization undertaking fieldwork can also help to influence behaviour in case such teams operate on the basis of democratic values. Long fieldwork and travel can strengthen personal relationships and help in better understanding and inculcation of team spirit. Sometimes incentives and rewards also provide a moral boost to appropriate behaviour.

REFERENCES

Chambers, Robert (1993). *Challenging the Professions Frontiers for Rural Development*, Intermediate Technology Publications, London.

—— (1997), *Whose Reality Counts? Putting the first last*, IT Publications, London.

Garvin, David A., A. C. Edmondson and Francesca Gino (2008). "Is Yours a Learning Organization?", *Harvard Business Review*. South Asia. March. hbrasia.org.

Kaplan, Allan (1996). *The Development Practitioners' Handbook*. Pluto Press. London.

Max-Neef. A. Manfred, Antonio, Elizalde and Martin, Hopenthayn (1991). *Human Scale Development: Conception. Application and Further Reflections*. The Apex Press, New York.

Mukherjee, Neela (1993). *Participatory Rural Appraisal. Methodology & Applications*, Concept Publishing Co., New Delhi.

Mukherjee, Neela (2002). *Participatory Learning and Action with 100 Field Methods*. Concept Publishing Co., New Delhi.

3

Community Voice Tools – An Overview

This chapter describes a range of community voice tools/mechanisms, key stakeholders involved in such tools and related institutional mechanisms. Towards mapping community voice, this chapter brings together 27 voice tools, which constitute two sets—one is for participatory assessments, while the other is for social accountability. Some of the tools have been described with the help of simple illustrations from the field, while others have been mentioned based on reference to literature in the field. The subsequent chapters in this book show how mapping of selected voice tools is emerging from different locations and places and how their integration at different levels can actually help construct larger pictures of such community voice.

Community voice when given space helps reveal community views and opinion; provide facts, issues, assessments and ideas; indicate people's analysis; and help towards learning, planning, exploring, monitoring, evaluating, owning and getting engaged in related actions. Participatory methodologies help community voice emerge and in that way embedded in diversity and pluralism, they can be important drivers and means to personal, institutional, professional and social change (Chambers: 2008).

As indicated above, the 27 voice tools listed below are of two generic types—(A) those related to Participatory Assessments; and (B) those related to Social Accountability. Both types can be combined as and when required.

(A) The voice tools related to *Participatory Assessments* have a much broader ambit and are applied for different objectives and purposes as required. Participatory assessments are flexible and relatively unstructured. They can be applied singly and/or combined depending on the context, location, group, theme, component, activity and sector to be assessed.

(B) The voice tools related to *Social Accountability* have a relatively narrow domain of 'accountability' dimension. By 'accountability' is meant relationship between bearer of a right or a legitimate claim and the agents or agencies responsible for fulfilling that right or that legitimate claim. Social Accountability involves transparency and openness in taking decisions and actions; answerability to justify those decisions publicly and controllability or checks and balances (Gloppen *et al.*: 2003).

Box 3.1: Tools for Participatory Assessments

(i) Participatory Poverty Assessment
(ii) Participatory Priority/Need Assessment and Problem Analysis
(iii) Participatory Planning and Action
(iv) Sustainable Livelihoods Assessment
(v) Participatory Empowerment Assessment
(vi) Participatory Assessment of Social Capital
(vii) Integrated Participatory Poverty Assessment
(viii) Participatory Process Assessment
(ix) Participatory Impact/Outcome Assessment
(x) Integrated Impact Assessment
(xi) Participatory Monitoring and Evaluation
(xii) Participatory Public Policy Making
(xiii) Constructing Picture/Word Picture
(xiv) Most Significant Change Tool

Tools related to Social Accountability when based on community voice through application of participatory tools help build synergy in terms of inclusion of multiple perspectives and objectives and also help achieve better results. The voice tools as per their generic types are listed in Boxes 3.1 and 3.2.

Each voice tool has been explained below and some of them have been illustrated from the field. Only four voice tools—(a) Participatory Poverty Assessment (b) Sustainable Livelihoods Assessment, (c) Integrated Participatory Poverty Assessment, and

(d) Voice Tool for Assessing Governance have been explained in detail in this book in Chapters 4, 5, 6 and 7, respectively.

Box 3.2: Tools for Social Accountability

(i) Citizens' Report Card
(ii) Citizen's Voice Card
(iii) Citizens' Participation in Public Policy Making
(iv) Participatory Budgeting
(v) Public Expenditure Tracking/Monitoring
(vi) Family Satisfaction Survey
(vii) Citizen Monitoring of Public Service Delivery
(viii) Citizens' Advisory Boards
(ix) Social Audit
(x) Special Accountability Institutions, e.g. Human Rights Commission
(xi) Lobbying and Advocacy Campaigns
(xii) Pro-Poor Public Interest Litigation
(xiii) People's Court

3.2. Tools for Participatory Assessments as listed in Box 3.1 are described below with field illustrations.

3.2.1 Participatory Poverty Assessment—Participatory Poverty Assessment is situational analysis of poverty mostly done by key stakeholders from the 'bottom'—the poor and marginalized groups of women and men in their own 'voice'. It helps flag important lessons and insights for furthering their cause and provides people's inputs, assessments and suggestions towards policy-making and practice. The PPA process helps involve key stakeholders in assessing development polices and programmes, in revealing their priorities and preferences, and in creating space for their "ownership" of the development process. For an illustration of PPA *see* Chapter 4.

3.2.2. Participatory Need/Priority Assessment and Problem Analysis—Participatory Need/Priority Assessment is a way in which people—men, women and children—reveal their own priorities and preferences, rank them, describe them and also suggest how and to what extent they can be fulfilled. It is a way in which people assess their own needs, analyze them, identify important factors and sometimes devise their own solutions to meet such needs. Table 3.1 is an example of a list of priority needs ranked by low income households from a commune in Cambodia during a priority needs' assessment.

Table 3.1: Priority Needs as Expressed by Low Income Rural Groups

Priority Needs of Low Income Groups	*Rank*	*Recommendation/Suggestion for External Development Authority*
Drought-Proofing	1	Drill well and rehabilitate ancient canal (start food for work programme)
Techniques to increase supply of food to overcome shortage (rice)	2	Drill well and also have measures for improvement of production technique
Better human health support	3	—
Better animal health support	4	Improve quality of village livestock and train farmers on improved animal raising technique
Inputs for soil fertility	5	Supply fertilizers to farmers at a reasonable prices

Notes: Field session facilitated by Sereyvath; the priority needs are ranked as the perspectives of the group.

Location: Commune Chrok Meas, Cambodia.

3.2.2a Participatory Problem-Solution Analysis—Through participatory problem solution analysis the voice tool helps profile problems, their prioritization and helps suggest ways to resolve such problems. Examples of community problem listing by different community groups from Commune Chrok Meas, Cambodia are given in Tables 3.1, 3.2 and 3.3. In Table 3.1, such problems listed also have description of the related issues concerned. Table 3.1 illustrates problem listing, its description, scoring to indicate priority of a problem and ranking of problems. Table 3.2 lacks description of the problems but has a list of problems (col. i), ranking of the problems (col. ii), ways to solve the problem (col. iii) and specific suggestions for local development authority (col. iv). Table 3.3 also provides people's insights into the problems concerned along with ranks and recommendations.

3.2.3 Participatory Planning and Action—Voice tools help community plan at local levels. Such micro-level planning is generally indicative and includes different issues in planning such as "why", "what", "where", "how much", "how" and "when", opportunity

Table 3.2: Problem Identification, Description, Problem Scoring and Ranking

Problem-Listing (Col. i)	Problem 1 (Col. ii)	Problem 2 (Col. iii)	Problem 3 (Col. iv)	Problem 4 (Col. v)	Problem 5 (Col. vi)	Problem 6 (Col. vii)
Problem categories	Irrigation re-habilitation	Rural road upgrading	Lack of capital	Disease prevention	Large areas of barren hill and waste land	Cultural-social problem
Problem description	Irrigation scheme has been damaged by typhoon, flood-subsidiary canals have not been built, so water has not flowed into fields in that area	Rural roads are still narrow and much eroded. The drainage system on the two side of roads remain to be done	Capital is needed for breeding of shrimps, crabs, cage fish • There is lack of capital for poultry/cattle breeding • There is lack of capital for undertaking agricultural service expansion	There is lack of technical staff and also technical support	Forest has got damaged; soil has become much eroded There are 200 ha of barren hill and waste lands	People's cultural standard is still low. Villagers still throw rabbits and dead animals into the roads. Rural roads are much muddy and dirty after rain and flood. All these cause pollution in the village.
Scoring	10	9	8	7	8	9
Rank	1	2	3	4	3	2

Note; The higher the score the greater is the weight of the problem concerned.

Table 3.3: Problem Ranking and Solutions, Commune Chrok Meas, Cambodia

Problems (Col. i)	*Rank (Col. ii)*	*Ways to Solve the problem (Col. iii)*	*Suggestions (Col. iv)*
Lack of food	7	Selling labour by migrating for jobs to Phnom Penh during dry season Do fishing to buy food in rainy season	It is requested that food for work scheme may start to dig a canal or a pond
Village flooded with rain water and occurrence of recurrent Droughts	5	The better off cultivate dry season rice by using tube-well irrigation.	A drainage system can be constructed A tube-well and a motor-pump can also be installed
Lack of rural road	4	—	A rural road needs to be constructed
Human illness	4	Need for private health worker and would pay for their services By use of traditional medicines	A health centre could be opened and a health staff could work in the village
Lack of security	3	Sometime they cannot sleep at night due to problems of insecurity	A permanent police post can be opened in the village
Low income	2	There was no discussion on this matter	There was no discussion on this matter
Lack of clean water	1	There was no discussion on this matter	There was no discussion on this matter
Lack of capital for buying chemical fertilizer	1	There was no discussion on this matter	There was no discussion on this matter

Note: Facilitated by Suon Seng.

Table 3.4: Problem Listing, Causal Analysis and Suggestions, Commune Chrok Meas, Cambodia

Problems	*Rank*	*Causes*	*Suggestions*
Drought for 7 years since 1996	0	• natural disaster • upland area • no water resource	Support food for work scheme to construct dam and reconstruct natural canal
Less land for rice production and low fertility	5	• lack of irrigated water • sandy soil structure • no techniques to improve soil quality • soil erosion	Provide technical skills training on agricultural management: plantation, making compost, land management Plant trees to protect soil erosion
No non-farm work	3	• no skills • no creative thinking	Provide technical skills training Provide vocational training with equipment support
Animal epidemic diseases	2	• no raising techniques • no hygiene • insufficient food • no vaccination for prevention and treatment • low quality of breeds	Provide animal raising techniques Provide vaccination and good breeds Appoint village vets with equipment support
Many children	0	• lack of education	Establish health centre and productive health
No cattle	5	• high mortality • no vaccination for prevention and treatment • no money to buy ox or buffalo	Provide animal raising techniques Support cow and buffalo banks Establish community raising of animals
Illiteracy	4	• no school and teacher in village • primary school is far from village • children work in farms	Establish literacy group Parents need to be conscious and allow their children to attend school
Lack of enough food consumption	0	• drought • soil infertility • low rice yield • no agricultural technique	Raise awareness about soil improvement and making compost
Many patients	4	• no health care centre • malnutrition • no sanitation in each family • no money to buy medicines	Establish health care centres Establish village health worker Promote comprehensive sanitation and family health

(*Contd.*)

(*Contd.*)

Problems	*Rank*	*Causes*	*Suggestions*
No irrigation system	4	• upland area • water resource is far from rice fields • no study from Provincial Department of Water Resources and Meteorology • existing canal eroded	Construct dam, village pond and reconstruct canal
No equipment and materials for rice production	2	• no money to buy materials and equipment	Establish cash credit and fertilizer bank
Violence in family	0	• Poor family • Low education • Not gender sensitive • Jealousy	Promote gender sensitivity

Note: Facilitated by Suon Seng

costs, risks, types of beneficiaries, related project activities, expected constraints, benefits, maintenance, mutual roles and activities and estimates. Such planning overviews can help draw detailed action plans as required. The following provides an illustration of participatory micro-level planning with local community for sand dune fixation and tree planting.

Table 3.5: Preliminary Participatory Micro-Level Plan on Sand Dune fixation, Quang Binh, Vietnam

Participatory Action Plan with Local Community	*Plantation Species-Acacia*	*Plantation Species-Coconut*	*Plantation Species-Eucalyptus*	*Plantation Species Tree such as Casuarinas*
Sand Dune fixation				
Wood				
Fuel Wood				
Fruit				
Why required to be planted? for sand dune fixation)	To avoid Drought	For humidity	Can suffer Drought	Can suffer Drought

(*Contd.*)

(Contd.)

Participatory Action Plan with Local Community	Plantation Species-Acacia	Plantation Species-Coconut	Plantation Species-Eucalyptus	Plantation Species Tree such as Casuarinas
Area to be planted	60 ha	10 ha	30 ha	150 ha
No. of Plants needed	300,000	4000	150,000	750,000
Where they need to be planted?	Foot hill	Valley	Hill top	Hill strip
How can they be planted?	1 ha is given to each household for plantation and maintenance			
When can they be planted?	In June and July the nursery can get started; Plantation could be done in the coming months of December and November			
What are the expected opportunities?	Labour force is available so jobs will get created;			
What are the expected difficulties?	At present there is lack of capital for seedlings and materials (cost of planting eucalyptus estimated); lack of techniques for plantation; complex geography; and some areas are distant.			
What options are available?	2.6 ha of nursery is needed & labour force can be mobilised from the locality			
What are the risks?	Unfavourable climate; diseases of plants; cows and buffaloes can destroy plants			
Activities by the project	Provision for polythene bags: 930,000 bags; Provision of seeds; Provision of Capital for fertiliser and pumps - 4 pumps @ 7.000.000 dong = 28.000.000 dong Wages for maintenance Wages for plantation = 135 labour @ 11.000 dong for 250 days = 337.500.000 dong			
Activities by others	Different commune allocate land to farmers; and forest department provides techniques			
Activities by farmers Protection and Maintenance Plan	Wages for nursery, plantation and protection: 1. Every household is responsible for maintenance and protection of 4 ha of sand dune fixation 2. Wages for protection in 3 years is 250 ha * 25 people * 12 months * 300,000 * 3 years = 273;750000 dong			
Who are the Beneficiaries?	1. Poor farmers will benefit from the nursery and forest 2. All the farmers will benefit from the planted forest			
What kinds of Benefits?	1. Wages for nursery 2. Wages for protection 3. Sand dune fixation 4. Catchment area protection 5. Fruit collection and fuel wood			
Estimates	A total of 952,250,000 dong is needed			

Note: Facilitator- Lam: Village Analysts - Women group of Thon Trung, Vo Ninh Commune, Quang Ninh District, Quang Binh Province, Vietnam.

For those areas with low literacy, such participatory micro plans can be done with the help of symbols[1], using cards, seeds and scoring, using interviews and emphasizing simple problem-solution approach.

3.2.4 Sustainable Livelihoods Assessment (SLA)—SLA aims to improve the lives of poor people and to strengthen their livelihoods. It is based on people's own perspectives and priorities for their livelihoods. SLA can be described as a way in which people discuss their assets related to livelihoods, the vulnerability conditions under which assets exist, the livelihoods preferences and the outcomes, the policies, institutions and processes which influence livelihoods and the do-ables thereby. SLA centres on people's livelihood-related activities and aims at mainstreaming environment within a broader framework.

The framework of SLA helps progress towards the following purpose:

- Define the scope and provide analytic base for livelihoods-related analysis.
- Help understand and manage the complexities of people's livelihoods.
- Become a shared point of reference for all those who are engaged in supporting livelihoods for making their contributions.
- The SLA framework explicitly links the micro level analysis with the macro picture and emphasizes that policy and institutional analysis must take place at all levels—from local to higher levels.
- No agency can work alone and hence partnerships are crucial.

For illustrations on the SLA tools and applications see Chapter 5.

3.2.5 Participatory Empowerment Assessment—People can assess their own degree/s of empowerment by means of participatory tools adapted to local situation. Such tools are flexible and their strength lies in the ways that they can be moulded to suit local context, circumstances and issues. In this section the issue of empowerment has been explored through Venn diagram (better known as 'Chappati' diagrams) based on field experience from India. In recent years, there has taken place innovation and adaptation in chappati/institutional diagramming at the field level so as to tailor them to measure "ownership", "empowerment", "decision-making", involvement", "relationship", "accountability", "participation" and other social aspects of institutional development. Such adaptations have taken place in the field during participatory sessions related to impact assessment/participatory evaluation of rural institutions in different projects. Such diagrams are explained below.

3.2.5.1 Venn ('Chappati') Institutional Diagramming—Chappati/ Venn diagrams are useful in study of relationships of institutions/ individuals with local communities. Venn/Chappati/Institutional diagramming is a "visual" method to represent the role of individuals/ institutions and their importance in decision-making. In such diagrams, circle/s of different sizes represent individual/s and/or institution/s, whose size shows its degree of importance in local decision-making and the overlapping of circles indicate overlapping in decision making. Overlapping of circles arises when one institution/ individual interacts with another institution or individual in which case the circles overlap on one another. Such overlaps may be large or small depending on the extent of interaction. If the circles are separate, the institutions have no contact and if they touch each other there is information passing between institutions. Strong/weak linkages between two institutions represented by two circles can also be shown by steady/broken lines/arrows.

> *"Ownership/ Empowerment" Chappati*—A variation of the usual Venn/Chappati diagram termed as Ownership/Empowerment Chappati (much depends on the aspect under discussion whether "ownership", "empowerment" or some other criteria) can be applied to different locations/groups/communities for studying relationships within members of local institutions such as self-help groups, user-groups and other village-based institutions. In such Ownership/ Empowerment Chappati, the participants construct their Chappati diagram (a single Venn diagram) on ownership/empowerment of each individual and identify the individual's socio-economic group based on indigenous criteria. As a "visual" output the advantage is that with proper facilitation, the control of the interactive process can be held by the local group members who are involved in constructing such Empowerment/Ownership diagram. It is best to use different labels in the diagram, depending on whether "ownership" or "empowerment" is being analysed.

3.2.5.1.1 *Illustration of "Ownership" Chappati*—In one village, for example, this tool was applied for learning about "ownership" aspects of members within the local self-help groups (SHGs). For this purpose, a big size chart paper was taken and the members of one local women SHG helped each other draw a circle with the aid of a round-shaped metal plate. The centre-point of the circle represented the highest degree of "ownership" and points away from it showed lower degree of the same. The names of the members of the SHG were written on small chits of paper and discussed in terms of individual feelings of ownership for such local institution. Based on this information the names of the members were then placed near the centre point or away from it depending on the degree of "ownership" revealed by each member based on local criteria. For informing the "ownership" Chappati the socio-economic status of households (whether poor, medium or rich) was also indicated against the names of the members with the help of symbols. This helped in self-assessment of "ownership" of different social strata in the village and also in terms of furthering project objective of involving poor people in that locality. See Box 3.3.

3.2.5.1.2 Some related points depicted by the 'ownership' Chappati as in Box 3.3 are indicated below:

(a) The degree of institutional ownership by its members and high/low ownership and the criteria for determining such ownership.
(b) Those who participated and benefited from institutions and the extent of their participation and benefit.
(c) The sense of responsibility and the degree of accountability of individuals towards institutions and the extent of participation in decision-making.
(d) The degree of empowerment accompanying the process of ownership, which has taken place through the institution in question.
(e) Names of the individual/s empowered and still to be empowered/not empowered.

3.2.5.1.3 Another field-based illustration of empowerment assessment from the village of Kheda Rasulpur, Kota, Rajasthan, India shows the following. It was a group-assessment done by the members of women self-help groups, (where each exercise was done in separate session and location) for a women's empowerment project. The group-evaluation was based on criteria, which evolved locally through discussion amongst its group members. It was to measure

Box 3.3: "Ownership" Chappati of Village-level Organization

Village Siriyo, Rishikesh, Uttaranchal (Now Uttarakhand), India:

One issue explored was about the sense of ownership of village level organization called Garema (a term used for village-based community organizations facilitated by the project) by its members. Whether the members owned Garema and its activities and if so to what extent? The members considered four aspects for constructing such an Ownership Chappati (a circular space) for Garema (see Chart 3.1) in which names of all members were ranked as per the criteria. The four aspects were in terms of four axes of Empowerment Circle (a circular space) namely,

- Attendance in meeting,
- Engagement in plantation work in the villages,
- Taking responsibility and volunteering, and
- Awareness level about role of village-level federation named Corema (a term used for inter-village-based organization representing federation of Garema).

About attendance in meetings only three members were attending them with utmost regularity while some other members had better attendance than the rest. About plantation activities, the members of Garema were ranked as per their involvement in such activities. About taking responsibility, only four members were good at discharging responsibility about Garema's activities. Regarding level of awareness about Corema only four members were aware and took interest in such activities.

Hence, as shown by the above indicators, the "ownership" of Garema varied amongst its members and was at a higher level for a limited number of members, who were enthusiastic, took initiative and responsibility and appreciated the utility of federated structure such as Corema.

Note: This tool was applied for assessment of Doon Valley Watershed Project, Dehradun, India.

Chart 3.1: Empowerment/Ownership Chappati

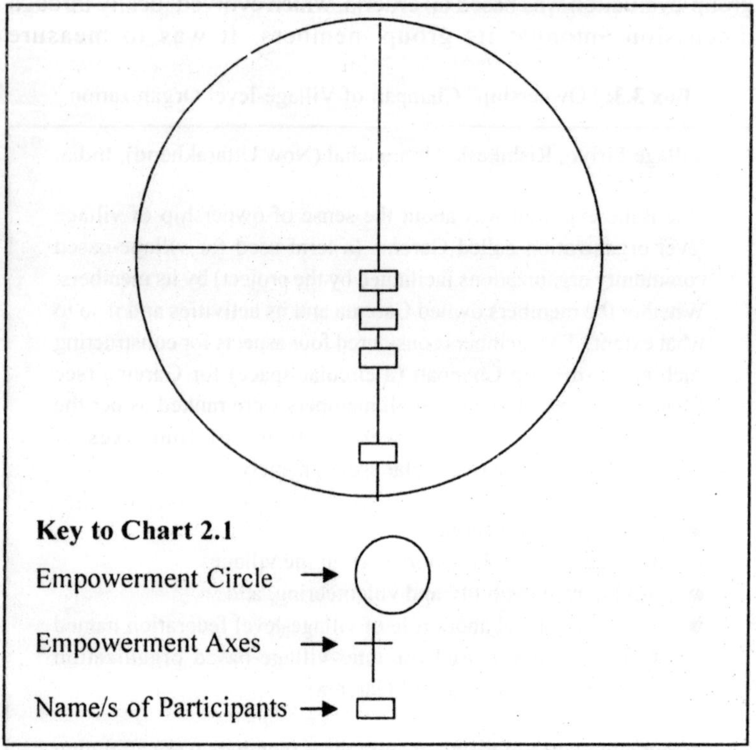

women's empowerment for which the "empowerment chappati" was applied by the members and the information generated was useful as lessons learnt in the course of end-of-project evaluation was carried out by the members themselves. The women found the tool empowering in the sense that they could evolve their own criteria based on their project objectives and then evaluate them in terms of what they thought was empowering and arrive at degree/s of such empowerment for each member.

At first, the members listed the objectives of the Mahila Mandal (self-help group of women) and then they together did the Empowerment Chappati based on such objectives. There were three Empowerment Chappati's constructed separately by the three self-help groups of women which showed how individual members of the three groups performed in their own groups. It had four axes, based on which women group assessed four aspects of their respective

SHGs from the central point of the Empowerment Chappati as indicated above. The four aspects were as follows:

- Number of persons they motivated for literacy,
- Number of persons motivated for family planning,
- Their income from (tailoring) skills acquired through project activities, and
- Increase in courage and confidence, on an individual basis.

Empowerment as measured by self-help group members included their achievement in terms of providing motivation for literacy and that for family planning. They thought that the self-help group movement had enabled them to reduce female illiteracy in that locality and also helped empower other women (non-members) in terms of having small families. Both indicators showed contribution towards women's progress by self-help group members. The three charts showing empowerment of individual members of different self-help groups of women were collated for gaining an overall picture as shown in Table 3.6. Summary results are indicated below:

Table 3.6: Overall Picture of Empowerment of Women Self-Help Groups

Names of Members	*Number motivated for literacy*	*Number motivated for family planning*	*Income generation (in Indian Rupees)*	*Increase in confidence and courage (Number of individuals)*
(i) Performance of Mahila Mandal 1. "Rajlakhsmi Sahayta Samuh"	265	355	83,000	High—3 Medium—2 Low—7
(ii) Performance of Mahila Mandal 2. "Anand Sahayta Samuh"	111	458	260,000	High—3 Medium—3 Low—5
(iii) Performance of Mahila Mandal 3. "Bajrang Sahayta Samuh"	235	348	157,000	High—3 Medium—1 Low—7
Total Numbers	611	1161	500,000	High—9 Medium—6 Low—19

Note: From the Field Notes of Neela Mukherjee, Participatory Health Assessment of Project on Reproductive Health, State Institute of Family Welfare, Rajasthan for Population Concern UK.

Table 3.6 shows wide variations in terms of empowerment of individual members of self-help groups across the three groups. The table shows that the members of self-help groups 1 and 3 had performed better in motivating others for literacy classes while those of group 2 had motivated higher number of individuals for family planning practices. In terms of generating income from skills acquired through the project, group 2 had performed better while members of group 3 had a slight edge with regard to increase in courage and confidence as compared to other groups.

- In terms of numbers, those motivated for family planning seems to be higher than those motivated to join literacy class, which is clearly pronounced in all the three self-help groups. One plausible reason was that there were not many individuals to be motivated for joining literacy classes since in that village the literacy rate was relatively high.
- In terms of income generation through skill building (e.g. sewing and tailoring skills) the range financial empowerment was between INR 60,000 to none. Skill building helped in sourcing of livelihood for many women and led to income generation.
- There were positive changes in courage and confidence of most women members though the change in position of individual members as placed in the Empowerment Chappati or Venn diagram showed wide variations. For few such positive change was high with a major increase in courage and confidence, while for some it was on a medium range and for many others such change was on the lower side.

3.2.5.1.4 Some lessons learnt from empowerment assessment exercises are listed below:

(a) The concept of using the symbol of "Chappati" or Indian wheat bread was dear to the heart of women. They prepared Chappati on a daily basis and served their family members as food. Men liked eating them and hence felt close to such food item.

(b) Placement/Ranking by members requires group discussion to be free of bias to the extent possible.

(c) There is a process of 'warming up' before the exercise is done. This generally involves discussion of objectives and activities of the institution/s under reference.

(d) Listing and then ranking/grouping of institutions in terms of their significance/relevance helps in construction of Empowerment Chappati by groups.

(e) Empowerment Chappati followed by analysis of criteria and possible action/s is generally more effective.

(f) Well being grouping after construction of Empowerment Chappati helps provide insight into the issue of "whose empowerment/ownership?" and "how much?"

3.2.5.1.5 Some limitations are indicated below:

- In case of institutions with large number of members such diagramming can become a time consuming exercise.
- Much discussion is required for placement of names of members on the Empowerment/Ownership Chappati and conflicts often arise, which need to be resolved amicably.
- Placement of names on the Empowerment Chappati becomes easier when considerable discussions have taken place amongst the participants.

3.2.6 Participatory Assessment of Social Capital—Uphoff (2000) writes all forms of capital can be understood as *assets* of various kinds, however, they were created. Assets are things that yield streams of benefit that make future productive processes more efficient, more effective, more innovative, or simply expanded. Social capital is an accumulation of various types of social, psychological, cultural, cognitive, institutional and related assets that increase the amount (or probability) of mutually beneficial cooperative behaviour. This is the behaviour that is productive for others as well as for one's self. Narayan (1999) states that the term 'social capital' "refers in general to the glue that holds groups and societies together through bonds of shared values, norms and institutions." The terms—social capital, social capability, social exclusion and social engagement are inter-related. Sen and Dreze (1995) are of the view that the term "social opportunity" can imply social capital. Sen (1997) defines social capability "as the ability to take part in the life of the community, to participate in social activities, to have a sense of belonging in the larger groups." Narayan (1999) defines social exclusion broadly to the societal and institutional processes that exclude certain groups from full participation in the social, economic, cultural and political life of societies. There are overlaps between the terms social exclusion and social capital.

Mutual trust and cooperation amongst members of communities is a significant factor explaining institutional performance (Putnam *et al.*: 1993). Drawing from Putnam *et al.* (1993) the features of social organization that enhance trust and cooperation increase societies' well being by making institutions more democratic and efficient in delivering public goods and services. Field evidence points out that when active involvement is sought of local communities for organizing themselves based on their knowledge and experience in planning and implementation of projects, the higher becomes the possibility of sustaining development initiatives (Cernea: 1991; Pretty: 1995; Pretty *et al.*: 2001; Mukherjee: 1997; Mukherjee: 2004 a,b, Uphoff:1992; Krishna and Uphoff:1999. Serra (2001) attempted measurement of social capital at the national level. Field results are indicative of the fact that social capital formation at the local level is crucial for natural resource management/protection. In a study of 64 villages in Rajasthan, India, Krishna and Uphoff (1999) found that an index of social capital variables is positively and consistently correlated with superior development outcomes in watershed activities.

Such measurement of social capital is important at the local level for reasons more than one. It provides an idea of the progress made by local institutions in terms of building social capital. Uphoff (2000) writes that if social capital is successfully understood then "it offers the prospect of our being able to create a stream of benefits that justify the expenditure involved". Uphoff (2000) adds that social capital is attractive to government and development agencies because it could enable decision-makers to make investments that increase the efficiency and chances of success for development initiative. Krishna and Uphoff (1999) conclude that purposive action to enhance social capital can be undertaken by acting on its constituent factors. Their field results show that though "history" of social capital matters, it does not determine much of stock of social capital of a household or village. It can also be applied as a participatory monitoring and impact assessment tool (Bond and Mukherjee: 2001) for finding out areas of weaknesses and strengths and undertaking mid-way corrections, if any, for strengthening social capital.

While analysing types of social capital, Uphoff (2000) distinguishes between structural and cognitive forms of social capital. Structural category is associated with various forms of social organization, rules, roles, procedures, and networks, which contribute to a stream of benefits resulting from social capital. Cognitive category of social capital derives from mental processes, norms, values, attitude and belief that contribute to collective action. Uphoff (2000) writes that both structural and cognitive forms are "the mechanisms by which social capital is built up and accumulated—stored, modified, expressed and perpetuated". He also mentions how structural and cognitive forms of social capital can erode fast and can be destroyed fairly quickly as compared to building up of such capital, which takes time.

Table 3.7: Criteria for Measuring Threshold Level of Social Capital

Criteria for Productivity	*Criteria for Equity*	*Criteria for Sustainability*	*Criteria of Empowerment*
1. Group membership, keenness, leadership and sense of responsibility 2. Group capacity and level of confidence 3. Status of financial capital base 4. External linkages, both vertical and horizontal 5. Technologies and improvement	1. Broad-based understanding of group activities and worldview 2. Group participation in decision-making 3. Equity in benefit-flows 4. Livelihood impacts and reduction in vulnerability	1. Vision/Ideas for future 2. Group-based resource regeneration/ conservation 3. Internal norms, mutual trust and role clarity 4. Group attachment/ ownership 5. Ability to raise issues and resolve conflict 6. Maintenance of asset	1. Social inclusion and emotional well being 2. Freedom to function as a group and power to influence decision-making 3. Power "within" and power "with" 4. Access to information and responsive governance 5. Transparent decision-making from 'above'

Source: Derived from Mukherjee (2002), Forest Protection Committees of West Bengal: *Measuring Social Capital* in Joint Forest Management, (see www.livelihoods.org)

In this context one oft-repeated question is why are some local level institutions relatively successful than others in managing localized resources. Do they have more social capital than others? What then could be the reasonable constituents of social capital and how do they influence management of resources? The core issue in this context is how to measure social capital. At the local level, the instrument of social capital, so critical to develop human freedom, is determined by a range of criteria, as indicated below, which in turn, influence the collective achievement of common goals/objectives by the community/group involved . Tables 3.7 and 3.8 provide a list of criteria for measuring social capital and some field estimates of social capital for self-help groups, respectively.

Table 3.8: Criteria for Assessing Social Capital of Self-Help Groups/ Communities: An Illustration

Criteria for Assessing Changes in Social Capital	*SHG 1 – Village W (Base Year: 2005)*	*SHG 2 – Village X (Base Year: 2005)*	*SHG 3– Village Y (Base Year: 2005)*	*SHG 4 – Village Z (Base Year: 2005)*
Productivity				
1. Group membership, keenness, leadership and sense of responsibility	1	1	3	4
2. Group capacity and level of confidence	1	1	3	4
3. Status of growth in financial capital	1	1	1	2
4. External linkages–vertical and horizontal	1	1	2	2
5. Technologies and improvement	1	1	1	1
Equity				
6. Broad-based understanding of group activities and worldview	1	2	3	4
7. Group participation in decision-making	1	1	2	2
8. Equity in benefit-flows	1	1	4	4
9. Livelihood impacts and reduction in vulnerabilities	1	1	5	2
Sustainability				
10. Vision/Ideas for future	1	1	3	4
11. Group-based natural resource regeneration/ conservation	1	1	4	4

(*Contd.*)

(*Contd.*)

Criteria for Assessing Changes in Social Capital	*SHG 1 – Village W (Base Year: 2005)*	*SHG 2 – Village X (Base Year: 2005)*	*SHG 3– Village Y (Base Year: 2005)*	*SHG 4 – Village Z (Base Year: 2005)*
12. Internal norms, mutual trust and role clarity	1	1	3	3
13. Group attachment/ownership	1	1	2	3
14. Ability to raise issues and resolving conflict	1	1	2	2
15. Maintenance of asset/s	1	1	3	4
16. Social inclusion and emotional well being	1	2	6	4
17. Freedom to function as a groups and power to influence decision-making	1	1	4	4
18. Power "within" and power "with"	1	1	3	3
19. Access to information and responsive governance	1	1		
20. Transparent decision-making from 'above'	1	1	3	3
Total score	20/120	22/120	57/120	63/120
Total score on 100	16.7	22.5	47.5	52.5

Note 1: Qualitative Scoring: Measurement of social opportunity is based on scoring on 20 criteria, as follows: 1=Negligible; 2=Low; 3=Medium; 4=High; 5=Very High; and 6=Excellent.

Note 2: There are 20 criteria for measurement of social opportunity. Each criterion with the highest score of 6, leads to a total score of 120. Any group or people's committee, which scores "excellent" on all criteria has a total score of 120 (6 multiplied by 20) while that, which scores "negligible" on all criteria has a total score of 20 (1 multiplied by 20).

3.2.7 Integrated Participatory Poverty Assessment—An Integrated Participatory Poverty Assessment is an integrated situational analysis of lives and living by the primary stakeholders covering different aspects such as (a) Social Group/Well Being Assessment; (b) Asset/Resource Assessment; (c) Vulnerability and Risk Assessment; (d) Livelihoods Assessment; (e) Problem-Opportunity Assessment; (f) Gender Assessment; (g) Institutional Assessment; and (h) Social Capital Assessment. For an illustrated Integrated Participatory Poverty Assessment, see Chapter 6.

3.2.8 Participatory Process Assessment—A participatory process is equally important as much as its outcome and hence stock-taking of such a process is an important prerequisite involving participatory exercises. The quality of participatory process is a major variable in determining its outcome and the better the quality of the process, the more is the enrichment of the process product. There are certain aspects to be observed in a participatory process, which generally help ascertain its degree, magnitude and quality. For tracking quality of participatory processes, a specific set of criteria is provided below based on various aspects of participation.

3.2.8a The set of criteria as in Box 3.4 is indicative (more process-related aspects could be added) as a means to strengthen the quality of participation of primary stakeholders, especially the poor and the disadvantaged and their engagement in terms of priorities, assessment and inclusion towards a more integrated approach. There are other aspects to be considered such as:

(a) Raising Awareness, Interest and Confidence of Poor Groups
(b) Levels of Participation
(c) The Breadth of Participation
(d) Active Participation
(e) Participatory Tools with Pro-Poor Focus
(f) Participatory Mechanisms to Engage Poor

Each aspect has been explored in terms of a checklist.

3.2.8a.1 Raising Awareness, Interest and Confidence of Poor Groups—Different groups within the poor when identified could have different stakes in any participatory process/exercise under reference. Usually one type of solution does not fit all the poor groups. It is a crucial task to start with how the poor groups have been identified. Their awareness levels could be raised by involving them directly and actively in the planning process. Those groups will have to be explained the process, the objectives, the approach, the expected outcome/s etc.

3.2.8a.2 Level/s of Participation—Some issues with regard to levels of participation include the following. At what levels is the participation of poor and disadvantaged groups? Whether only at the local level, or also at higher level/s? Whether participation of poor is

Box 3.4: Aspects of Quality of Participatory Process

- Whose participation counts?
- Which are those stakeholder groups actually involved in a participatory exercise?
- And on what basis have they been identified? How is their participation solicited?
- Who is being represented from which stakeholder groups?
- What mechanism exists in any participatory exercise for making the marginalized and excluded groups to actively engage them selves, noting that such groups could require space and time to interact actively and also be able to understand the objectives and purposes at hand and the expected outcomes.
- What could be some specific reasons for non-participation or limited engagement of poor and marginalized groups?
- What steps need to be taken to fill gaps in those stakeholder groups which reveal limited engagement?
- What are the ways to involve the marginalized group/s?
- How are different groups of stakeholders actually participating in the related assessment process?
- Which stakeholders are participating more than others noting that men's participation could be generally at a much higher level than that of women?
- What steps have been taken to demystify the concepts of people's participation, assessment, social accountability, planning, appraisal, monitoring for the common people, especially the marginalized group/s, to enlist true participation?
- Have the concepts of ownership, transparency etc. been further de-mystified for engagement of those who may find these concepts not easy to understand/appreciate?
- Whether needs and priorities of poor groups are noted and documented as much as the other groups involved?
- Whether such needs and priorities get listed, incorporated and integrated with those at higher levels?
- What are the remaining gaps in such a process? How are they being overcome or met?

mostly at the data collection stage and not so much at the need assessment stage, planning and action stage or monitoring stage? How difficult is it for the poor to be heard at the local or higher levels? What can be done to avoid or offset influential people or elitist biases at the local and higher levels? Those representing the poor at different levels—how effective are they in supporting poor to reflect their issues and priorities?

3.2.8a.3 The Breadth of Participation—Some issues include the following. How wide is the participation of the poor? How many women and men are engaged? And how many actively participate? What about participation by different categories of poor groups? What steps are there to solicit participation of women groups? Which groups participate more than others and why? What are the constraints in soliciting participation of different poor groups and how are they overcome and by what means?

3.2.8a.4 Active Participation—Some related issues include the following. Who spoke during the assessment sessions and who (or which groups) could not find space to express her/his views (their)? Whose views were taken into consideration and why? Whose views were not considered and for what reasons? Who was being dominated and what measures were taken to avoid or offset such dominance? How effective was such participation in terms of pro-poor stance of the assessment? How effective was such participation in terms of gendered assessment? Did the poor groups and individuals have opportunities to express their dissent or different opinions? How were those handled in the assessment process? Is there evidence that such dissenting views got ignored in the assessment process? If so, what could be the reasons?

3.2.8a.5 Participatory Tools with Pro-Poor Focus—Some issues in this context include the following. What tools were used to facilitate the poor and in what manner? Are these tools poor-friendly? Do these tools have a literacy bias? To what extent poor women's and men's knowledge were utilized with regard to application of such tools? Do they feel empowered to express their views in the assessment process? What levels of clarity are there in terms of the objectives and content of assessment? In terms of social mapping are all the key social aspects of the poor groups covered? Also, how is it in comparison to non-poor groups? What tools are being utilized for prioritization of issues and reaching consensus, if any? Are the tools for prioritization suitable for soliciting participation of the poor groups, the women, the deprived and the marginalized sections of the community? How is such assessment exercise cross-checked and validated so that it actually supports mainstreaming poor people's concerns, issues and ways of resolving them?

3.2.8a.6 Participatory Mechanisms to Engage Poor—Some issues in this context include the following. What kinds of mechanisms are being utilized to help the poor own the assessment process? How are they supported to have a bigger and better voice in the assessment process? What steps are being taken to organize them and to what extent will they prove effective and why? What other ways of empowerment have been used in the process of decision-making? Is there any feedback mechanism for the poor groups to voice their suggestions or grievances related to participatory exercises in which they are engaged? Have these been incorporated into the assessment framework? How and in what manner? Which groups can be called as gainers in the assessment process?

3.2.9 Participatory Impact/Outcome Assessment—A Participation Matrix can be used for such assessment. Such participation matrix can be applied to a wide variety of situations for assessing criteria, which are pro-poor and also for checking how much have the poor groups benefited, e.g. from a programme or project. In a participation matrix, the different social groups are listed on one side, while the criteria for impact/outcome assessment are listed on the other side of the matrix. A simple example is given below in Table 3.9. The matrix can be adapted for achieving different social assessment objectives as required.

Table 3.9: An Illustration of the Participatory Impact/Outcome Matrix

Social Groups/ Criteria	*No. of women beneficiaries under household asset creation, e.g. sanitary latrine*	*No. of children to be immunized*	*No. of persons receiving micro credit*	*No. of poor women actively involved*
Destitute				
Ultra poor				
Poor				
Middle class				
Better off				

3.2.10 Integrated Impact Assessment—Participatory evaluation is a frontier research area in participatory approaches. It is in striking contrast to the conventional approach, where the job of evaluation is mostly specialized with emphasis on "numbers". "materials" and "targets". Such emphasis fails to capture the nuances of the development process, and the "worldview" of project beneficiaries that participatory evaluation can account for. One participatory method by the name of "Project Benefit-Impact Matrix" (PBI Matrix) was applied as one of the tools for a project at Maldives for conducting ex-post evaluation.

The project benefit-impact matrix was one base tool used for post-evaluation of the project in Maldives. Each session lasted between one and a half and three hours, depending on the group size, the number of project activities, the time taken to recollect past project activities, etc. The number of participants interacted in each island community varied between 10 and 70 and included both women and men, who were approached in separate groups.

3.2.10.1 In each case, groups of participants were provided with small cards and pens for listing, drawing and writing, as well as wide sheets of paper. They were first requested to remember and list the project activities to start with (for details *see* Table 3.10). The participants then described the project activities and scored each of them in terms of their impact on individuals, the group or the community. For example, generation of electricity impacts upon the whole community while handicraft training activity impacted only on selected individuals. After scoring, the participants discussed the impacts of each of the project activities and wrote them on cards as shown in the fourth column of Table 3.10. This was followed by discussions on the current status of each activity and reflections on its sustainability (fifth column). Finally, participants were asked to make suggestions and recommendations for follow-up action. When the matrix was completed, the facilitators summarized the findings and presented them back to the participants for cross-checking and correction of errors and omissions.

3.2.10.2 As facilitators, one practical limitation of the PBI matrix was that with large groups of participants there arose many views where consensus building became an arduous task. Before arriving at a group score, the participants were encouraged to do proper group discussion. Often a tentative score was placed against a project activity and was altered based on group consensus. In case of difficulty faced by the participants in arriving at a single score, the participants were encouraged to score differently from the group and then discuss

Table 3.10: Project-Benefit Impact Matrix (Women), Maldives

Name of Activity (*Col.1*)	*Year of Activity* (*Col.2*)	*Score*[*] (*Col.3*)	*Impact of Activity* (*Col.4*)	*Status and Sustainability* (*Col.5*)	*Recommendations* (*Col.6*)
1. Health awareness programme	1993/94	10	Community awareness has grown as a result of inputs in child care, food, child spacing and family planning. Such knowledge is also getting applied.	The community with health worker's support continues to practice the imparted information.	For further sustainability the women suggest preparation and distribution of reference materials. Other recommendations include: • Sewing courses should be included in any project. • here should be emphasis on planning and implementing income generating activities like shop or hotel.
2. Handicraft training	1994	9	8 women took the training and can make small items like hand bags, lamps and hats with local materials.	Though the women are interested they cannot practice it since there is no market for the product.	
3. Honey bee-keeping	1993	7	The island women committee members have gained some knowledge in bee-keeping	The members found it difficult to continue since training was incomplete. For example, when the bees flew away they lacked knowledge about ways to get them back.	
4. Credit scheme	1994	8	4 women borrowed money for sewing activities and still continue with loan repayment.	The scheme is useful but repayment is problematic due to no frequent local arrangement for repayment.	

(*Contd.*)

(*Contd.*)

Name of Activity (*Col.1*)	Year of Activity (*Col.2*)	Score* (*Col.3*)	Impact of Activity (*Col.4*)	Status and Sustainability (*Col.5*)	Recommendations (*Col.6*)
5. Electricity	1995	7	24 hours electricity available to island community with manifold increase in regular income of Island Development Committee (IDC) from electricity charges.	The island women's committee helps in cleaning the powerhouse while maintenance is looked after by IDC.	• raining courses in home gardening should have follow up sessions. • arketing linkages should be included for handicraft training.
6. Home gardening	1993	7	A specialist taught the women and school children for 8 months in preparing horticulture beds and applying fertilizers which resulted in women planting banana, papaya, tomato and pumpkins.	The women found it difficult to continue except for growing banana plants, since they lacked knowledge on plant disease and treatment.	Island Analysts: Amira, Aneesa, Faheema Aminath, Mariyam, Ihusaana, Aminath, Aminath Ismail, Haseena Eesa, Mariyam Hussein, Arifa Eesa, Aishath Eesa, Aishath Mohammed, Lucky Star, Kashmeeru, Alivaage, Murigu, Femoaraage, Queen.
7. Entrance deepening	1993	6	Has increased accessibility to the island where local fishermen are able to enter the island even after sunset.	Once a year the men clean the entrance while the women prepare special food for them.	
8. Training in electric wiring	1994	5	Only one man was trained and applies his knowledge as and when required, though he does not charge for it.	More men should be trained.	

(*Contd.*)

(*Contd.*)

Name of Activity (Col. 1)	Year of Activity (Col. 2)	Score* (Col. 3)	Impact of Activity (Col. 4)	Status and Sustainability (Col. 5)	Recommendations (Col. 6)
9. Training in household furniture making	1993	8	11 men were trained who make cupboards, chairs and tables for income generating activity.	Men are earning good income and advance training course would be helpful.	Venice, Muraka, Riverside, Venus, Saveyra and Paris.
10. Training in engine repair & maintenance	1993	6	A total of 26 men participated with one person each from the local fishing vessels. They are now skilled in handling engine problems thus saving large expenses on maintenance.	The course is very useful and advance course would be an added advantage.	Facilitator: Aminath Latheefa
11. Training in English language	1995	10	The teacher taught English for a month and left.	The community arranged for a teacher trained from India who is being paid by parents of the children.	

Note: * stands for scores allotted for impact prioritization, which is out of 10, where higher score means higher impact; Col. stands for column. Location: Island: Badidhoo, Dhaalu Atoll, Maldives.

amongst themselves so as to reach consensus. Another point observed by the evaluation team was that group recall of project activities took time since the project activities had got over years back. Since, most participants were literate they wrote their points on small cards that were arranged in appropriate columns of the matrix (though in case of participants with low literacy it is possible to use symbols of various types to record their views).

Since both women and men groups were approached separately for participatory evaluation, the results showed clear differences in gender-based perspectives. The evaluation matrix showed different relevance of project activities to gender groups. The women group gave more weight to those activities, which were important from their viewpoint and sometimes missed out on listing other activities of the project as listed by men. The status and sustainability of project activities were also perceived differently by gender groups and the recommendations also differed. Evaluation by gender groups led to gender-specific information and, on the whole, generated more information as lessons learnt for bettering future projects.

One of the objectives of such participatory evaluation as explained to the island-communities was that the lessons learnt from the project could be utilised for formulating new projects for other island-communities. The participants were sent prior information about such evaluation and were candid about their views regarding which activities worked and which did not. They took considerable interest in discussing them since the activities started by the project were important to the community. During evaluation sessions, the participants were motivated to write on cards and they felt that their views were important.

3.2.10.3 Some strengths of the PBI matrix, based on field experience, were as follows:

- PBI matrix is a "visual" method that has the flexibility to provide a compact evaluation of the project. It is both transparent and flexible for it enables the participants to evaluate project activities as a group, and change their group scores and decisions as required.
- To encourage wider participation, each participant is given few cards, pens and seeds for scoring. The cards help those participants who are generally shy to talk and are willing to write their views.

- Once the method is explained to the participants, they are able to construct their own PBI matrix without much of outside facilitation. The process involved in the PBI matrix is to that extent self-sustaining.

3.2.10.4 As facilitators, a practical limitation of the project benefit-impact matrix was that with large groups of participants, many views arose and consensus building became an arduous task. Before arriving at a group score, the participants were encouraged to have a full group discussion. Often a tentative score was placed against a project activity and was altered, based on group consensus. Where difficulties were faced by the participants in arriving at a single score, they were encouraged to score separately and then discuss the issues raised in order to reach a consensus. As most of the participants were literate, they wrote their points on the cards that were arranged in appropriate columns of the matrix. However, greater use of symbols could be made with groups having low skills in literacy.

3.2.10.5 Since both women's and men's groups were approached separately for the participatory evaluation, gender-based perspectives were articulated. For example, the women's group emphasized those activities which directly affected them and did not always list the range of project activities that the men listed. The status and sustainability of project activities were also perceived differently by different gender groups and thus the recommendations also differed.

3.2.11 Participatory Monitoring and Evaluation (PM & E)—In simple terms, evaluation is assessing appropriateness of design and implementation methods for achieving objectives and recommending necessary changes. While monitoring is a regular, systematic, periodic assessment and its purpose is to determine whether programme/project is being implemented as planned and to provide information during the life time of the project, so that adjustments and/or modifications can be made if required.

3.2.11.1 There are two broad types of evaluation exercises: (a) Efficiency evaluation and (b) Impact evaluation. Efficiency evaluation is for assessing and improving performance and effectiveness. Impact evaluation is for assessing/estimating impact and identifying those factors determining them and recommending changes. Some aspects of evaluation include:

- What are the objectives? Whether the objectives are general/ immediate/long-term?
- How much has been achieved? And to what extent is that sustainable?
- What are the impacts?
- What are the factors influencing impacts?
- Whether design, planning and implementation and cost in terms of objectives are appropriate?
- Whether objectives need to change?

3.2.11.2 Monitoring is regular data collection system to feed into planning, decision-making and implementation whereas evaluation is periodic review of achievements against targets feeding back into management system. Monitoring involves continuous process of checking whether project activities are as per schedule and whether project inputs are being used by targeted population. Evaluation focuses on periodic assessment of the relevance, efficiency and impact of project in terms of project objectives. Monitoring is generally an internal project activity whereas evaluation can be internal and external and may involve comparisons based on external information in terms of time, area and population. Some similarities between monitoring and evaluation are that both make all participants accountable and are integral parts of the whole project. Both are learning activities to improve qualities of decision-making and changes envisaged through projects.

3.2.11.3 Monitoring and evaluation can be conventional based on questionnaire survey while application of participatory methods make for participatory monitoring ánd evaluation. Participatory M & E is more group/community-oriented, relatively unstructured and based on people's views and assessment. A comparison of participatory M & E and conventional M & E is given below in Table 3.11.

3.2.11.4 The types of indicators emphasized in participatory M & E include the following:

(a) Indicator/s of Availability
(b) Indicator/s of Relevance
(c) Indicator/s of Accessibility
(d) Indicator/s of Utilisation
(e) Indicator/s of Coverage

Table 3.11: A Comparison of Conventional M & E and Participatory M & E

Monitoring and Evaluation through Conventional Survey	*Participatory Monitoring and Evaluation*
Based on multi-topic survey with help of questionnaire	Based on Group Interactions through PRA/PLA in different locations
Whose Reality counts? Outsiders as Experts	People's Reality with people as analysts—People explain complex things in their way and with their emphasis
Closed-ended Inquiry – Questionnaires fielded by field investigators	Open-ended Inquiry – Field-based PRA/PLA –type sessions with minimum of closed questions
Top-Down Process – All questions cannot be anticipated	Bottom-Up Process – Questions-Answer-Question-One leading to the other
Looking for "Average" picture and solutions	Looking for Diversity-Differential Pictures and Solutions
Emphasizes Quantitative aspects	Has both Qualitative and Quantitative Aspects
Individual as unit with little scope for group work	Group analysis and group presentation
Tends to overlook gender aspects	Gender aspects are important

(f) Indicator/s of Quality
(g) Indicator/s of Effort
(h) Indicator/s of Efficiency
(i) Indicator/s of Impact
(j) Indicator/s of Process
(k) Indicator/s of Sustainability/Maintenance
(l) Indicator/s of Equity

3.2.12 Participatory Public Policy Making— Participatory Policy Making is another tool where different groups of stakeholders (cutting across gender, class, caste, interest groups) etc. are engaged in area or topical planning, reviewing and/or monitoring and are consulted for reviewing existing policies and suggesting policy changes and providing inputs to new policies. To exercise broad-based participation, citizen forums and associations could be met as small groups for discussing/reviewing any aspect of public policy making such as area-planning and/or resource allocation for example, decisions relating to resource allocation at a meso level. They could also be met as bigger group/s for proposing/reviewing meso plans. This also includes consultation with an expert committee which represents such citizens' groups. Proposed decisions by higher authority could be presented to larger citizen groups whether to arrive at final decision/s or to seek validation of policy decisions.

This tool is also effective for gaining social accountability and this has been mentioned later in section 3.3.3. It is important to point out that participatory public policy making is rather a huge field with a variety of rich experience and it also does overlap with tools of social accountability. In this context, Burgess and Malek (2005) write that one common form of public participation is that of public hearing where government representative give a presentation on a proposed decision and the public is asked to react and provide short comments (1-3 minutes). Such a form may not be much effective in problem solving. Rather, Burgess and Malek (2005) hold that citizens' advisory committees are more effective though they need much commitment from their constituent members and also to overcome in-fighting. Other forms of public participation also include ballot initiatives for proposed constitutional amendments, which are then voted by the public.

The International Association for Public Participation lists seven standards for public participation[2]:

1. To have a say in decisions about actions that affect their lives.
2. To have the promise that the public's contribution will influence the decision.
3. To have a process encompassing the interests and needs of all participants.
4. To include involvement of people potentially affected by the proposed decision/s.
5. To involve participants in defining how they will participate.
6. To provide participants with necessary information to participate in a meaningful way.
7. To communicate to participants how their input affected the decision.

In many countries, there are instances of different stakeholder groups engaged for selected policy-making exercises. For example, in India the draft on National Rural Employment Guarantee Act was discussed and debated by different stakeholder/advocacy groups before it was finally passed by the Parliament as an Act. However, it is also important to recognize that such opportunities for policy-changes can attract many people to be engaged though decisions about actions get postponed (Clark: 2001) or not much changes happen in terms of action. Again, field experience shows that though such public participation bring decision-making closer to local people, the public may not have enough influence over policy-making and local and national interests can often contradict (Sudirman and McGrath: 2005).

3.2.13 Constructing Word/Visual Picture—Construction of picture/word picture (Bond & Mukherjee: 2001) is a visual/verbal method for creating description of any topic under consideration. Such picture or word picture helps in depicting a scenario or situation or state of living or extent of progress with words/picture chosen by the group/individual interacted with. The word picture is a method for creating "word" or "visual" description of any topic, examples of such word picture can be description of vulnerable household, subsistence living, state of ill-being/well-being, etc. Such word pictures help paint a scenario with words chosen by participant groups interacted with. Such word pictures evolving from key stakeholders in a participatory manner are practical and realistic and also help in their involvement and ownership. They are quite handy for monitoring purposes and the stakeholders can monitor their own situations through such pictures/word pictures. Word pictures evolved separately for women and men help focus on gender issues and reveal gender perspective. When word pictures are scaled up from the local level to the macro level, they help generate composite variables for tracking and monitoring.

3.2.13.1 For illustration purposes, given below are two word pictures (Development Tracks: 2000, 2004-5)—the 'worst' picture and the 'best' picture for monitoring the status of street children as in Table 3.12. They can be adapted and applied as per locality, gender, age and other variables. Appropriate visualization (pictures, drawings, objects, narrative, story and other form/s) of different criteria is important for small and young children to participate for their own situational assessment so that they can relate to them freely in their own ways and through their own individual/group experience. Two illustrative scenarios for picture/word picture construction are described in Table 3.12.

3.2.14 Most Significant Change (MSC) Tool—The Most Significant Change (MSC) was invented by Rick Davies (1996) to overcome some challenges associated with monitoring and evaluating

Table 3.12: 'Word' Picture for Participatory Monitoring of Street Children: Illustrations of the 'Worst' Picture and the 'Best' Picture

Worst Picture	*Best Picture*
• Living on the street • Doing hazardous jobs	1. Empowerment and 'Power With' and 'Power Within' Freedom from the clutches of the musclemen/ middlemen Life skills to tackle musclemen/ unscrupulous people Power to resist unjust pressure and unjust demand
• Absence of well being • Depressed • Scared • Stressful life	2. Positive Discrimination Confidence to talk with elders/ strangers and tackle unjust acts/demands Can challenge strangers and demand better behaviour Can resist mean and dirty jobs/acts
• Mentally insecure • Lack of self esteem • Lack of confidence	3. Right to Shelter and safety and Practical Access Get access to a proper shelter Access to a safe place to keep cash and other items such as clothing, sandal etc. as required
• Lack of trust in others • Traumatized • Lack of access to basic amenities • Sexually abused • Socially excluded and deprived	4. Emotional Well-Being, Social Inclusion Have developed a basic sense of security Have a sense of bonding with peer group Have developed a process generating social capital and partnership with others Have organized themselves for exercise of their basic rights and freedom
• Avoids human being • Acute food insecurity • Exploited • Cheated and repressed by musclemen, police, employers and other unscrupulous people	5. Responsive Governance/Society with Accountability and Voices and Choices of Street Children for inclusive Development Have been able to develop self-esteem Have been able to develop self-confidence Can resist ill treatment and injustice Have developed basic knowledge of rights and relevant laws of the land. Legal aid available and able to register case/s at the police station for effective action. Able to take part in discussions and decision-making to flag their own issues and local level development Have access to an active forum for redressing grievance/s
• Physically tortured • Have no access to justice • Drug addict • Scavenging for food	6. Well being and Stress Reduction There is decline in the sense of ill being There is sense of freedom from injustice and exploitation There is feeling of security There is decline in stress burden Able to distinguish between good and bad, right and wrong
	7. Improved Livelihoods Freedom from child labour Learning vocational courses and basic education For children above 15 years, there is increase in practical and vocational skills

(*Contd.*)

(*Contd.*)

Worst Picture	Best Picture
	Freedom from exploitation by middlemen and employers Able to negotiate just wage Work conditions are less extractive Food security and get food at regular intervals
	8. Freedom from Hunger and Right to Food Get nutritious food Do not have to beg for food Freedom from scavenging
	9. Access to Better Health Knowledge and Services Ability to access medical treatment as and when required Have acquired good knowledge of preventive health practices Able to Practice preventive health measures Quality of physical health has improved
	10. Improved Sanitation Standards Have facilities for proper toileting Have facilities for bathing and washing clothes. Sanitation standards are better in the surroundings

Source: Development Tracks RTC (2000, 2004-05).

complex programmes, both in terms of implementation and outcomes. MSC is a tool for participatory monitoring and evaluation. Such tool helps monitor on a regular basis and provides data on impact and outcomes which help assess changes and performance of projects. It is participatory since it helps involve many stakeholders in deciding change to be recorded and in data analysis. It is a process whereby significant stories are collected at the field level and the most significant story of change is then arrived at by a panel of stakeholders or project staff. The answer to "what changes?" are often in the form of stories of who did, what, when and why and the reasons why the event is important (Davies: 1996 and Davies and Dart: 2005).

The MSC tool has been widely applied for monitoring and evaluation for studying social changes in different sectors including business. For further details see the manual by Davies and Dart: 2005, web pages of Government of South Australia: 2008, Clear Horizon: web pages, Exchange: 2005, Anecdote: 2007, Health Link Worldwide and Lydia *et al.*: web pages. Application of the tool has also been documented through videos (*see* The Participatory Video Revolution web pages).

3.3. Tools for Social Accountability

Social Accountability mechanisms refer to a broad range of tools (beyond voting) that citizens, communities and civil society organizations can apply/use to hold government officials, bureaucrats and politicians accountable. Such tools include a broad range of actions (with implications in terms of direct and/or indirect, legitimate/not legitimate political space) to hold government and politicians responsible.

3.3.1 Citizens' Report Card—The citizens/communities/groups provide their views, opinions, scores on selected aspects for example, performance of government related to quality, coverage, efficiency, responsiveness of public/private services, say for example, in the area of providing drinking water or say primary schooling. The views and opinions are organized from different participants/user-groups, based on certain criteria/questions. Such responses to questionnaires are then collated to provide the 'larger picture'. Citizen Report Card tool is mainly prepared through a structured questionnaire (*see* Adikeshavalu: 2004; Buhl *et al.*, 2004a; 2004b; World Bank, 2001; 2004). In this book a Community Voice Tool (CVT) for assessing governance has been described in Chapter 7, which is a voice tool based on participatory group interactions rather than on any structured questionnaire. Outcomes in forms of Citizen's Report Card or CVT can present larger picture/s, both quantitative and/or qualitative. Both can help to indicate the areas of progress and areas of concern.

3.3.2 Citizens' Voice Card—This tool is generally meant for assessing service delivery and is mainly a tool for social accountability purposes. However, it can be combined with participatory assessments as and when required. Such a tool based on interactive meetings with local communities tends to reduce investigator's bias as present in questionnaire surveys. It enables excluded and weaker segments of the population to participate in assessment of service delivery organizations, express their views and to have better grasp of the issues discussed in small group meetings. For further details see Chapter 7 of this book.

3.3.3 Citizens' Participation in Public Policy Making—In practice, citizens' participation in the context of social accountability can range from the more "traditional" forms such as public meetings to the more novel approaches such as consensus conferencing, and from mechanisms that seek responses from participants acting alone (surveys) to those involving deliberation between different members of the public working in groups (www.scotland.gov.uk/Publications/2005/09/16120247 - 15k)

E-governance is becoming an important tool for social accountability. About e-governance and using ICTs for citizens' participation in public policy-making, Caddy (2002) points out that ICTs can lower barriers (e.g. cost, time, distance). However, there are limits depending upon citizen access to ICTs (i.e. bridging the digital divide) and the capacity of governments to use ICTs effectively in policy-making. Engaging citizens online has five main challenges: Scale (many voices); Capacity (of citizens and civil servants); Coherence (throughout the policy cycle); Learning (from local level, other countries); and Evaluation (of costs, benefits, impacts) (Caddy: 2002); and access to resources, and the level of technology. Hence, such limitations have to be kept in mind for usage of tools for evaluating government performance in informing, consulting and engaging citizens in policy-making.

There is a wide range of literature available on the net including concepts, methodologies and country experience, both at local and national level (*http://www.ids.ac.uk/ids/particip/research/socpol.html*; Citizen Participation in Social Policy; Warfield: 1993, www.scotland.gov.uk/Publications/2005/09/16120247-15k; *http://www.epa.gov/publicinvolvement/* US Environmental Protection Agency: Public Involvement; Also see references in section 3.2.12 as above.

3.3.4 Participatory Budgeting—Participatory Budgeting (PB) links budgets, policy-making and participation of citizens. It is a participatory public expenditure management process—management of public resources involving mechanisms to directly involve ordinary citizens, communities and civil society organizations in the process of allocating, disbursing, monitoring and evaluating the use of public resources. There is no blueprint for PB. It can vary from situation to situation. Citizens have opportunities to allocate resources, prioritize social policies and monitor public spending in public forums. It started in Brazil (in Alegre and Belo Horizonte) and is still practised as a part of urban governance.

There is no blueprint for PB. It can vary form situation to situation. (Wampler: 2000)—Citizens have opportunities to allocate resources, prioritize social policies and monitor public spending in public forums. PB started in Brazil and many other countries are picking up from such experience. Broader political environment is necessary for success of PB. Networks of social movements, NGOs, CBOs can provide critical support for undertaking exploratory PB. Citizens not only choose but also provide legitimacy to government policies, programmes and reform efforts. Higher the rate of citizen's participation, higher could be the legitimacy. Government must have resources to initiate public works selected by the participants. Brazil municipalities have 12 to 15 per cent available for new public works (Wampler: 2000). PB programme also focus on taxes and how to improve tax collection rates. There are neighbourhood meetings and city meetings—capacity building and awareness creation as parts of PB.

Distribution of resources under PB is based on two criteria (Wampler: 2000) as indicated below:

(i) *Quality of life index*—Each region receives percentage of budget depending on its overall needs.
(ii) *Mobilization processes within the region*—Organized groups compete, mobilize, negotiate and deliberate within their own region over available resources. All projects cannot be supported so groups form alliances to promote particular projects. Project implementation takes place according to previously established criteria with approval of technical plans.

In case of Brazil municipalities, there is consensus that PB stimulates participation since decision by citizens' results in policy changes. Participation can grow from year to year.

Communities are able to define their own development scenario through PB on public works. Citizens are better able to understand the division of authority in the government and conditions for better working. This serves to educate the population and also demonstrate the limited powers of the government. However, in recent literature (Chavez: 2008) it has been stated that even well developed processes of local participation could be highly affected by institutional changes produced by party politics...." the watering down of participatory budgeting—which contradicts previous assumptions about its strength and even its 'irreversibility'—highlights the need for further research on the objective quality and social roots for citizen participation."[3] Applicability of PB, experience from UK shows that PB can inspire and help people to see where and when they can get involved[4]. One important lesson learnt for organizers and participants is to create opportunities in each process for local engagement which is genuinely empowering (Blakey: 2008).

3.3.5 Public Expenditure Tracking/Monitoring (PET/M)—Civil societies/NGOs/ CBOs set up mechanisms to track specific areas of public expenditure and related public activities and inform public and media. In Nepal, the PETS/Service Delivery Survey carried out as a part of the process monitoring of targeted programmes (Development Vision: 2004).was indeed a much fruitful attempt at monitoring and flagging the lacunae in the process of targeted programmes such as Free Textbook Distribution and National Scholarship Programmes in Doti and Banke Districts. The PETS/Service Delivery Survey of education services covered both supply and demand sides of educational services. The scope of the PETS/Service Delivery Survey was made applicable to three broad components:

(i) Expenditure tracking;
(ii) Monitoring output and quality; and
(iii) Monitoring process of the programmes to achieve outputs.

On the demand side, it had a structured questionnaire covering the following:

(a) Knowledge and awareness level of parents about the two educational programmes which were being monitored;
(b) Perception of students/parents on the educational services;
(c) Impact of these services on the quality of education; and
(d) Problems encountered and suggestions for improvement.

The survey was also based on case studies and focus group discussions with both beneficiary and non-beneficiary households based on a checklist for inquiry on the number of children, education level, reason/s for not sending children to school, etc. In terms of tools, the PETS/Service Delivery survey was mainly based on structured questionnaire.

3.3.6 Family Satisfaction Survey—Family satisfaction survey questionnaire could be considered a part of well-being survey and is a quick way of gaining overviews on two aspects—level of satisfaction from different items of consumption of goods and services and assessment of performance of government services delivery. The questionnaire provides a cursory view of 'satisfaction' and need not contribute towards any analytical basis for such satisfaction. It may not help resolve what could have gone wrong and how situation can be retrieved or bettered. Such questionnaire may be of limited use in the sense that it is good in tracking public views/symptoms related to standard of living but fails to go beyond that. It need not help capture forces behind those symptoms, which are important factors to explain levels of satisfaction/dissatisfaction.

In case of Nepal, the family satisfaction survey questionnaire was applied as a part of Nepal's NLSS questionnaire survey (Central Bureau of Statistics, Nepal: 2002) to help inquire about the level of satisfaction regarding different items of consumption, which constituted standard of living such as housing, food, clothing, health care and schooling. The other aspect of probing on family satisfaction was related to the performance of government service delivery in health, education, drinking water, electricity, road, postal and telephone services. The questions related to the level of satisfaction for different items of consumption for living had four categories of responses:

(i) whether less than adequate;
(ii) whether just adequate;
(iii) whether more than adequate; and
(iv) whether applicable or not applicable.

In terms of human development framework, the questionnaire on family satisfaction is generally limited to levels of satisfaction with physical assets such as housing, food and clothing; and selected access such as schooling and health care. Satisfaction with assets such as natural assets, financial assets and socio-political assets are mostly excluded in the questionnaire although they easily constitute intrinsic part of any well-being or satisfaction survey. In general, the family satisfaction survey questionnaire often proves to be a limited tool for it excludes a larger part of the entire gamut of satisfaction or well-being related to the capability framework and criteria. Such satisfaction survey when made much wider and analytical help flag relevant issues and also to arrive at ways to resolve such issues based on citizens' knowledge and experience. The conventional satisfaction survey generally taps only a limited part of the entire set of citizens' satisfaction level, knowledge and experience though the possibilities are immense and worth exploring.

In the health sector, usage of family/consumer satisfaction surveys is quite common. For instance, the Department of Public Welfare in

Pennyslvania, U.S. requires primary contractors to implement a comprehensive approach for the measurement of consumer/family satisfaction. Consumer and Family Satisfaction interviews help in "early identification and resolution of problems related to service access, and timeliness of service delivery, appropriateness of services and treatment outcomes. Additionally, satisfaction surveys assist in determining the level of satisfaction with respect, dignity and hopefulness as integral components of the entire service delivery system."[5] Some other such surveys include Consumer Satisfaction Survey[6], Review of Approaches to Satisfaction Surveys of Clients of Disability Service Consultancy Report[7], Agency-wide client satisfaction Survey Report[8] and People for change[9].

3.3.7 Citizens' Monitoring of Public Service Delivery—Civil societies/NGOs/ CBOs/interest groups form action squads to monitor public service delivery in selected fields; and become engaged in advocacy and information sharing. This helps respond effectively to concerns on delivery and outcomes on public services, increase community ownership and often helps contain cost and increase efficiency, *see* also Chapter 7 of this book and *www.idea.gov.uk/idk/aio/1118552*, Stipak (2008), O'Neil *et al.* (2007), *unpan1.un.org/intradoc/groups/public/documents/un/unpan027075.pdf*

3.3.8 Citizens' Advisory Boards—Citizen Advisory Boards can be set up by civil society, court of law or government to monitor and advise public service delivery agencies or other specific issue/s related to public interest. Such Citizen Advisory Boards are constituted for a variety of purposes such as health, environmental quality, infrastructure, water supply, watershed, disability, child abuse and others. Citizens' Advisory Boards help inform in terms of citizens' knowledge and ideas and also make space for their involvement. Much depends on the powers grated to such Boards in terms of engaging in decision-making processes. For further discussion and different country experience see *www.law.indiana.edu/ilj/oldsite/volumes/v73/no3/applegate.html*, *www.infrastructure.gc.ca/research-recherche/results-resultats/rn-nr/rn-nr-2007-08-eng.html*, *www.mass.gov/dcr/waterSupply/watershed/documents/quabbinaccessch3.pdf*

3.3.9 Social Audit—As defined in "Social Audit Resource" web page[10] "Social Accounting and Auditing is a way of measuring and reporting on an organization's social and ethical performance. An organization which takes on an audit is transparent and makes itself accountable to its stakeholders." Social audit "supports an organization to monitor, account for, report on and improve its social, ethical and environmental performance"[11]. It helps narrow gaps between vision/goal and reality, between efficiency and effectiveness. It is a technique to understand, measure, verify, report on and to improve the social performance of the organization (Jain and Polman: 2003). Social audit is undertaken for the purpose of enhancing quality of local governance, particularly for strengthening accountability and transparency of local bodies. It creates an impact upon governance. It helps value the voice of stakeholders, including marginalized/poor groups whose voices are rarely heard.

For further reading on concepts of social audit, its framework, stages and illustration of social audit manual see VICTO Social Audit Project's manual[12]. For relationship between social accounting and auditing, role of social auditor and social compliance auditing see *http://www.interpraxis.com/social_audit_resources.htm*. For civil society views on principles, scope and process to be followed in application of social audit, in case of India see Nayak:*http://orissarti.com/socialaudit/social_audit.htm*. For value of social audit, impact, methodology and policy development see Brown (2001).

3.3.10 Special Accountability Institutions, e.g. Human Rights Commission—Human Rights Commission at a national level is generally an autonomous body with a mandate to safeguard human rights and monitor cases of its violation. There is a range of literature available on the web and country experience with regard to human rights institutions including assessment reports by International Council on Human Rights Policy and UN High Commissioner for Human Rights (2005), Amnesty International (2001) and Commonwealth Secretariat (2001).

3.3.11 Lobbying and Advocacy Campaigns—Some civil society organizations/NGOs/ INGOs as well as donors may involve themselves in lobbying issues with sub-national, national or international inter-governmental agencies and organize campaigns to organize and/or inform the public. Building the capacity of marginalized people to express their voice for change is an important part of advocacy in a rights-based approach. There could be different strategies and tools for such advocacy campaign/s (for a detailed guidebook see Veneklasen and Miller: 2002). Some illustrations in this case include save childhood campaign (www.savethechildren.org.uk/en/41_4234.htm), lobbying against child labour such as save childhood or *bachpan bachao andolan* by advocacy groups (*www.bba.org.in/*), Jonathan Gabay's brand communication blog at *www.brandforensics.co.uk/wordpress/archives/60* for bridging the child labour fashion credibility gap and *www.everyhumanhasrights.org/learn-more-about-the-every-human-has-rights-campaign.*

3.3.12 Pro-Poor Public/Social Interest Litigation—Some civil society organizations or some groups of citizens or a single citizen could file public interest litigation in a court of law to support interests of poor groups. Public interest litigation may not be defined in any statute or in any act. It has been interpreted by judges to consider the intent of public at large. Although, the main focus of such litigation is only "Public Interest" there are various areas where such litigation could be filed (www.helplinelaw.com/docs/pub-i-litigation/index.php-18k), for example, violation of basic human rights of poor; conduct of government policy; compelling government to perform a public duty; and violation of religious rights or basic fundamental rights.

This tool has been applied with much success in case of India since the Eighties[13]. The Supreme Court of India gave all individuals in the country and the newly formed consumer groups or social action groups, easy access to the law through a broad public interest perspective (*see* Vadivel in Legal Services India.com, www.legalserviceindia.com/articles/pil.htm-30k).

The court is now seen as not only providing relief to its citizens but also venturing into policy formulation that public authority must follow (Desai and Murlidhar: 2000). Within the last two decades, India has not only enacted specific legislation on environmental protection but has also virtually created a new fundamental right to a clean environment in the Constitution. It shows the activist role of the Indian judiciary (Abraham: 1999).

However, the development of Public Interest Litigation (PIL) in India has seen many pitfalls (*see* Jha, G. Problems facing Public interest Litigation in India, Legal Services India.com, www.legaiservicesindia.com/articles/pil_ind.htm-37k). Also see *Halisbury Law Monthly*, August, 2001). The genuine causes and cases of public interest have in fact receded to the background and the abuse of PIL has become more rampant than its use. Suspicion has been generated by spurious causes mooted by privately motivated interests in the disguise of the so-called public interests. Weakness for publicity affects judges, lawyers and litigants alike. Again, the attempt by the judiciary through PILs to enter the area of policy making and policy implementation has caused concern in political circles. The credibility of PIL process is being questioned in terms of whether the judiciary is overstepping the boundaries of its jurisdiction and that it is unable to supervise the effective implementation of its orders.

3.3.12 Citizens' Jury/People's Court—A Citizens' Jury/People's Court often has same implications in terms of social accountability. It could be set up by civil society to deliberate/settle issues related to public injustice and grievances. It is perceived to have advantages such as making policy-makers review and think through their policy arguments; engaging ordinary people relating policies to their own experience; and bringing an alternate set of values to public policy issues. Issues in this context include the 'representativeness' of the juries, their value added in terms of expenses and their power to influence decisions (www.scotland.gov.uk/Publications/2005/09/16120247-15k).

Other issues emerging from the field include engaging with power at different levels; opening political space with marginalized stakeholders; developing long-term strategy and scaling up; ignoring and suppressing voices; reaching consensus between multi-stakeholders and flagging voices of dissent; democratizing policy-making and interventions; maintaining upstream public engagement; and gaining authority and power (for case studies on citizens' juries see Kuruganti, Pimbert and Wakeford: 2008, Bryant: 2008, Singh: 2008, Kashefi and Keene: 2008, Eady *et al.*: 2008, Fitzduff *et al.*: 2008, Wakeford, Murtuia and Bryant: 2008, Right 2B heard Collective: 2008 in IIED: 2008).

3.4. Tools in the Toolbox for Listening to Voice

There is a wide range of participatory monitoring/planning tools/methods, which have evolved in recent years and have been applied in many countries in different contexts. One main advantage of such methods/tools is that they are quite flexible and can be customized as required. Another strength of some of these participatory tools, especially those based on PRA/PLA, is that they are relatively process-oriented and often the process become equally or even more important than the product. The emphasis on the process in which the tool/method is applied also helps provide credibility and trustworthiness of the output. Tables 3.13 and 3.13A contain overview of the method/tools for participatory social assessment and social accountability.

Table 3.13: Participatory Social Assessment and Social Accountability: A Comparison of Selected Tools

Name of Method/Tool	*Summary Description*	*Field/s of Application/s*	*Selected Aspects*
Tool/s for Social Account-ability	Social Accountability mechanisms refer to a broad range of tools/techniques and methods/ actions (beyond voting) that citizens, communities and civil society organizations can apply/use to hold government officials and bureaucrats accountable.	The tool/s can be applied to seek public opinion, user-views, client -reports on any specific social policy, programme or project.	Tools for Social Accountability with clear focus can prove handy to provide quick feedback on current programme/theme. It can provide quick results and help to flag issues from people's perspectives for future corrective measures. However, in the presence of negative public mood such tools need to be handled with care. As compared to PPA these snap–shot tools have limited analytical content.
Participatory Poverty Assessment (PPA)	PPA, a situational analysis of poverty mostly done by key stakeholders from the 'bottom' – the poor and marginalized groups of women and men in their own 'voice'. It helps to flag important lessons and insights for furthering their cause and provides space for people's inputs and assessment for pro-poor policy-making and practice. The PPA process helps to involve key stakeholders in assessing development polices and programmes, in revealing their priorities and preferences and in creating space for their "ownership" of the development process.	PPA could be designed from the 'bottom' and/or from the 'top' as required; and is widely applicable for field inquiry into different themes, social groups and areas for seeking people's assessment/mandate on a range of themes/ issues.	PPA can provide assessment with people's analysis. However, it presumes skilled field facilitators with appropriate behaviour and attitude. It also implies synthesis of data with analytical content based on people's perspective. It can raise public expectations and it is important to manage such expectations. Often, the poor groups are too busy to give time for discussion and hence the time factor needs to be handled appropriately.

(*Contd.*)

(*Contd.*)

Name of Method/Tool	*Summary Description*	*Field/s of Application/s*	*Selected Aspects*
Participatory Need Assessment (PNA)	Participatory Need Assessment is a way in which people assess their own needs, analyze them, identify important factors and devise their own solutions to meet such needs.	PNA is generally applicable for any need assessment involving communities/groups in any field in both rural and urban areas.	PNA needs to be done with care and caution since it can raise people's expectations for quick action. Often, the poor groups are too busy to give time for discussion and hence the time factor needs to be handled appropriately.
Participatory Priority Assessment	Participatory Priority Assessment is a way in which people – men, women and children reveal their own priorities and preferences, rank them, describe them and also suggest how and to what extent they can be met and who can meet them and why.	Participatory Priority Assessment is generally applicable for any need assessment involving communities/group/s in any field in both rural and urban areas.	Participatory Priority Assessment could be at a meso or at a macro level. There could be many stakeholder groups with contrasting priorities and negotiating with them is a skilful process. For any negotiating process one has to safeguard the interests of the poor, which may not be easy in societies with high inequalities. One needs to have good facilitation skills to manage the process of consultation in a transparent manner and to flag pro-poor agenda.
Participatory Livelihoods Assessment	Participatory Livelihoods Assessment is a way in which people discuss their assets related to livelihoods, the vulnerability conditions under which assets exist, the livelihoods preferences and the outcomes, the policies, institutions and processes which influence livelihoods and the do-ables.	Participatory Livelihoods Assessment focused on livelihoods is widely applicable to both rural and urban areas.	Participatory Livelihoods Assessment starts at the grassroots and requires good facilitation skills and understanding of the context. Often, the poor groups are too busy to give time for discussion and hence the time factor needs to be handled appropriately.

(*Contd.*)

(*Contd.*)

Name of Method/Tool	Summary Description	Field/s of Application/s	Selected Aspects
Participatory Policy Making	Participatory Policy Making is another tool where different groups of stakeholders (cutting across gender, class, caste, interest groups) are engaged and consulted in reviewing existing policies and suggesting policy changes and new policies.	Participatory Policy Making could be a consultation process of stakeholders on selected policies, which impact upon people's lives	For any policy review, it is important to have small group discussions on policy overviews and other information as required. Warming up sessions add to meaningful policy review/s and contributions from the stakeholders.
Participatory Impact Assessment	Participatory Impact Assessment is widely used as a tool to explore and appreciate impacts from the perspectives of key stakeholders. Interactive sessions are held with stakeholder groups to identify what impacts have been made by policies, programmes and projects under reference, of what magnitude and which way the impacts are moving.	Participatory Impact Assessment is widely applicable to any project/programme/policy for which impacts need to be assessed. It is applicable to both urban and rural scenarics and when gendered provides meaningful pictures. Differential analysis of impacts in terms of different social groups provides insights into the distribution of impacts in terms of equity dimensions.	For target groups with many programmes and projects in operation, it is not easy to differentiate impacts and establish a one-to-one correspondence between a project activity and its impact. Again, for small-sized programmes/projects, it is not easy to isolate specific impacts and often a mixed picture emerges, which at best is merely indicative. Interactions with controlled groups help to assess impacts better. Some impacts take relatively longer time to show up and post-programme/project analyses have proved useful for such impact assessment. Still complicated are those impacts, which are erratic and whose patterns cannot be determined beforehand.

(*Contd.*)

(*Contd.*)

Name of Method/Tool	*Summary Description*	*Field/s of Application/s*	*Selected Aspects*
Constructing Word/Visual Picture	Constructing Word/Visual Picture – The word/visual picture is a method for creating description of any topic under consideration, whether through words or visually. Examples of such word picture can be a description of vulnerable household, subsistence living, status of ill being/well-being etc. Such word/visual picture help in painting a scenario with words (and/or visually) chosen by participant groups interacted with. Such word/visual pictures evolving from key stakeholders in a participatory manner are practical and realistic and also help in better engagement and ownership. Word pictures evolved separately for women and men help to focus on gender issues and to reveal gender perspectives. When word pictures are scaled up from the local level to the macro level, they help to generate composite variables for tracking and monitoring.	Word picture construction has better applicability for programmes/projects, which cover large areas and where it can be assumed that some part of the impact on people's lives is attributable to the programme/project under reference. This tool has better applicability for projects, which are more integrated and holistic.	The construction of word pictures needs to be participatory involving key stakeholders in a series of workshops. It is desirable that the word pictures meant for monitoring are generated from the bottom. Workshops conducted for constructing word pictures take time and patience and need to be broad-based and transparent. The word pictures are handy tools for impact monitoring. For illiterate or semi-literate participants the word pictures can include drawings, pictures and illustrations, which can then help to relate impacts in a visual manner for monitoring purposes.
Most Significant Change	MSC is a tool for participatory monitoring and evaluation. Such tool helps to monitor on a regular basis and provides data on impact and outcomes which help to assess changes and performance of projects. It is participatory since it helps to involve many stakeholders in deciding change to be recorded and in data analysis.	Any project or programme in development.	Monitoring and evaluation.

Table 3.13A: Tools/Methods for Social Accountability

Tools for Social Accountability	*Summary Description*	*Field of Application/s*	*Selected Aspects*
Citizen Report/Score Card	The citizens/communities/groups provide their views, opinions, scores on selected aspects for example, performance of Government related to quality, coverage, efficiency, responsiveness of public/private services, say for example, in the area of providing drinking water or say primary schooling. The views and opinions are collated from different participants/user-groups, based on certain criteria/questions. These are then aggregated or made into indices to provide the 'larger picture'. It can be both quantitative and/or qualitative. It could help to indicate the areas of progress and areas of concern.	Applicable to any programme or any public concern.	Often, it is conducted through a questionnaire survey, which is mostly structured through closed questions such as 'yes' or 'no' and then the data is processed for arriving at averages and proportions and other numerical estimates. It is important to have an independent and neutral organization engaged in doing Citizen Report Card for then people tend to have more faith and trust in the outcome. Factors such as transparency in activities undertaken to prepare the Citizen Report Card, the credibility of the organization doing it, the type of sampling and its coverage, who is being included and excluded, the size of sampling and the analysis – all go to determine the quality of the report card. Citizen Report Card is an advocacy tool and follow up action on such citizen report card is equally important to make it meaningful and effective for responsive and good governance. (one latest variant of citizen report card is polling through mobile phones and messaging linked to radio/TV channels and outcome shared/advocated through the same channels and newspapers).

(Contd.)

(*Contd.*)

Tools for Social Accountability	*Summary Description*	*Field of Application/s*	*Selected Aspects*
Citizen participation in public policy making,	In this tool different citizen forums and associations are first met as small groups for discussing area planning and resource allocation concerns for example, at a meso level and later as a big group to propose meso plans to different authority.	Any policy domain, which impacts many citizens.	It is mainly engaging civil society in a consultative process.
Participatory budgeting (PB)	Participatory Budgeting links budgets, policy –making and participation of citizens. It is a participatory public expenditure management process – management of public resources involving mechanisms to directly involve ordinary citizens, communities and civil society organizations in processes of allocating, disbursing, monitoring and evaluating the use of public resources. There is no blueprint for PB. It can vary from situation to situation. Citizens have opportunities to allocate resources, prioritize social policies and monitor public spending in public forums. It started in Brazil (Alegre and Belo Horizonte) and is still practiced as a part of urban governance. Many other countries are picking it up.	Applicable to any budgeting process at a micro, meso and/or macro level	Experts have pointed out that many of the beneficial effects of PB could depend on sufficient resources for investment, a responsive legislature, and an active civil society. Where these conditions do not exist, there is possibility that participatory budgeting process is captured by a narrow and elite-oriented segment of society, or arouse little public interest.

(*Contd.*)

(*Contd.*)

Tools for Social Accountability	*Summary Description*	*Field of Application/s*	*Selected Aspects*
Public expenditure tracking/ monitoring,	Civil societies/NGOs/CBOs set up mechanisms to track specific areas of public expenditure and related public activities and to also inform public and media.	Applicable to any public expenditure, which is decided to be tracked.	Much of it could be tracking within the public service delivery agency system and there could be constraints in tracking budget and expenditure lines. Proper maintenance of records of receipts and expenditure is not always forthcoming and there could be resistance by insiders and outsiders in completion of the process of tracking public expenditure. It also presumes enough technical knowledge and subject-specific knowledge in the activities related to such tracking.
Citizens' monitoring of public service delivery	Civil societies/NGOs/CBOs/interest groups form action squads to monitor public service delivery in selected fields; and to engage in advocacy and information sharing.	Applicable to any public service delivery, which is decided to be tracked.	Similar as above.
Citizen advisory boards	A Citizen Advisory Board can be set up by civil society, court of law or government to monitor and advice public service delivery agencies or other specific issue/s related to public interest.	Public complaints and public grievances relating to denial of justice from government, private sector and others come under its purview.	Maintaining credibility and transparency in the eyes of the public is important.

(*Contd.*)

(*Contd.*)

Tools for Social Accountability	*Summary Description*	*Field of Application/s*	*Selected Aspects*
Special accountability institutions, e.g. human rights commission	Human Rights Commission at a national level is generally an autonomous body with a mandate to safeguard human rights and monitors cases of its violation.	All violations of human rights	Maintaining credibility and transparency in the eyes of the public is important.
Lobbying and advocacy campaigns	Some civil society organizations/NGOs/INGOs may involve them selves in lobbying issues with sub-national, national or international inter-governmental agencies and undertake campaigns to organize and/or inform the public.	Any public issue, whether regional, national and inter-national.	Maintaining credibility and transparency in the eyes of the public is important.
Public/social interest litigation in favour of poor	Some civil society organizations or some group of citizen or a single citizen could file public interest litigation in a court of law.	Any public issue.	The litigation can be prolonged.
People's court	A people's court can be set up by civil society to deliberate/settle issues related to public injustice and grievances.	Public complaints and public grievances related to denial of justice from government, private sector and others could come under its purview.	Maintaining credibility and transparency in the eyes of the public is important. Often it is difficult to bring the concerned parties together in the court. There is also the issue of legitimacy.

Following from the discussion on voice tools, as above, chapter 4 explains and illustrates participatory poverty assessment from the field and related learning process.

NOTES

1. See Mukherjee (1993) and (2002) for details on symbols, cards and other means to plan with people having low or no literacy.
2. IAP2 Core Values, *http://iap2.org/displaycommon.cfm?an=4*
3. page 60, Chavez, Daniel (2008), "The watering down of participatory budgeting and people power in Porto Alegre, Brazil", in IIED's (2008), Participatory Learning and Action, 58, towards empowered participation: stories and reflections, International Institute for Environment and Development, June.
4. UK Government's Neighbourhood Renewal Programme focuses on engaged of deprived communities in generating social outcomes.
5. Pennyslvania Department of Public Welfare Office of Medical Assistance program www.dpw.state.pa.us/Omap/rfp/SEStndsReq/omapSESRappL.asp - 30k, (Appendix L) Guidelines For Consumer/Family Satisfaction Teams and Member Satisfaction Surveys), also see for details see Advancing Excellence in America's Nursing Homes, *www.nhqualitycampaign.org/files/im/6_Satisfaction_TAW_Guide.pdf.*
6. *Consumer Satisfaction Survey 2003 Final.doc View as HTML* depts. washington.edu/.../Adult%20and%20Famil %20Consumer%20Surveys/Consumer%20Satisfaction% 20Survey%202003%20Final.pdf ;
7. Review of Approaches to Satisfaction Surveys of Clients of Disability Services, Consultancy Report, 1998, www.pc.gov.au/gsp/reports/consultancy/disabsvc - 17k.
8. *AGENCY-WIDE CLIENT SATISFACTION SURVEY REPORT*
   A total of 559 *family* members or friends of Adults with mental health problems. participated in the *Family Satisfaction survey.* www.dcf.state.fl.us/publications/docs/staterpt1.pdf
9. Family Service, Toronto, People for change, 14 May 2008 Development of the Client *Satisfaction Survey*, www.familyservicetoronto.org/whatsnew/survey.html
10. *http://www.interpraxis.com/social_audit_resources.htm.*
11. *Source*: Social Audit, New Zealand 159 Palmerston Streets, PO Box 145, Westport, New Zealand.
12. www.coopdevelopmentcenter.coop/Good%20Practices/SocialAuditManual.pdf -
13. Within the last two decades, India has not only enacted specific legislation on environmental protection but has also virtually created a new fundamental

right to a clean environment in the Constitution. The distinguishing nature of this jurisprudence shows the nature of the new Indian constitutional law regime accords greater importance to public concerns than protecting private interests and the activist role of the Indian judiciary (Abraham: 1999).

REFERENCES

Abraham, C.M., (1999). *Environmental Jurisprudence in India*, p. 331, Martinus Nijhoff Publishers.

Adikeshavalu Ravindra (2004). "An Assessment of the Impact of Bangalore Citizen Report Card on the Performance of Public Agencies", ECD Working Paper Series 12, The World Bank Evaluation Department, The World Bank Washington D.C. June.

Amnesty International (2001). "National Human Rights Institutions: Amnesty International's Recommendations for Effective Protection and Promotion of Human Rights", Amnesty International, October.

Anecdote (2007). "Putting stories to work, Most Significant Change—A Primer", September, www.anecdote.com.au/archives/most_significant_change/ - 28k

Blakey, Heather (2008). "Participatory budgeting in the UK: a challenge to the system", in IIED's (2008), Participatory Learning and Action, 58, towards empowered participation: stories and reflections, International Institute for Environment and Development, June.

Bond, Richard and Neela Mukherjee (2001). *Livelihood Asset Status Tracking (LAST) A Case From Rajasthan*, Impact Assessment for Sustainable Development Unit, Working Paper Series, Institute for Development Policy and Management, University of Manchester, March.

Brown, L., (2001). "Social Auditing and Community Cohesion: The Cooperative Way (A Report to the Cooperative Secretariat and Canadian Heritage), February.
http://www.agr.gc.ca/rcs-src/coop/index_e.php?page=brown&s1=pub

Bryant, Peter (2008). "Mali's Farmers' Jury: an attempt to democratize policy-making on bio-technology", in IIED's (2008), *Participatory Learning and Action*, 58, Towards empowered participation: stories and reflections, International Institute for Environment and Development, June.

Buhl, Solveig, Qian Wei and Wang Xuixeong (2004a). Report Card—Satisfaction Survey, An initial Observation from China, Technical Report 2, GTZ, July.

Buhl, Solveig, Qian Wei and Wang Xuixeong (2004b). Towards Comprehensive and participatory Poverty Monitoring and Impact Evaluation in Jiangxi Province, China.

Burgess, Heidi and Cate Malek. "Public Participation." *Beyond Intractability*. Eds. Guy Burgess and Heidi Burgess. Conflict Research Consortium, University of Colorado, Boulder. Posted: September 2005 <*http://www.beyondintractability.org/essay/public_participation/*.

Cabannes, Yves "Participatory Budgeting: Conceptual Framework and Analysis of its Contribution to Urban Governance and the Millenium Development Goal". Concept Paper, see *www.googles.com*

Caddy, J. (2002). Information, Consultation & Public Participation in Policy-making: Mapping the experience of OECD countries, OECD, June, E-governance: Agenda-setting workshop Council of Europe, 10-11th June.

Central Bureau of Statistics (2002). *Nepal Living Standards Survey II 2002/03*: Household Questionnaire, CBS, Thapathali, Kathmandu.

Cernea, M.M. (1991). *Putting People First*, (Second Edition) Oxford University Press

Chambers, R. (2008). *Revolutions in Development Inquiry*, Earthscan, London.

Chavez, Daniel (2008). "The watering down of participatory budgeting and people power in Porto Alegre, Brazil", in IIED's (2008), *Participatory Learning and Action*, 58, Towards empowered participation: stories and reflections, International Institute for Environment and Development, June.

Clay, David (2008). "The changing face of community participation: The Liverpool black experience", in IIED's (2008), *Participatory Learning and Action*, 58, Towards empowered participation: stories and reflections, International Institute for Environment and Development, June.

Clark, Cindy, (2001). "*Making Change Happen: Advocacy and Citizen Participation*," Institute for Development Studies-Participation Group, *http://www.justassociates.org/MakingChangeReport.pdf*

Clear Horizon, Most Significant Change Technique Overview, www.clearhorizon.com.au/page.php?pid=24 - 13k

Commonwealth Secretariat (2001). "National Human Rights Institutions, Best Practice", Commonwealth Secretariat, London.

Davies, R. and J. Dart (2005). The "Most Significant Change" (MSC) Technique-A Guide to Its Use. April, www.mande.co.uk/docs/MSCGuide.pdf

Davies, R (1996). "An Evolutionary Approach to Facilitating Organizational Learning: An Experiment by the Christian Commission for Development in Bangladesh", htpp://www.mande.co.uk/docs/ccdb.htm.
depts.washington.edu/.../Adult%20and%20Famil%20Consumer%20Surveys/Consumer%20Satisfaction%20Survey%202003%20Final.pdf
Consumer Satisfaction Survey 2003 Final.doc View as HTML

Desai, A. H. and Murlidhar, S. (2000). Public Interest Litigation: Potential and Problems, published in B.N. Kirpal *et al.* (ed.), (2000) "Supreme but not Infallible—Essays in Honour of Supreme Court of India, International Environmental Law Research Centre, Oxford University Press, New Delhi, www.ielrc.org/content/a0003.pdf

Development Vision (2005). Community Groundwater Irrigation Sector Project (CGISP): Socio Economic Impact Study, Development Vision, Nepal Pvt. Ltd.

Development Vision (2004). Process Monitoring of Targeted Programmes, Free Textbook Distribution and National Scholarship Programmes—Doti and

Banke Districts, Final Report, Submitted to the National Planning Commission by Development Vision, Nepal Pvt.Ltd, Kathmandu.

Development Tracks (2000, 2004-5). Typescript, Field Notes on Street Children of Delhi, Development Tracks in Research, Training & Consultancy, New Delhi.

Dreze Jean and Amartya Sen (1995). *India, Economic Development and Social Opportunity,* Delhi, Oxford University Press.

Eady, Nigel, Jasber Singh, Alice Taylore-Gee and Tom Wakeford, (2008). "Community x-change: connecting citizens and scientists to policy makers", in IIED's (2008), *Participatory Learning and Action*, 58, Towards empowered participation: stories and reflections, International Institute for Environment and Development, June.

Exchange (2005). Most Significant Change: "An Evolutionary Approach to Monitoring that Facilitates Organizational Learning", February. www.healthcomms.org/comms/eval/le02.html - 20k

Fitzduff, Niall, Peter Byrant, Gwen Lanigan and Catherine Purvis (2008). "Hearing the real voices: exploring the experiences of the European Citizens' Panel", in IIED's (2008), *Participatory Learning and Action*, 58, Towards empowered participation: stories and reflections, International Institute for Environment and Development, June.

Gloppen, Siri L. Rakner, A. Tostensen (2003). "Responsiveness to the Concerns of the Poor and Accountability to the Commitment to Poverty Reduction", WP 2003:9, Chr. Michelsen Institute, Development Studies and Human Rights, Bergen, Norway

Government of South Australia (2008). The Most Significant Change, Department of Education and Children's Services, 10th September www.learningtolearn.sa.edu.au/learning_workroom/a8_publish/modules/publish/content.asp?id=13795&navgrp=441 - 14k

Halsbury's Law. Monthly (2001). Sponsored by Lexis Nexis, August Judicial Activism in Public Interest Litigation, t www.halsburys.in/judicial-activism.html - 14k

Haq, Jackie (2008). Community participation: 'activists' or 'citizens', in IIED's (2008), *Participatory Learning and Action*, 58, Towards empowered participation: stories and reflections, International Institute for Environment and Development, June.

HealthLink Worldwide, Networking and Learning, How Stories Help us to Learn, www.healthlink.org.uk/we-do/network_msc.html - 19k

International Council on Human Rights Policy & UN High Commissioner for Human Rights (2005). Assessing the Effectiveness of National Human Rights Institutions, Versoix.

IIED (2008). *Participatory Learning and Action*, 58, towards empowered participation: stories and reflections, International Institute for Environment and Development, June.

Jain, S.P. and Wim Polman (2003). *A handbook for trainers on participatory local development: The Panchayati Raj model in India*, Food and Agriculture Organization of the United Nations Regional Office for Asia and the Pacific, Bangkok, 2nd Edition.

Kashefi, Elham and Chris Keene, (2008). "Citizen juries in Burnley, UK: from deliberation to intervention" in IIED's (2008), *Participatory Learning and Action*, 58, Towards empowered participation: stories and reflections, International Institute for Environment and Development, June.

Krishna, Anirudh and Norman Uphoff (1999). Mapping and Measuring Social Capital: A Conceptual and Empirical Study of Collective Action for Conserving and Developing Watersheds in Rajasthan, India, *Social Capital Initiative Working Paper No. 13*. Washington: World Bank.

Kuruganti, Kavitha, Michel Pimbert and Tom Wakeford (2008). "The people's vision—UK and Indian reflections on Prajateerpu" in IIED's (2008), *Participatory Learning and Action*, 58, Towards empowered participation: stories and reflections, International Institute for Environment and Development, June.

Lydia Fehring, Jenny Pettenon, Ann Fagan, Kathryn Goyen, andJessica Connor, Evaluation: Land Learn's most significant change, www.regional.org.au/au/apen/2006/refereed/5/3083_fehringlr.htm - 37k

Mukherjee, Amitava (ed.) (2004a). *Participatory Rural Appraisal, Methods & Applications in Rural Planning*, Concept Publishing Company, Delhi.

Mukherjee, Amitava (ed.) (2004b). *Participatory Monitoring*, Concept Publishing Company, Delhi.

Mukherjee, Neela (1993). *Participatory Rural Appraisal, Methodology & Applications*, Concept Publishing Co., Delhi

Mukherjee, Neela (1997). *Participatory Appraisal of Natural Resources*, Concept Publishing Co., Delhi

Mukherjee, Neela (2002). *Participatory Learning and Action with 100 Field Methods*, Concept Publishing Co., Delhi.

Mukherjee, Neela (2002). *Forest Protection Committees of West Bengal: Measuring Social Capital in Joint Forest Management*, (also see www.livelihoods.org)

Narayan Deepa (1999). "Bonds and Bridges: Social Capital and Poverty", Poverty *Research Working Paper No. 2167*, The World Bank D.C. July.

Nicholson, L. (2005). *The Research Shop*, March, www.scotland.gov.uk/Publications/2005/09/16120247 - 15k.

Nayak, B., *http://orissarti.com/socialaudit/social_audit.htm*

Nicholson, L. (2005). The Research Shop, March, www.scotland.gov.uk/Publications/2005/09/16120247 - 15k.

O'Neill, T., Foresti, M. and Hudson, A. (2007). *Evaluation of Citizens' Voice and Accountability: Review of the Literature and Donor Approaches*. London: DFID.

Pennyslvania Department of Public Welfare Office of Medical Assistance program www.dpw.state.pa.us/Omap/rfp/SEStndsReq/omapSESRappL.asp - 30k. (Appendix L) Guidelines For Consumer/Family Satisfaction Teams and Member Satisfaction Surveys), *also see* for details see Advancing Excellence in America's Nursing Homes, *www.nhqualitycampaign.org/files/im/6_Satisfaction_TAW_Guide.pdf*

Pretty, J. (1995). "Participatory learning for sustainable agriculture", *World Development*, 23(8), 1247-1263

Pretty, Jules and Hugh Ward (2001). "Social Capital and the Environment", *World Development*, Vol. 29, No.2, pp.209-227.

Putnam, Robert D., Leonardi, R., & Nanetti. R.Y. (1993). *Making Democracy Work: Civic Tradition in Modern Italy*, Princeton University Press, Princeton N.J.

Right 2B heard Collective and Swingbridge Video (2008). If we have time, motivation and resources to Participate, does that mean we gain authority and power?, in IIED's (2008), Participatory Learning and Action, 58, Towards empowered participation: stories and reflections, International Institute for Environment and Development, June.

Sen Amartya (1997). Social Exclusion: A Critical Assessment of the Concept and Its Relevance (mimeo), Asian Development Bank, September.

Serra, Renata (2001). "Social Capital: Meaningful and Measurable at the State Level?" *Economic and Political Weekly*, February 24, 2001.

Singh, Jasber (2008). "The UK Nanojury as 'upsteam' public engagement" in IIED's (2008), *Participatory Learning and Action*, 58, Towards empowered participation: stories and reflections, International Institute for Environment and Development. June.

Social Audit New Zealand 159 Palmerston Streets, PO Box 145, Westport, New Zealand.

Stipak, B. (2008). Towards more thoughtful and responsible use of public opinion data by local administrators, *Journal of Urban Affairs*, published online, vol.5, issue 3, 14th February.

Sudirman, D. W. and S. McGrath (2005). "Public Participation in Local Forestry Policy-Making after Decentralization: Uncertainties, challenges and expectations in Tanjung Jabung Barat District, Jambi Province, Forest and Governance Programme, No. 3, January.

The Participatory Video Revolution, Combining Participatory Videos with the Most Significant Change Approach, www.insightshare.org/case_study_msc.html - 25k.

The World Bank (2004). Citizen Report Card Surveys—A Note on the Concept and Methodology, Social Development Notes, Participation & Civic Engagement, *Note No. 91*, February.

The World Bank (2001). Philippines Filipino Report Card on Pro-Poor Services, Environment and Social Development Sector Unit, East Asia and Pacific Region, *Report No. 22181*—PH, May 30.

The World Bank (2004). *Making Services Work for Poor People, World Development Report.* The World Bank, Washington D.C.

Uphoff, N. (1992). *Learning from Gal Oya: Possibilities for participatory development and post-Newtonian Science,* Cornell University Press, Ithaca.

Uphoff, N. (2000). "Understanding Social Capital: Learning from the Analysis and Experience of Participation." In Partha Dasgupta and Ismail Serageldin, eds., *Social Capital: A Multifaceted Perspective,* 215-249, World Bank, Washington, D.C.

Vadivel, V. S., Public Interest Litigation: A Boon or Bane, Legal Services India.com, www.legalserviceindia.com/articles/pil.htm - 30k.

Veneklasen, Lisa and Valerie Miller, (2002). *A New Weave of Power, People and Politics, The Action Guide for Advocacy and Citizen Participation,* Co-Editors, Debbie Budlender and Cindy Clark, published by World Neighbours, Oklahoma, USA, The Asia Foundation, San Francisco and Lisa Veneklasen, Washington D.C.

VICTO Social Audit Project, Social Audit Manual, Canadian Cooperative Association and CIDA, www.coopdevelopmentcenter.coop/Good%20Practices/SocialAuditManual.pdf.

Wakeford, Tom, Bano Murtuia and Peter Byrant (2008). Ignoring and suppressing grassroots participation in a northern English town, in IIED's (2008), *Participatory Learning and Action,* 58, Towards empowered participation: stories and reflections, International Institute for Environment and Development, June.

Wampler, Brian (2000). A Guide to Participatory Budgeting, October, *www.internationalbudget.orf/resources/library/GPB.pdf*

Warfield, Wallace P., (1993). "Public-Policy Conflict Resolution: The nexus between culture and process." In *Conflict Resolution Theory and Practice.* Edited by Sandole, Dennis J.D. and Hugo van der Merwe, (1993) Manchester, U.K.: Manchester University Press.

www.coopdevelopmentcenter.coop/Good%20Practices/SocialAuditManual.pdf

www.dcf.state.fl.us/publications/docs/staterpt1.pdf

Family Service, Toronto, People for change, 14 May 2008 Development of the Client *Satisfaction Survey,* www.familyservicetoronto.org/whatsnew/survey.html

www.epa.gov/publicinvolvement/: U.S. Environmental Protection Agency: Public Involvement

www.idea.gov.uk/idk/aio/1118552, Innovations in Public Services, Literature Review

www.ids.ac.uk/ids/particip/research/socpol.html: Citizen Participation in Social Policy

www.infrastructure.gc.ca/research-recherche/results-resultats/rn-nr/rn-nr-2007-08-eng.html

www.interpraxis.com/social_audit_resources.htm

www.law.indiana.edu/ilj/oldsite/volumes/v73/no3/applegate.html, "Beyond the Usual Suspects: The Use of Citizens Advisory Boards in Environmental Decision making" by John S. Applegate

www.legalservicesindia.com : Jha, G. Problems facing Public interest Litigation in India, www.legalservicesindia.com/articles/pil_ind.htm - 37k-

www.mass.gov/dcr/waterSupply/watershed/documents/quabbinaccessch3.pdf

www.pc.gov.au/gsp/reports/consultancy/disabsvc - 17k Review of Approaches to Satisfaction Surveys of Clients of Disability Services, Consultancy Report, 1998.

Agency-wide Client Satisfaction Survey Report

www.scotland.gov.uk/Publications/2005/09/16120247 - 15k

www. unpan1.un.org/intradoc/groups/public/documents/un/unpan027075. pdf, *Public Governance Indicators: A Literature Review*

www.blackwell-synergy.com/doi/abs/10.1111/j.1467-9906.1983.tb00040.x

4

Participatory Poverty Assessment (PPA) at Local Level: A Field Illustration

This chapter explains and illustrates Participatory Poverty Assessment (PPA) and the related learning process. It provides practical illustration from the field at the micro level.

4.1 What is a Participatory Poverty Assessment?

Participatory Poverty Assessment (PPA) is a situational analysis of poverty mostly done by key stakeholders from the "bottom"—the poor and marginalized groups of women and men—in their own "voice" which helps flag important lessons and insights for furthering their cause and provide space for people's inputs and assessment for pro-poor policy-making and practice. The PPA process helps involve key stakeholders in assessing development polices and programmes, in revealing their priorities and preferences and in creating space for their "ownership" of the development process.

4.1.1 PPA

PPA is a tool for situational assessment of poverty from the perspectives of the poor people. It is a tool to arrive at an integrated picture of poverty assessment and its reduction constructed mainly from the perspectives of the poor people. It is a tool to map poverty assessment from the local level to a higher level and to produce synthesis pictures of poverty mapped by local stakeholders. However, the aspects of poverty assessment and integration could vary across studies. PPA's broader objectives, goals, scope and methods could also vary. Many institutions view PPA more as a policy-research exercise for understanding poverty from the perspective of poor people and their priorities and possible actions to improve their lives. In this context, one useful definition of PPA by DFID is that "Participatory Poverty Assessment" (PPA) is an instrument for including the perspectives of poor people in the analysis of poverty and the formulation of strategies to reduce it.

4.1.2 Country Experience in PPA

While Bangladesh (UNDP: 1996) mainly focused on dimensions of poverty, vulnerability assessment, problem-solution assessment and assessment related to service delivery, the World Bank's Project on "Consultations with the Poor" in 23 countries for feeding into the World Development Report 2000-01 aimed at understanding poor people's perspectives on four key themes:

- Ill being and well-being,
- Problem and priorities,
- Institutional relationships, and
- Gender issues.

The PPA in Guangxi Province, China (ITAD/DFID/World Bank: 2004) aimed at social group assessment and assessment of thrust areas such as education and health. The scope of PPA in West Bengal (Development Tracks/Asian Development Bank: 2005) was still broader and all inclusive such as assessment of social groups, resources, vulnerability, livelihoods, prioritized problems-solutions, gender-related issues, issues related to policies, institutions and processes and people's best and innovative practices at the grassroots. One important purpose of PPA is to improve the effectiveness of actions aimed at poverty reduction. There could be multiple topics/aspects/components assessed through PPA depending on the situation.

4.2 Field Illustrations of PPA

First a group of facilitators oriented themselves with participatory principles and voice tools and undertook purposive sampling of villages to select a village for conducting their first PPA exercise.

Village Selection for PPA—Village Chekka was selected based on poverty criteria, low literacy level, interior location of the village, rain-fed agriculture, interior location and predominance of *beedi* making as a source of local livelihood. There are 156 villages in area concerned of which at least 40,000 villagers from 80 to 90 villages are engaged in *beedi* rolling as their main source of livelihood.

4.2.1 Overcoming Biases and Building Rapport

The PPA team visited Chekka village equipped with participatory methods and principles and a checklist of issues, made efforts to build rapport with the community in Chekka for soliciting their participation for PPA. Visual items and diagramming were used for involving participants who were not literate. Along with rapport building, the objectives and purpose of PPA were explained. Care was taken to mainstream gender by interacting with both women and men groups. Interactions with different social groups were also carried out and results cross-checked. Some standard rural development biases minimized by the PPA team were 'location' bias, gender bias, 'tarmac' bias, 'elite' bias, 'time' bias (avoiding migration period/s) and professional bias (outside facilitators as inter-disciplinary teams).

4.2.2 Background of Chekka Village

Chekka village was quite large and widespread with much wasteland. There were nearly 3000 households residing in the village, where most were landless. Almost all the households were engaged in *beedi* rolling as a source of livelihood. The PPA team met different social groups in three locations and interacted on their living conditions and life and their perspectives on the poverty situation and pathways out of poverty. Many of them are *kumor* by caste (those who make earthen pottery) though most of them have abandoned their traditional pottery work in favour of *beedi*-rolling due to reasons such as shortage of space to keep earthen materials, problems in acquiring earth etc.

The women were able to roll *beedi* (say between 200-500 *beedis*) which were much less in quantity than men who rolled (say between 700 -1000). One bundle of *beedi* of 1000 fetched INR 30. However, many were just able to roll 500 *beedi* per day for Rs. 15 worth of goods such as 1 kg rice, 250 grams potato and some salt procured from the *beedi* trader. Many small children, both girls and boys, were busy making *beedi* and not having a chance to attend schools. Some children (20%) studied till the primary level and very few continued until the high school. Many women including the elderly, suffered from various ailments like weak eyesight and body aches due to the rigorous activities involved in *beedi* making. Nor were they able to get proper medical treatment/medicines from the local doctor nor were they stop making *beedi*. Sudden closure of *beedi* factory due to reasons such as high inventory of *kutcha beedi* adversely affected local livelihoods.

4.2.3 Social Groups in Village Chekka

After primary introduction and explanation of the objectives of the village study, the local people were asked to define who were the poor and the non-poor and why so. The women replied that those households were better off, which had men, land, food security and education—this being the basic difference between the rich and the poor.

The residents of the Chekka village were able to divide the village society into four distinct social groups based on criteria such as living conditions, land ownership, health conditions and others. The following paragraphs provide a description of each of these groups. (also see Chart 4.1).

- *Middle Income*: The villagers in this category owned about 1 or 2 *bighas* of land with most of their houses being made of clay walls and tiled roofs. There are some houses with tin roofs and brick walls as well. Their household assets comprised steel utensils, watches, cycles and radios while the livestock in their possession was quite limited. They did managed two square meals a day and mainly had rice or *chappati* in winter, with vegetables. Education was restricted effectively to the primary level with very few children going to the high school. The health centre was located nearby but the facilities available were of very poor quality, forcing the villagers to opt for distant hospitals and doctors at nearby cities and other places at high cost.
- *Poor Households*: This group did not possess any agricultural land with most of the houses made of clay and tin roofs. Their household assets were restricted to aluminium vessels

Chart 4.1: Social Grouping

Social Group	*Food taken*	*Physical assets*	*Type of house*	*Land ownership*	*Education levels*	*Health facilities*	*Livelihoods*	*Livestock or poultry*
Middle Class (19%)*	Have rice twice a day. In winter, *chapati* with vegetables	Steel utensils, watch, cycle, radio, TVs	Most houses have tiled roofs and clay walls. Some have tin roofs and brick walls	1–2 bighas dependent on rainfall	Most go to primary schools but very few go to the high schools.	Health centre is nearby but has poor facilities. During emergencies, villagers have to go far away while most cannot afford it.	*Beedi* trader (*mahajon*), One teacher of primary school	1 or 2 cows or goats
Lower Income or Poor (37.5%)*	Rice, starched rice, *saag* and vegetables available, twice a day	Aluminium utensils	Houses with tiled roof and clay walls	No agricultural land	Children go to primary schools and ICDS centres	Health centre is nearby but has poor facilities.	Throughout the day, women and men roll *beedis*, some engaged in *beedi* factories	Some have goats or cows
Deficit Households (37.5%)*	Starched rice and boiled potatoes twice a day	Earthen vessels and aluminium utensils.	Broken clay walls, half portion of roof is tiled patched with polyethene	No land	Children cannot go to school as they work in *beedi* making	Rolling beedi gives them headaches, stomach problems and eye problems	Roll *beedi*	None
Destitute (6%)*	Whatever food is available, from time to time	Very few aluminium utensils and earthen vessels	Broken clay house with tiled roofs.	No land	Children do not go to school	Stomach problems, weak eyesight, back-aches	Roll *beedi* and beg	None

Note: * = % estimates by villagers of different social groups.

while livestock ownership was also minimal. They had two meals a day consisting of rice, starched rice, cooked and boiled vegetables as available. Their children attended primary school and child development centre. The local health centre was of limited value as the medicines available were of very poor quality. The men and women worked throughout the day in the *beedi* factories.

- *Deficit Household*: They did not own any form of land or livestock while their housing conditions were also very poor—the clay walls were broken and the roof was covered with polythene and tiles. Household assets were limited to mostly earthen/a few aluminium vessels. The food intake consisted of starched rice and boiled potatoes while the children had no education as they were also made to work in *beedi* rolling. The health of this group was not good as the *beedi* rolling activities led to poor eyesight and other ailments. The *beedi* trader was their chief source of financial support.
- *Destitute* : This group was the poorest of all and did not own any land, livestock or household assets. They lived in broken clay/thatched houses with polythene roofs and ate whatever they could manage on a daily basis through *beedi* rolling and even begging. The children did not go to school but rolled *beedis*. There were several health afflictions like stomach aches, back aches, weakening eyesight, TB, etc.

4.2.4 Resources and Access in Chekka Village

The major natural resources (*See* Chart 4.2) were all related to the supply of water for different purposes. They included the local river adjoining the village, all small and large ponds along with the check dam built on the same river. Chekka village had no prominent social resources while the loans or wages paid by the *beedi* trader and the rearing of livestock and poultry were the major sources of income for the villagers. Of a total of 3000 households in the village, a mere 20 people had studied up to the graduate level and formed the miniscule supply of educated human resources the village had. As far as physical resources were concerned, the village had a fair amount of the same—the primary school, the local health care centre, the post office, the ICDS centre, the children education centre and the village administration.

Chart 4.2: List of Village Resources

Natural resources	*Physical resources*	*Human resources*	*Social resources*	*Financial resources*
• Small pond • Local river • Check dam • Large pond	• Primary school • Health care centre • Post office • Child development centre • Child education centre • Village administration	• There are 20 graduates among almost 1200 households	• Often the trader lends money to the villagers when in need	• The trader • Poultry • Goats

4.2.5 Trends in Chekka Village (See Chart 4.3)

Wage rate, food patterns, household assets, agriculture, social milieu in different years are listed below:

- *1990* : The labour wage rate was INR 8 plus 1 kg of rice per day while a kilogram of rice cost INR 5. The wages for *beedi* making were Rs. 10 per 1000 *beedi* rolled. The staple diet consisted of 100 grams of starched rice and boiled or roasted potatoes. There were very few household assets while sanitation facilities were absent. There was no agricultural progress while the respect for the poor was abysmally low. Alcoholism and crime were rampant. The amount paid as dowry ranged from INR 5,000 to INR 10,000. Although rainfall levels were high, there were no natural calamities like floods.
- *1995*: The labour wage rate increased to about INR 15 per day with the price of rice touching INR 7 per kilogram. The staple diet was chapatis, vegetables, saag and 2 kg of rice for 7 in a family. Natural calamities stayed away while rainfall remained high—drinking water came from the wells. Household assets were limited to steel utensils, cycles and watches. Agriculture progress happened at low levels. Dowry payments were in the range of INR 20,000 plus other household items.

- *2000*: In this year, the labour wage rate was INR 20 while rice was priced at INR 8 per kilogram. The staple diet of the people now included *chapati* made of wheat, starched rice, vegetables and roasted potatoes. Natural disasters, agricultural progress, ownership of household assets and sanitation did not register any rise while the amount to be paid in dowry reached the mark of INR 30,000 along with other household items. Some children from poor households became educated and there was respect for the educated poor.
- *2003* : The labour wage rate and the cost of rice were INR 25 and INR 10, respectively. The diet mainly comprised of rice, pulses, vegetables and fish from the river. The household assets in middle class households now included radios, televisions and cycles but for others, in general, there were not much change from the previous period considered. There was increased regard for the poor, especially the educated poor, while the level of dowry had increased to about INR 40,000 in cash plus other household items.

4.2.6 Seasonal Patterns in Chekka Village

Selected seasonal aspects emerged from the session on the seasonal patterns of living conditions in the village (*See* Chart 4.3).

- During the months of April-June and August-October with acute scarcity, there was hardly much work available for the village in terms of *beedi* rolling or agriculture with the wages dwindling to INR 15 to INR 18 per 1000 *beedi* rolled. This extreme hardship period forces many youngsters to theft and crime, mainly petty thefts. The little savings were used up for subsistence purposes.
- In June-July-August and October to February, work was available for the villagers to make a living. *Beedi* making and farm work still remained the main sources of livelihoods with men, women and children engaged in such activities.
- February and March were better months of the year when much work was available for men, women and children. Even the remuneration touched a high of about INR 30 for every 1000 *beedi* rolled.

Chart 4.3: Inter-Temporal Variations

Year	*Labour wages*	*Price of food*	*Quantity of food/ diet contents*	*Assets owned*	*Natural calamity*	*Rain fall*	*Dowry system*	*Respect for the poor*	*Improvement in Agriculture*	*Sanitation facilities*
1990	Rs. 8 and 1 kg of rice *Beedi* wages was Rs. 10 per 1000 *beedi*	INR 5 for 1 kg of rice	Starched rice—100 gms, Boiled or roasted potatoes	Tin utensils	Was less	High rain fall Drank captured water	INR 5000—INR 10000	Low respect for the poor. Alcoholism and theft prevailed	Negligible	Negligible
1995	*Beedi* wages Rs. 15 General wages also same	INR 6 —Rs. 7 per kg	2 kg for 7 people, *Saag*, *Chapati*, Vegetables sometimes	Steel utensils, Cycle, Watches	Was less	Drank well water. High rainfall	INR 20000 plus other household items	Low respect for the poor. Alcoholism and theft prevailed	Present only for those who own land	Negligible
2000	*Beedi* wages Rs. 20 General wages also same	INR 7 – INR 8 per kg	starched rice, Roasted potatoes, leafy vegetables, *chapattis* at times, 3 kg rice for 9 people	Steel utensils, Cycle, Watches	Was less	Drinking water from tube well	Lack of money resulted in stalling of several marriages INR 30000 plus furniture	Increase in thefts Slightly higher level of respect, especially for the educated poor	Dependence on rainfall No improvement for agriculture	Negligible
2003	*Beedi* wages was Rs. 25 per 1000 *beedi* General wages also same	INR 10 for 1 kg of rice	4 kg of rice for 11 people, pulses, vegetables, Catch fish from the river and eat	Radio, tape, cycle	Nil	Drinking water from tube well	Money plus other items INR 40000	Higher respect for the poor	Nil	Negligible

Chart 4.4: Seasonal Calendar

April-May	*May-June*	*June-July*	*July-August*	*August-September*	*September-October*	*October-November*	*November-December*	*Decem-ber-January*	*January-February*	*February-March*	*March-April*
This is a period of scarcity. Employment In Agricultural and *beedi* work are not available Poverty forces many to theft and crime The *beedi* wages fall to Rs. 15 – Rs. 18 for 1000 *beedis*		Farm work available for both men and women		Acute period of scarcity as all savings are finished in the previous 2 months		Farm work like paddy harvesting is available. *Beedi* work is also available		Paddy harvest-ing and *beedi* making work are available	Men, women and children roll *beedi* INR 25 per 1000 *beedis* is the rate	Roll *beedi* at INR 25 per 1000 *beedi*	

4.2.7 Decision-making and Gender Aspects in Chekka Village

A discussion with the group of villagers on decision-making presented a very interesting picture for Chekka (See Chart 4.5). The major decisions taken in a village household have been listed in column (i) of Chart 4.5. It was mentioned that apart from deciding on what to cook on a given day, the women remained the weaker actors in the process of making any decision in the household. All decisions relating to agriculture, taking loans, livestock rearing and selling and others were the prerogative of the men in the house. Most decisions, especially the ones which directly involved the family unit, were jointly taken by the men and women such as decision on marriage of children, education and health of children, working in the *beedi* mills and the sale of land amongst others.

Chart 4.5: Gender Role in Decision Making

Various Tasks *Column (i)*	*Women* *Column (ii)*	*Both* *Column (iii)*	*Men* *Column (iv)*
Beedi making after taking *beedi* leaves from the mahajon		**	
Agriculture			**
Cooking decisions	**		
Marriage of daughter		**	
Marketing for household			**
Education of children		**	
Taking children to the doctor		**	
Selling of land		**	
Taking loans			**
Rearing and selling poultry and livestock			**

4.2.8 Problems in Chekka Village

Chart 4.6 provides a list of problems of the villagers and also indicates possible solutions as suggested by the villagers.

- The main problem was that of the houses of the villagers being of poor quality where the roofs were broken and water seeped in during the rains, making it difficult for the inmates to live. It was suggested that the village administration should build houses for the villagers, similar to those provided under the subsidized housing scheme—Indira Awas Yojana—in different locations within the village itself.

- The wage they received for *beedi* rolling was inadequate to make two ends meet for their families. The wages needed to be increased and also their timely payment. The *mahajon* should keep aside a fund from where these payments could be made.
- Further, many villagers were landless. They could not grow their own food and hence felt constrained. They suggested that the government, through the district authority, should provide them land and also get more wastelands under the cultivable area.
- Health problems were acute in the village despite the presence of a health centre, basically, due to the low standard of the facilities available there. The villagers went far to procure good treatment and medicines, which was expensive for most of them. In the process, many sold their assets to find surplus money for good treatment. They suggested that the village administration should try to improve these facilities and also build a better health centre in the village.
- A severe water scarcity plagued the village affecting drinking water facilities as well as irrigation systems. The solution suggested was that the village administration should arrange for better irrigation facilities and also start harvesting rainwater in ponds dug especially for the purpose. The villagers could cooperate in this process.

Lack of employment opportunities was leading several young men to become criminals by night. To curb this growing menace, the villagers said that a bank should be setup in that area for giving loans to these youngsters which would enable them to start a business of their own.

- The villagers also cited a problem of getting firewood from a long distance which took a lot of time and energy. It was suggested that the village administration could collaborate with the villagers with the former providing the saplings and the latter doing the work of planting them.
- Amongst other problems were included lack of social security, lack of a common space to roll *beedis* and the mistargeting of the "below the poverty line" (BPL) list. They are described below in Chart 4.6.

Chart 4.6: Problem-Solution Analysis

Primary problem	*Nature of problem*	*Possible solutions*	*Who should be responsible?*	*Where to implement the solution*
Problem of dwellings	Tiles are broken water seeps in during rains and huts get flooded. Children can't study. The huts are too small and it is difficult to make beedis; there is not much space to rear livestock.	Provide houses like the ones given under Indira Awas Yojana	Village administration Villagers and village administration together reconstruct the houses	Houses to be redone in their own paras
Shortage of funds	Get minimal work in rolling *beedi* which does not yield adequate incomes	They should get higher wages and timely payment	Owner of *beedi* factory (mahajon) Funds should be arranged in time	Near continuous work from the *beedi* factory for the labourers
Landlessness	Don't have own agricultural land Have to buy food and eat	Government should provide land for possession; wasteland should be utilized	District authority and villagers together need to solve the problem	For those villagers who are landless
Health problems and inadequate health facilities	This is due to *beedi*-making. Many are suffering from TB but try to hide it. "If they do not make *beedi* then what do we eat?" There is not enough arrangement for treatment. The child always inhales the gas of tobacco leaves. Treatment and medicines provided by health care centre are not adequate. Forced to travel far for treatment and medicines which is expensive. There is a hospital for beedi workers but there is no powerful treatment available. Elementary treatment is available and treatment is not in pace with the incidence of sickness. One needs to go to Ranchi for treatment and	The health worker should be more efficient Villagers should get more medicines	Village administration	Open a high standard health centre near the village

(*Contd.*)

(Contd.)

Primary problem	*Nature of problem*	*Possible solutions*	*Who should be responsible?*	*Where to implement the solution*
	spend INR 150 (travel cost) + INR 200 /INR 300 (doctor's fee) + INR 700/800 (medicines). Some people are forced to sell their house/land			
Water problems	No drinking water facilities are available nearby No irrigation facilities, which is hampering agriculture	Irrigation facilities should be provided. Rainwater should be harvested in large ponds.	The residents of the village with co-operation from the panchayat	In the whole village
Lack of employ-ment opport-unities	No work leads to boost in crime among the young boys due to frustrations	Open a small bank which gives them loans to start a small business	With the help of Panchayat	For the unemployed educated young boys
Scarcity of Firewood	Have to get firewood from very long distance.	Plant trees in the barren courtyards of the old buildings	Plantation by villagers with the help of the panchayat as the latter gives them the trees	For those dependent on firewood
Lack of social security	Few *beedi* companies have arrangement for Provident Fund for their beedi workers. Others do not provide any facility	Provident fund scheme in *beedi* needs to be started by all *beedi* companies	*Beedi* companies and District authority	For those who roll *beedi*
Lack of a common space to roll *beedis*	There is no place to roll *beedi*; huts are small and there is no extra space	A common space is required in the village to roll *beedi*	Can be arranged by village administ-ration	For those who roll *beedi*

(Contd.)

(*Contd.*)

Primary problem	*Nature of problem*	*Possible solutions*	*Who should be responsible?*	*Where to implement the solution*
BPL list mis-targeted	There are 3000 households in this village, of which 2000 households fall within BPL. Roughly 1000 households in BPL are mis-targeted	Those poor households left out from the BPL list needs to be included	By the Government	For those poor households whose names are left out from the BPL list

4.2.9 Institutions in Chekka Village

A discussion of the institutions that functioned in the village revealed that Chekka had some local institutions (*See* Chart 4.7) to support the villages but they were not without their share of problems.

- The primary school in the village has enough students but the quality of teaching was not up to the mark. The teachers came from a great distance and, often, did not come at all. The villages needed to ensure that the staff of the school was regular as only then would the quality of education improve. Some government help in this regard was most welcome.
- The Integrated Child Development Scheme (ICDS) centre suffered from the common problem of the quantity of food distributed to the children being below the villages' expectations and needs. Several children did not go to the centre for the same reason. The obvious solution to this situation was to increase the amount of food that each child received at the centre.
- As mentioned earlier, the local health centre was not of much help as the quality of medicines provided at the centre was very poor. Moreover, not all medicines were available with the doctors there. This issue needed to be addressed quickly.
- The village had a post office but it did not open on most days of the week.
- The SSK operated from under a tree in the village as it did

not have a proper structure to house it. This exposed it to several natural hindrances, prime among them being the vagaries of monsoons. Further, the number of students was too large, which prompted the villagers to suggest the establishment of a second SSK in the village itself.

Chart 4.7: Institutional Analysis

Institution	*Problems faced*	*Possible solutions*
Primary school	Teacher has to come from far off and often do not turn up. Quality of education is not good. There are 4 men and two women as teachers but they are not regular.	Villagers should ensure that the teachers are regular and arrive at 10-30 AM and go home from duty at 4 PM. They should teach well Government help is required for better management of teachers and schools.
ICDS centre	There are 4 ICDS centres in the village. They are all constrained due to lack of space. Food quantity is considerably less, which discourages children from going to school.	If the quantity of food given were to be increased, all would become interested. Rice provided as mid-day meal is distributed at a pace of 3 months. This can be done after every 7 days to reduce food deficit amongst children.
Health centre	Doctors do not treat patients well and are available only for an hour or so. There are not enough medicines available. There are no good doctors and no beds for treatment. Medicines and treatment standards provided are not adequate.	The doctors should perform their duty and be available full time. The treatment standard needs to be improved. The medicines provided need to be of better quality and quantity.
Post office	It is closed on most days.	It should be open on all working days
Shishu Shikha Kendra (Child Education Centres)	It is organized under a tree which exposes them to nature's problems such as heat, rain etc. There are too many students.	There is a need for one more SSK in the village.

4.2.10 Livelihoods Analysis

Charts 4.8 and 4.9 indicate problems in existing livelihoods and the preferred sources of livelihoods, respectively.

Chart 4.8: Problems and Options: Existing Livelihoods

Problem	*Prioritisation – (Voting)*		*Possible Options*
	Men	*Women*	
(i) Health problems due to beedi-making; get aged much before time; the hospital for *beedi* workers does not have arrangement for proper treatment and the doctors are also not equipped well and need better attitude.	2	10	They start making beedi at the age of 8 and 9 (the child is inhaling the *beedi* has right from her childhood) or even earlier and get old quickly at the age of 40-45 years when their speed slows down and their health gets debilitated. Many have T.B. Yet the hospital meant for *beedi* workers has no proper arrangement for treatment of *beedi* workers. There are 40,000 *beedi* workers in Jhalda-2 and only 150 of them come to this hospital. They need to borrow money for going to Ranchi for medical treatment. The *beedi* employer provides no facility for medical treatment. The hospital meant for *beedi* workers needs to be upgraded and doctors need to attend more efficiently.
(ii) Unable to procure *beedi* leaves in time	8	2	Other sources of livelihoods required besides *beedi*-rolling.
(iii) A proportion (20% to 30%) of *beedi* rolled are rejected arbitrarily by *beedi mahajon*	—	—	The beedi workers should be supported to form their own Self-Help-Groups so that their bargaining power increases. They cannot start selling their own packaged *beedi* in the market due to Government rules (they need government permit for selling *kattcha beedi* and they also need permit for labeling). There is no local market for raw beedis and they have little or no ability to bargain with beedi traders for marketing their own *beedis.* The government imposes excise duties and other taxes on beedi, which is of no benefit to the *beedi* workers.
Eyes easily get cataract	1	5	Require periodic arrangements for cataract treatment.
No cash to treatment and buy medicines	Not scored	8	All *beedi* employers can provide provident fund facilities and the workers can then be allowed loans against such fund. At present only one or two do it.
No space to roll *beedi*	Not scored	Not scored	A common space with a roof is required to be constructed for beedi making
Not enough work for each of us	Not scored	Not scored	Other sources of livelihoods required.

Some preferred livelihoods as suggested by the poor are indicated below:

Chart 4.9: Preferred Sources of Livelihoods

Preferred Livelihoods	Suggested Steps
Rearing ducks	If rainwater could be held in ponds, ducks could be reared in them.
Rearing hens and goats	Better quality hens are needed. Training will enable women to rear poultry.
Doing pisciculture in the ponds	If ponds are dug, pisciculture can be carried out in them.
Rearing milch cattle	For those who have cows, better breeds are required. Also training is needed to breed such cows.
Working in brick kilns	Financial aid is needed. Bank loans will help build kilns.
Tailoring	Training is needed as well as loans. Village administration or block can provide help in this regard.
Vegetable and paddy farming	Irrigation facilities will help in farming activities.

In absence of other opportunities, *beedi* rolling was the predominant source of livelihood of women, men and children of village Chekka. Some of the preferred livelihoods that the villagers of Chekka were looking for are listed in Chart 4.9 given above. They include rearing of poultry and milch cattle, vegetable farming, paddy farming, tailoring, working in brick kilns and breeding fish in the local ponds.

Several steps were suggested to improve upon the existing livelihood/s. If new ponds were dug where rainwater would be captured, it would help in the rearing of ducks and also provide the opportunity of fish-breeding by the villagers. In terms of rearing livestock and poultry, the villagers were looking for access to better breed and training on the technical aspects of the processes involved. Women could be trained to play an active part in such livelihoods. Some form of financial assistance from banks and other institutions would help in such activities, especially in building brick kilns and tailoring pursuits. The provision of irrigation facilities would provide invaluable support to the various farming options that the villagers preferred to undertake.

4.3 Lessons Learnt

The lessons learnt by the facilitators' team from PPA in Chekka village are indicated below:

(i) The better is the rapport building with the villagers the better is the participatory process. Patience is a big factor for outside facilitator/s. Once the outside facilitators are accepted by the villagers and their credentials looked into, participatory inquiry becomes much easier. The more the time spent in establishing rapport the less is the noise in the primary data. Rapport building and its quality influences the kind of information generated during participatory inquiry. It is not easy to conduct PPA amongst fear, suspicion and disbelief amongst the villagers.

(ii) Peer reviews on a daily basis help in improving quality of PPA process and output and sustaining the tempo of the team. It also provides an opportunity for group-sharing, learning and reflection.

(iii) Social mapping helps in identification of locational issues and providing social overviews. Visual diagramming methods help those who are not literate and those who are reluctant to talk.

(iv) Conflicts amongst local people arising during participatory sessions need to be sorted out amicably.

(v) Management of expectations of the people is important in a participatory process.

(vi) Inappropriate locations for PPA infuse noise in the data and makes it biased.

(vii) Women participate actively when interacted as separate groups rather than combined. Those lacking confidence to talk before groups are better approached through case studies or on one-to-one interactive basis. Case study method provides opportunities to destitute and other marginalized/weaker groups to participate. Some disadvantaged people when met in smaller groups or individually are able to express their views and priorities. Often the poor lack courage and confidence to speak on their issues. It is important to create space for their views to emerge. Poor may have empty boxes in terms of local sensitive issues and their solutions. They would also like to know the end-result of PPA.

(viii) Group exercises are important and generate transparency, ownership, involvement, exchange of views and group validation. It is important to engage different actors in the community to resolve their doubts. In a dependency relationship, the poor would remain at the back and the 'better off' will take initiative to talk with outsiders.

(ix) Community time is limited and outsiders need to respect community time.

(x) It is important for facilitators from outside to have primary assessment of the local situation based on their experience. Skills for observation are very important. It is also important to remember that PPA sessions can generate both qualitative and quantitative data.

5

Participatory Livelihoods Assessment as Community Voice Tool

In this chapter I have described the components of Sustainable Livelihoods' Assessment (SLA) Framework, its application in a field study, an SLA-type micro picture and an SLA-type 'larger picture' of community voices at a sub-national level. To be specific, the present chapter includes the following four sections.

(i) Components/Elements of SLA Framework[1]
(ii) Background of SLA-type Field Inquiry
(iii) Micro-level SLA-type picture based on local community voices
(iv) Evolving larger SLA-type Sub-National level picture based on micro-level community voices

5.1 SLA Framework

SLA framework aims to improve the lives of poor people and to strengthen their livelihoods. A livelihood comprises of the capabilities, assets[2] and activities required for a means of living. A livelihood is sustainable when it can cope with and recover from stresses and shocks and maintain or enhance its capabilities and assets, both now and in future without undermining its natural resource base[3]. Based on people's own perspectives and priorities for their livelihoods, SLA could be described as a way in which people discuss their assets related to livelihoods, the vulnerability conditions under which assets exist, their livelihoods preferences, livelihoods-related outcomes, the policies, institutions and processes which influence their livelihoods and their recommendations thereby. SLA starts with people and aims to mainstream environment within a broader framework. Development agencies can contribute by increasing the opportunities available to individuals/groups/communities by building up their asset base; and helping to ensure that the policies, institutions and processes, which define people's options are working in favour of the poor.

5.1.1 SLA Components

SLA framework includes five components of complex livelihoods:

- Capital Assets
- Vulnerability Context
- Policies, Institutions and Processes (PIPs)
- Strategies
- Livelihoods-related Outcomes

There are five different types of assets upon which individuals draw to build their livelihoods. These are:

- Natural Capital
- Social Capital
- Human Capital
- Physical Capital
- Financial Capital

5.1.1.1 Description of the five Capitals

The five capitals are briefly described below:

(i) *Natural Capital*—Natural resource stocks from which flows are useful to livelihood such as land, water, wildlife, biodiversity, etc.
(ii) *Social Capital*—Social resources such as networks, membership of groups, trusts etc.
(iii) *Human Capital*—Skill, knowledge, ability to work, good health.

(iv) *Physical Capital*—Basic infrastructure — transport, shelter, water, energy and communications.

(v) *Financial Capital*—Financial resources available to people whether savings, credit, remittances, etc.

The different types of capital assets indicate a useful starting point for thinking about how and in what combination assets do translate into sustainable livelihoods. The SLA framework suggests that there is a close correlation between people's overall asset status, the resources that they can draw upon and their robustness. Building up assets is thus a core component of empowerment. The underlying principle is that of multi-dimensional approach to understanding poverty and well-being. There is first the social analysis for distinguishing different social groups. This is followed by analysis of capital assets for different social groups. In SLA, some relevant issues are as follows:

- How has asset status been changing over time?
- Have there been upward or downward changes in the assets?
- What are the root causes of changes and how do they vary between different social groups?
- What changes are anticipated in the next few years and why?

5.1.2 Vulnerability/Risk Context

There is a need to understand the vulnerability/risk context in which assets exists, in terms of the trends, shocks, seasonality and local cultural practices, which affect livelihoods.

5.1.3 Transforming Policies, Institutions and Processes

It is important to understand how public policies, institutions/ organizations such as Government, NGOs, community based organizations, private sector, etc. and processes such as laws, rules, customary rights, incentives, etc. define people's livelihood options. Their expected impacts are as follows:

- They are critical in determining who gains access to which type of asset and what the effective value of asset is.

Table 5.1: Some Related Aspects of Livelihoods and Vulnerability Context

Component	*Some Key Issues*	*Examples*
Trends		
Resource Stocks	What is happening to natural resource stocks and quality?	Deregulation/Renewal trends; Loss of resources to rural/urban use.
Population Density	What is current density and how is this changing?	Density figure; Population growth figure; information on out-migration.
Technology	What technologies exists, which are likely to benefit the people of this area?	Technology database; local knowledge/varieties, technologies in use.
Politics	How are people in this area placed in terms of political representation?	Ethnic origin; distance to nearest seat of Government
Economics	How do economic trends affect livelihoods?	Price trends of locally produced goods; Percentage of local goods, which are traded
Shocks		
Climate	How does climate affect people's livelihoods/well being?	Annual rainfall, rainfall variability, Climate disasters
Conflict	Is there any civil or resource conflict (or likelihood of such conflict) in the area?	Accounts of conflict, legal cases pending
Seasonality		
Difficult Months	How do the difficult months affect people's livelihoods/well being?	Deficit months, coping strategies
Culture		
Culture	What effect, if any, does culture have on the way people manage their assets and the livelihood choices they make?	Unexplained differences between this and other area; accounts of the way things are done (and) constraints

Note: Adapted from DFID materials/notes on SLA and also from www.livelihoods.org

- Together with people's asset status, they help define which livelihood strategies or activities natural resource-based or otherwise—are open and attractive.
- Again, markets and legal restrictions have a profound influence on the extent to which one asset can be converted into another type of asset (e.g. natural capital into financial capital).

Thus, the SLA framework explicitly links the micro with the macro and emphasizes that policy and institutional analysis must be considered at all levels.

5.1.4 Livelihood Outcomes and Indicators

Drawing from participatory principles, it is crucial that we should listen to those with whom we are working and learn from them about their own objectives, own understanding of poverty and their own beliefs about the root causes of poverty. The main caveat relates to environmental sustainability. Often short-term survival rather than sustainable management of natural capital (soil, water, genetic diversity, etc.) can be priority of many poor. Hence, working with people to help them understand the contributions (positive or negative) that their livelihoods are making to the environment and to promote sustainability is a long-term objective. It is also important to discuss and include indicators of sustainability.

5.1.5 From Analysis to Action

What can be the entry points for support and action at the field level? In the course of a learning exercise, a set of practical issues and suggestions on SLA are expected to evolve from local community perspectives, based on their knowledge and experience.

5.1.6 SLA Objectives

The broad objectives of SLA include supporting livelihoods of poor through the provision of:

- A more supportive social environment.
- Improved access and better management of natural resources.
- Improved access to financial resources.
- Improved access to high quality education, information, technologies and training, and better nutrition and health.
- Improved access to facilitating infrastructure.
- A policy and institutional environment which supports multiple livelihood strategies and promotes equitable access to competitive markets for all.

5.2 Illustration from SLA-Type Field Inquiry

In order to derive a larger sub-national picture of community voices on sustainable rural livelihoods, an SLA-type field study can have different objectives, as illustrated below:

- To learn about ways in which the poor organize their livelihoods.
- To learn about the opportunities and constraints, which poor face while securing livelihoods.
- To learn about the role of different actors in supporting livelihoods of poor communities.
- To learn how to enable the poor to secure their preferred livelihood opportunities and overcome constraints and exclusionary processes.

Some key steps involving SLA-type field inquiry include the following:

- Consensus of stakeholders to conduct SLA and set objectives
- Capacity building for SLA team
- Selection of sampling/area coverage, focus groups etc.
- Preparation of a checklist of issues for field inquiry
- Informing local communities, both women and men groups
- Rapport building and group interactions based on participatory principles and tools
- Sharing of findings and review by local communities
- Cross-checking of data
- Analysis and synthesis of field inquiry
- SLA write ups and arriving at a SLA-type 'larger picture' and policy doables
- Sharing of findings with policy-makers and practitioners
- Options and follow ups in terms of policy changes

A practical field study on SLA undertaken in the year 2003 is given below primarily for purposes of illustration of selected aspects of such study. The illustration below is a compressed one being mainly illustrative in nature. However, SLA-type study needs to have enough depth for organizing people's voices and for arriving at a 'larger picture'.

5.2.1 Choice of Villages and Sampling Aspects

The choice of villages is quite important for arriving at a larger sub-national picture and needs to be undertaken carefully based on selected criteria, sampling objectives and budgetary constraints. The field illustration described here is for a province, which has different agro-ecological zones and based on them the livelihoods of rural poor vary. For the field study under discussion, the sampling was a 3-staged process where 4 districts (sampling of districts covered 22.2 per cent of total number of districts) covered 4 distinct types of agro-eco-socio zones. The 4 districts included were:

(i) District no. 1 or 'forest-based' district,
(ii) District no. 2 or 'rice bowl' district,
(iii) District no. 3 or 'flood plain' district, and
(iv) District no. 4 or the '*terai*' district.

Within the 4 districts, a total of 15 blocks were selected which had higher incidence of rural poverty as per province-related indicators. Within the 15 blocks, a total of 22 villages were selected. The villages studies included consultation with local authority and there was spot-selection of some villages to reduce any selection-related bias.

5.2.2 Field Inquiry

Field inquiry for SLA included some generic steps (as listed below) though there was scope for enough flexibility and, hence, deviations from the steps were expected in the normal course of fieldwork depending on local situation at hand. Following review of secondary data, some generic steps for participatory sessions at local level were as follows:

- Rapport building, warming up
- Exploratory interactive sessions with communities/groups of women and men
- Exploratory overviews
- Topical probing
- Probing for gap filling
- Validation of outputs and processes
- Sharing with different stakeholders

Field inquiry for the study was based on the methodology and the principles of Participatory Rural Appraisal/Participatory Learning and Action (PRA/PLA). A generic checklist for SLA-type field inquiry was prepared on a pilot basis, which was complemented by a topical checklist, tested and improved upon based on insights gained through field exercises. Fieldwork based on SLA framework was done *in situ*, through participatory sessions with over 500 village participants, of which, 60 per cent were women, on an average.

5.3 Micro-level SLA-type Picture

Based on local community voices, a sample illustration from Photik village is given below. Two SLA facilitators[4] interacted with the villagers. It took some time to break ice and to elicit people's interest in expressing their views.

5.3.1 Photik Village, located near a river bank, had 130 resident households and five caste-based hamlets. The villagers constructed four social groups in the village, according to their criteria of land holding, occupation, housing, etc.

Table 5.2: Estimates of Social Groups in Photik Village based on Local Criteria

Social Groups	Estimated Proportion of Total Village Households (%)	Criteria for Social Grouping
Group 1: Middle Class	12.5 % (16 households)	Households had, on average, land holdings of 40 bigha[5] and their livelihoods were dependent mainly on agriculture. They lived in brick houses with tinned roofs. They had food throughout the year. Some of the family members had migrated outside village for work. They possessed consumer durables such as furniture, radio, etc.
Group 2: Lower Middle Class	37.5 % (48 households)	The average land holding of this group was 8 bigha[5] which they used for agriculture. They lived in mud houses with straw or asbestos sheet roofs. They somehow managed their food and living.
Group 3: Agricul-tural Labourer	37.5 % (49 households)	This group consisted mostly of daily agricultural labourers. They worked in others houses. They had land on government-donated land and lived in mud houses with straw roofs.

(*Contd.*)

(*Contd.*)

Group 4: Ultra Poor	12.5 % (17 households)	The people in this group begged for living. They had little or no space to live. They either lived in dilapidated huts or in the courtyards of others. They had very little possession or utensils. They somehow managed to live and all days were not the same for them. There were some women in this group who got old age pension from local government. For this group 9 subsidized houses had been built under the government scheme of Indira Awas Yojana.
Total = 4 Social Groups	Total = 100 % Total = 130 households	

5.3.2 Assets People Accessed and Used

As expressed by local groups, there was natural capital in the form of a river and other water bodies such as ponds. In a social map drawn by the villagers, there were seven ponds shown. There was local aforestation drive by local government and trees planted by local villagers. The human capital was in the form of initiatives taken towards educating their children and trying to change local sanitary habit (of open defecation) mainly through the influence of such school-going children who had carried such message home. The groups were also of the opinion that their village did not have enough social capital to bind them together and women's consciousness and decision making abilities had much scope for improvement.

The physical capital status of the villagers varied with different social groups. Such physical capital was being strengthened through some government schemes like subsidized housing, construction of sanitary toilets etc. Limited access to financial capital was supported by local banks and other funds such as Rural Irrigation Development Fund. With increase in irrigation facilities, crops such as potato and paddy were being grown which generated income for the landholders and also for the labourers who worked on those lands.

5.3.3 Vulnerability Context

Food was available up to some extent throughout the year. There was food scarcity during the months of August-September-October, but the villagers somehow managed. Their diet consisted mainly of rice, vegetables and small quantities of fish and during festivals they tried to have chickens. Animal diseases were prevalent during the months of May, June and July. Human diseases such as fever and stomach related problems existed all round the year.

5.3.4 Poor People's Livelihoods

The local livelihoods were mainly dependent on agriculture, daily labour, milch cow rearing and other activities like making puffed rice, boiling paddy, working as domestic help in others houses. Agricultural work was done mostly by men. Daily wage labour was done both by men and women. Milching of cows was also shared as the men milked the cows while the women prepared milk products like cottage cheese to be sold in the markets. Other activities like making of puffed rice, paddy boiling and working as domestic help in others, houses were done by women only.

Some women working as wage labourers indicated that they had preference for tailoring and sewing activities provided they were able to have sewing machine. They also preferred making of puffed rice, poultry-breeding and making plates from 'sal' leaf collected from nearby forests. Their most preferred livelihood source was rearing good quality cattle for milk production. Groups of women villagers indicated their livelihood preferences as in Table 5.3.

Table 5.3: Preference Ranking of Livelihoods by Women Groups

Livelihood Activity	*Preference Ranking*
Rearing good quality cattle	1
Sewing work after taking training	1
Making puffed rice with machine	1
Making sal leaf plates	2
Rearing poultry birds	3

This group also indicated gender-wise division of access and control in different matters. The discussions were summed up as given in Table 5.4.

5.3.5 In What Ways Policies/Institutions Help/Restrict People's Livelihoods?

The role of the local government through *gram panchayat* was positive and some government schemes were being implemented in the villages.

Table 5.4: Gender-wise Responsibilities, Access and Decision-Making

Activity/Decision-Making	*By Women (%)*	*By Men (%)*	*Total (%)*
Agriculture work in fields	25	75	100
Agriculture work at home	37.5	72.5	100
Vegetable growing	100	—	100
Poultry work	100	—	100
Work related to cattle	50	50	100
Decision about purchasing	25	75	100
Decision about spending	—	100	100
Decision about children education	100	—	100
Decision about marriage of children	50	50	100
Decision about number of children	37.5	72.5	100
Decision about women working	100	—	100
Decision about loan repayment	50	50	100

Nine houses had been constructed under subsidized housing scheme for ultra poor households. The villagers had sent a proposal to their local government for increasing the number of such subsidized houses by 4 or 5. Under the IRDP scheme, the villagers got bank loans for purchase of goats, cows, establishing shops, business of puffed rice, etc., which were mostly repaid, though a few were defaulters. A system of farmers' credit card had also started where 25-30 farmers were given such cards. Some villagers were of the view that with start of full-fledged banking operations like lockers and mortgage loans, they would be saved from the clutches of the village money-lenders.

The local governance had made significant contributions. In Photik village, there was 95 per cent sanitation. For setting up sanitary toilets, the beneficiary contributed INR 200 and an equal amount was contributed by the local body. The sanitary material was prepared by the Sanitary Mart run by a local NGO, which employed many people to prepare sanitary pan and the concrete slab. The sanitary latrines for the poorer households had been constructed by local authority at its own cost. However, only 50 per cent of the latrines were being used on account of certain local beliefs. Some villagers expressed that the consciousness for using sanitary toilets would come gradually and much through the children who brought the message of sanitation home to their families.

There were local schools constructed by the local governance—one old building and a new one. The older building was being used as a centre for children below 5 years of age. They gave mid-day meal in the form of rice and pulses and also provided medicines. In the new building, the school ran up to class IV. The students were given 3 kilos of rice per head per month, school uniform and books though the boy students were not given books and uniform.

The local governance could set up 10 tube-wells in the village. With improvement in water quality, the health of the villagers had improved. The maintenance was overseen by a local beneficiary committee of 7-8 members, mostly women and any repair work was done by local authority. Of the 10 wells, 2 needed to be repaired. The local governance had constructed a bridge, though its railings were broken. Aforestation activities helped grow trees such as Sesum, Eucalyptus and Acacia.

The district level government had a River Irrigation Development Fund Scheme, under which there were 6 submersible wells which supported local agriculture activities. The villagers remarked that at least 6 more wells were needed to fully meet the irrigational needs of the village. The wells were looked after by a local beneficiary committee of 7-8 farmers which also levied a charge for the water during the agriculture seasons. The district level government had started construction of village roads but the same was incomplete. Many villagers felt that without specific funds allotted for this purpose, not much progress could be envisaged. Under the government scheme for self help groups (SHGs), there were 2 SHGs of 6 men members, each running for one year and had been supported once by the local authority for one-time revolving fund. The village had electric cables though the poor households could not access due to lack of funds. There was a health centre and polio camps had been organized. There was also a veterinary doctor who visited the village occasionally and the treatment of livestock was therefore not easy. Though there was a Sub Divisional hospital at the block level, the village was in the need of a doctor and also medical equipments which were costly.

The villagers also mentioned about the Government provident fund scheme for agricultural labourers. The agricultural labourers deposited INR 10 every month in the bank and the local government deposited an equal amount for each individual in the bank. The scheme was open to agricultural labourers between the ages of 18-50 years, both male and female. This deposit continued up to the age of 50 years of age, after which a lump sum deposit of INR 40000-42000 accumulated per individual account. The amount including the principal and the interest thereon was received by the individual. A passbook for this purpose was issued to the individuals concerned.

5.3.6 What were the Livelihoods-related Outcomes?

The facilitators enquired about the investments required for each livelihood-related activity, the risks involved and the income generated.

In agriculture, different types of investment were required depending on the crops grown on a seasonal basis. Risks foreseen in agriculture included natural calamities, lower fertility of land and lack of proper irrigational facilities. Daily labour needed no investment and the villagers earned INR 55 per day with which they maintained their livelihoods. The other risk was that of illness affecting health of villagers. For some better off families, which undertook milch cow related business, the investment was mainly in terms of cost of the animal to the tune of INR 4000 to INR 8000 per cow. The risk was in the form of the cow contracting a disease and dying. Other problems such as shortage of water to wash the cows and lack of good quality cows were also there.

5.3.7 Selected Observations by SLA Facilitators

During the field sessions on sustaining livelihoods, it was observed that the women were not very clear about what activities they could undertake to improve their livelihoods-related opportunities. Every time they were prompted by the men to say something and it appeared that through them the opinion of the men was being voiced. The women later interacted as separate group/s for voicing their views.

It was also observed that there was a sand quarry nearby the village and the trucks carrying sand passed through the village. The roads were in bad shape and there was a lot of dust which affected the health of the people. It was mentioned by local people that the condition of the roads worsened during the rainy season.

As mentioned by local groups, much of the outside work was done by local men. The role of the women was more in housework, cooking, paddy related work at home, etc. It was also observed that the women needed to raise their awareness levels and confidence so that they could become more self-reliant. There was need for SHGs of women to be formed in the village. The local people and authority could motivate the women and support them to form their own groups for organizing their preferred livelihoods-related activities.

Table 5.5: Some Livelihoods-Related Investments and Outcomes in Photik Village

Activity	*Investments*	*Duration of Activity*	*Constraints*	*Support Received*	*Selected Outcomes*
Agriculture	For one agriculture crop season an investment of INR1500 per bigha[6] was required. For second agriculture crop season an investment of INR 3000 per bigha[7] was required. For potato crop investment of INR 3000 per bigha[8] was required.	One harvest was available during July-April. Second harvest was available between January-April	There was lack of irrigation facility, incidence of diseases and loss of fertility of land	Loan was received up to INR 3000	Income from one crop was INR 2500 per bigha.[9] Income from second crop was INR 4500 per bigha.[10] Income from potato crop was INR 8000 per bigha[11]
Daily Labour		All round the year	Susceptibility to diseases		Daily wages of INR 55
Milk Business	Calf cost was INR 2000 to 4000 minimum cost was Cow costs INR 8000 to 10000	All round the year	Diseases afflicting cattle, lack of water to bathe, lack of good quality cows		The household need for milk was met

5.4 Evolving Larger SLA-type Sub-national Picture

The larger sub-national picture on sustaining livelihoods was organized based on micro-level community voices. The community voices from the 22 study villages were put together to arrive at a sub-national picture. Some steps and details for the synthesis picture are provided below.

5.4.1 Who are the Poor?

Poor households lived in different localities under diverse agro-ecological-social conditions. However, such deficit households demonstrated many similar patterns with regard to access to physical/social/natural assets, livelihood composition, food availability, social exclusion and governance issues. In the study villages, the poor groups were facilitated to do their own social analysis of the village and come out with criteria for differentiating poor groups from those non-poor. Since the poor groups owned few assets, the emerging criteria included size of land owned, period of food availability from one's own land, type of house, period of wage labour, etc.

A synthesis picture of such social groups is presented in Table 5.6, where 5 categories of social groups are described in terms of different poverty indicators. While doing the social analysis most participants thought that it was important to distinguish between destitute households and destitute women-headed households. All groups did not exist in all study villages though in many villages it was not difficult to find all the groups as described in Table 5.6.

Table 5.7 provides a glimpse of poor and non-poor groups in the study villages. As per indigenous criteria, some study villages had 100 per cent poor groups in at least two study districts. Large chunks of poverty existed in all the four districts studied. Proportion of poor groups ranged from 44 per cent to 100 per cent in the study villages of one district where forests predominate though such a case was relatively less in other districts.

Table 5.6: Social Grouping Based on Participants' Criteria—The Larger Sub-National Picture

Social Groups (Col.1)	*Type of Dwelling (Col.2)*	*Food Security (Col.3)*	*Land Holdings and other Resources (Col.4)*	*Main Livelihood Activities and Coping Mechanisms (Col.5)*	*Health, Education and Social Status and Access (Col.6)*
(ia) Destitute household with thatched hut Ultra-Ultra poor	Small thatched hut	Low food security, go hungry when sick or no work, also face seasonal shortage of food, get food as alms. High dependence on wild food of those having local Sal forest.	No land, no asset have/not have homestead land, not received patta land. Those with access to local forest have high dependence on NTFPs.	Sell twigs, branches, leaves, dry wood, NTFPs; exchange fish for food/paddy, some beg work as labourers, sell advance labour, work in others' homes.	Some have handicapped and sick family members - socially invisible - isolated from mainstream government programmes and NGO activities. Very few are covered under IAY. Health of family members is a recurring problem. Children do not attend school and adolescent girls cannot be married due to lack of funds for dowry etc. Sometimes they are married by raising money through charity.
(ib) Destitute women with no house Ultra-Ultra poor women (especially	No land, no house, live in other's houses	Low food security, go hungry when sick or no work, also face seasonal	No asset have/not have homestead land, received/ not received patta land. Those with	Wage labour, sell firewood, beg collect and sell dry leaves, Work as midwives, work in others' homes Very few covered under government housing scheme for poor and Annapurna Yojana	Sick, aged, incapable of work, elderly women. Some handicapped persons, deserted/divorced. Health of family members is a recurring problem. Children do not attend school

(Contd.)

(Contd.)

Social Groups (Col.1)	Type of Dwelling (Col.2)	Food Security (Col.3)	Land Holdings and other Resources (Col.4)	Main Livelihood Activities and Coping Mechanisms (Col.5)	Health, Education and Social Status and Access (Col.6)
widowed, deserted and elderly unmarried women)		shortage of food, get food as alms. High dependence on wild food by those having local Sal forest.	access to local forest have high dependence on NTFPs.		and adolescent girls cannot be married due to lack of funds for dowry etc. Sometimes they are married by raising money through charity. -socially invisible -excluded from local development process and mainstream development programmes.
(ii) Wage labourer and poor producer –Ultra poor with little/no farm land	Live in mud houses with thatched roofs	2-3 months food available from farming and rest is from wage labour, seasonal scarcity. Those having access to	10 kathas of land, mostly upland with little or no irrigation facility many do not have patta land, some have patta land (cultivated/ not cultivated). Those with	Daily wage labourer, produce and sell many items, make Sal leaf plate, weave mat, make handicrafts etc., get negligible return from their land. Some coping mechanisms include dependence on NTFPs in food deficit periods and migration. Work in fields, sand quarries and brick fields throughout the year. Many also sell trees and sell fish to buy food.	Health status is problematic from time to time, also affected by seasonal diseases. Many children do not attend school and those attending easily drop out. Mostly not part of mainstream development process. Social status is low and no influence on decision-making at local level.

(Contd.)

(Contd.)

Social Groups (Col.1)	Type of Dwelling (Col.2)	Food Security (Col.3)	Land Holdings and other Resources (Col.4)	Main Livelihood Activities and Coping Mechanisms (Col.5)	Health, Education and Social Status and Access (Col.6)
		local Sal forest collect wild food mainly in off seasons.	access to local forest depend on NTFPs.	They take advance payment for labour from farmers, brick-field owners, mining construction contractors for work to be done at a later date.	
(iii) Moderate Poor	Live in mud houses with thatched/tinned roof	Ordinarily 6-9 months food available from farming. Those having access to local Sal forest collect some wild food.	Around 1 to 4 bighas of land. Those with access to local forest depend on NTFPs.	Since farming does not sustain throughout the year this group is also engaged in wage labour of different types. Some lease land/ take land on lease for cultivation. Many women are engaged producing different items, such as Sal leaf plate making, mat weaving and making handicrafts, cultivate vegetables etc. They collect fuel from the forest in the form of dry twigs, branches, leaves etc. both for domestic use and for selling them in the market.	Can take care of health expenses when necessary though recurring expenses become difficult to bear. Mostly send children to primary and to middle schools. Participate in mainstream development processes and are beneficiaries of different schemes, both government and NGOs. Many are members of SHGs and cooperatives and producer/user groups.

(Contd.)

(Contd.)

Social Groups (Col.1)	Type of Dwelling (Col.2)	Food Security (Col.3)	Land Holdings and other Resources (Col.4)	Main Livelihood Activities and Coping Mechanisms (Col.5)	Health, Education and Social Status and Access (Col.6)
(iv) Middle Class and Lower Middle Class	Mud/pucca houses with tin roofs	Have access to food throughout the year	Over 4 bighas of land. They collect NTFPs and also buy them from the poor groups as required.	The middle class depends on agriculture, grows vegetables, run shops and other multiple activities. Many lease their land and livestock to poor groups. While some take land on lease for cultivation. They employ wage labour for farm-related activities. Some also have maids helping with household work. The lower middle class cultivates crops, vegetables, sell fish and work as daily labour. Some are engaged in petty trade, small production and business and hawking of merchandise.	Health status is good except for those with terminal illness or disability. Children attend schools and many join colleges. Many are politically active and are leaders in local governance and political parties. They participate in local level decision-making and are in a position to influence it.
(v) Well off	Pucca house	Good food security	Self-reliant, owns land (around 20 bighas or more), owns shallow machine	Grows jute, paddy, wheat, many are service-holders, face less uncertainty and have ability to make investment and cope with risks. Many lease lands and livestock to others.	Health status is good and can undertake medical treatment as and when required. Children attend good schools including boarding schools and also go for higher studies. Many live in

(Contd.)

(Contd.)

Social Groups (Col.1)	*Type of Dwelling (Col.2)*	*Food Security (Col.3)*	*Land Holdings and other Resources (Col.4)*	*Main Livelihood Activities and Coping Mechanisms (Col.5)*	*Health, Education and Social Status and Access (Col.6)*
			They buy NTFPs from the poor groups as and when required.	Employ wage labourers for farm work and producing different items. Employ maids to work in their households.	towns and cities and return to the village from time to time. Some have caretakers to attend to day-to-day affairs. As elite group, they wield considerable influence in local governance and decision-making.

Note: The local terminology—English equivalent used by village participants for identifying different households within the social groups are indicated in parentheses.

Source: Collated from field notes on different study villages.

Table 5.7: Comparative Picture of Poor/Non-Poor Groups: Based on Villagers' Perspectives

Village and District	No. of HHs	(1) Destitute (%)	(2) Wage labour (%)	(3) Moderate poor (%)	Poor (1+2+3) (%)	Non-Poor (%)	Total (%)
District No. 1							
Village 1	1029	6.25	15.45	51.5	73.2	26.8	100.0
Village 2	45	8.9	68.9	17.8	95.6	4.4	100.0
Village 3	440	5.0	57.3	—	62.3	37.7	100.0
Village 4	670	5.4	24.6	30.0	60.0	40.0	100.0
Village 5	45	25.1	50.0	24.9	100.0	—	100.0
Village 6	40	—	87.5*	12.5	100.0	—	100.0
Village 7	140	—	50.0*	50.0	100.0	—	100.0
Village 8	240	6	12.5	25.0	43.8	56.2	100.0
District No. 2							
Village 9	120	12.5	37.5		50.0	50.0	100.0
Village 10	75	12.0	53.3	13.3	78.6	21.4	100.0
Village 11	560	6.3	37.5	25.0	68.8	31.2	100.0
Village 12	27	7.3	26.0	66.7	100.0	—	100.0
Village 13	35	8.7	57.1	17.1	82.9	17.1	100.0
Village 14		25.1	43.7	—	68.8	31.2	100.0
Village 15	1500	12.5	50.0	25.0	87.5	12.5	100.0
District No. 3							
Village 16	85	3.5	40.2	31.2	74.9	25.1	100.0
Village 17	35	—	62.5*	25.0	87.5	12.6	100.0
Village 18	60	—	37.5*	50.0	87.5	12.5	100.0
Village 19	276	—	62.5*	25.0	87.5	12.5	100.0
District No. 4							
Village 20	500	—	50.0*	25.0	75.0	25.0	100.0
Village 21	250	—	71.4*	22.8	94.2	5.8	100.0
Village 22	750	—	56.2*	43.7	100.0	—	100.0

Note 1: The estimates are based on the social grouping method applied by local communities.

* Stands for data inclusive of destitute households.

Note 2: Village participants in the study villages applied a PRA method for social grouping where they discussed and identified social categories of households based on local criteria. Once the social categories emerged they were placed on ground/chart paper with the help of symbols and/or in writing. Then the participants were facilitated to arrive at proportion of households in each social category by using 16 betel nuts/seeds (equivalent to 16 anna = one Rupee), representing total number of households in their village. The participants arrived at estimated proportions and accordingly apportioned betel nuts (a popular food item taken with betel leaves) against different social categories. In case of representing fraction/s betel nuts were broken in pieces and then placed against the social group.

Source: Collated from field notes on different study villages.

5.4.2 Poverty Trends

Regarding poverty trends in the study villages, there were broad indications of both inter- and intra-group movements within the social groups in the study villages with reference to Table 5.7. In many study villages, the participants mentioned that new livelihoods opportunities created as a result of multi-crop cultivation, construction of roads, national highways, etc. helped many poor households progress forward. Situation regarding food security and nutrition had also improved over time. With increased irrigation facilities, those cultivating off season paddy crops, jute and vegetables had improved their lot. So have the poor households whose work opportunities had increased due to cultivation all year round.

However, there were also indications of sliding down of households from less poor to more poor status. Some trends showed that in one village many landed households had sold off their land (this included those provided by the government) to meet contingencies and were now employed as labourers on the same land. Poverty was on the rise in the 'flood plain' and the 'terai' with dampened markets for sericulture, *aman* paddy, tea cultivation, etc. Due to lack of demand, poverty trend was also on the rise for poor households engaged in weaving textiles and making handicrafts. Though enterprises such as food processing, floriculture and pisciculture appeared promising, the poor groups were unable to access necessary finance and support for inputs and infrastructure.

On balance it could be remarked that though the situation had improved for many poor households, there was increased feminization of poverty with rise in the number of women-headed households as destitute and ultra poor group/s due to breaking down of the conventional safety net. With socially depressing forces such as high cost of medical treatment and dowry payment, breaking the vicious circle of poverty was not easy. A kind of thumb rule provided by the women participants from some villages showed that on average, household incomes of INR 25 per day and INR 50 per day met subsistence needs of ultra poor and poor households, respectively. Continuous flow of such income was difficult and only those households who earned more than subsistence level were able to save for difficult times.

5.4.3 Livelihoods Pursued by Poor Groups

An overall sub-national picture on the existing livelihoods' pattern emerges from the synthesis of livelihoods ranking as shown in Table 5.8. It shows that in the study villages, poor people's livelihoods mainly revolve around wage labour [see row (iii) in Table 5.8], which is primarily agriculture labour (rank 1) and also non-agriculture labour (rank 1) followed by livestock rearing [see row (ii) with rank 2], a small initiative supplementing main livelihoods. Livelihoods are generally season-specific whether it is agricultural labour in the cropping season or non-agriculture labour in the off-season. Both types of labour—agriculture and non-agriculture—can involve migration within the district, or across districts and states. Livestock includes goat/sheep, chicken, duck, cattle and pig.

Table 5.8: Existing Ranking of Livelihoods in Study Villages

	Livelihoods	*District No. 1*	*District No. 2*	*District No. 3*	*District No. 4*
(i)	Cultivation of one's own land	7	2	6	3
(ii)	Livestock rearing	2	3	2	1
(iii)	Wage labour	1	1	1	2
(iv)	Tea Garden worker	—	—	—	4
(v)	Skill-based IGA	—	—	14	—
(vi)	Selling country liquor	—	—	—	5
(vii)	Weaving handlooms	—	—	9	—
(viii)	Silk thread making	—	—	10	—
(ix)	Making bamboo craft	4	—	5	8
(x)	Working as maid	—	3	8	—
(xi)	Making Sal leaf plates	5	—	—	—
(xii)	Making Muri (puffed rice)	—	3	—	—
(xiii)	Catching fish	—	5	13	6
(xiv)	Homestead gardening	8	—	—	—
(xv)	Selling fuel wood	6	—	—	7
(xvi)	Coal mines labour	—	4	—	—
(xvii)	Cultivating pineapple	—	—	—	7
(xviii)	Beedi rolling	—	—	4	—
(xix)	Out migration	3	—	3	—
(xx)	Petty trade	—	—	12	—
(xxi)	Work in mango orchard	—	—	11	—
(xxii)	Begging	—	—	7	

Note: The ranks on livelihoods have been estimated based on the scoring/ranking method of PRA which was applied during field study for village participants to rank their different sources of livelihoods-related activities in terms of their local significance based on the number of poor people engaged in such activities.

For study villages in district No. 2, agriculture on one's own land was ranked 2nd, which was relatively important in comparison to that in district No. 4 (rank 3rd), district No. 3 (rank 6th) and district No. 1 (rank 7th). For the study villages in district No. 3, out-migration and *beedi* rolling were ranked as 3rd and 4th while bamboo craft emerged as the 5th source of livelihoods. In district No. 2 which was also a mining district, work in coal belt was ranked as 4th (influenced by participants from the study villages in the coal belt).

In district No. 1, both bamboo craft and Sal leaf plate-making were important activities for ultra poor followed by selling fuel wood and dry leaves from forest and agro-forestry. In district No. 3, many ultra poor women worked as maids in better off households, while many destitute households survived through begging. In district No. 3, work in mango orchards was no longer remunerative and hence low in terms of rank while fishing, petty trade and tailoring were not enough to involve many poor households as sources of livelihoods. In district No. 3, weaving activity (rank 9th) and sericulture (rank 10th) had lower ranks since they were facing increased uncertainties due to sagging markets and falling prices.

Some characteristic features of poor people's livelihoods based on the study villages are listed below. Poor groups' livelihoods' activities were broadly categorized as shown in Table 5.9. Some key opportunities and constraints are also indicated.

- Agricultural labour was the main livelihood activity. However, in the forest villages forest-related livelihoods were quite common. Though least preferred, the most common livelihood-related activity was wage labour whether in agriculture, plantation, construction activities, mining and/or stone cutting.
- Most livelihoods-related activities were highly seasonal in nature and induced vulnerability in poor households mainly in terms of food insecurity and health care. In rain-fed farming areas, seasonal migration was a pronounced strategy during non-farming season/s.
- As for forest-dependent livelihoods, there were qualitative differences in household living conditions depending on access to local forests. The differences were significant in case of access to thick Sal forest or Acacia forest, the latter being considered to be an inferior option as stated by local people

since it mostly provided dry leaves/twigs on a daily basis and timber at a later stage. Those poor households with access to dense Sal forest were generally in a better position during the difficult seasons. They were able to harvest a variety of food items and other products from the forest for selling them and/or for household consumption. The Sal leaf plate making was an important activity for women in poor households, especially in the 'forest-based' district No. 1 and also in district No. 2.

Table 5.9: Selected Categories of Livelihood-Related Activities by Poor Households

Categories	*Livelihood-related Activities*	*Key Opportunity*	*Constraint*
Agriculture-related	Soil preparation, paddy planting, de-weeding, paddy harvesting, paddy de-husking, making puffed rice for selling, cultivating wheat, *moong, mashur, arhar* and other pulses; Babui and other grass cultivation, cultivating jute, collecting, snails, catching fish, snake etc. from doba, water pools, ponds, rice fields, gleaning etc.	Irrigated areas under multiple cropping provided opportunities for wage labour round the year.	Agriculture was seasonal and markets were not picking up. There was little scope for ware-housing arrangements. With rise in chemical inputs traditional wild food of ultra poor from farmer's field had declined
Forest/Micro Environments, e.g. home gardening	Collecting Sal leaves and making Sal-leaf plate; collecting dry leaves and putting them in bags and selling, collecting dry wood in bundles and selling, collecting babui grass for rope-making; collecting NTFPs such as *kendu pata, kurchi; piyal, binchi, bhela* and others; collecting flowers – *mahul*; collecting gum such as *barha*, collecting mushrooms; collecting *kachra*, ledhachaal, etc. collecting, snails, catching fish, snake etc. from water bodies and micro environments, doing home-gardening.	Those villagers with mixed forest in the locality were able to access a range of NTFPs, which they could sell. Others with mono forests such as those of Accacia could access mainly fuel.	NTFPs were seasonal and available in small quantities. Forest guard allowed limited harvesting.

(Contd.)

(Contd.)

Categories	*Livelihood-related Activities*	*Key Opportunity*	*Constraint*
Mining and Quarrying	Cutting stones, digging morrum mines, working in coal mines, helping in loading and transporting mined materials.	This provided work opportunities and higher wages especially during off-seasons.	Incidence of lung disease was high in the colliery belt due to pollution.
Livestock rearing	Goat-rearing, cow rearing, sheep-rearing, chicken-raising, pig-raising, raising of goat, duck, rabbit and other livestock.	Livestock rearing was preferred by the poor and was potentially a profitable venture with good backward and forward linkages.	Incidence of disease in livestock was considerably high, especially chickens and veterinary support was limited.
Craft/Artisan-related	Sericulture, handloom weaving, carpentry, tailoring, black smith, selling grocery, mat making, basket making, making bamboo craft, weaving talai etc.	Upgradation of skills in bamboo craft making, weaving mats and baskets could help in accessing better markets.	With falling demand sericulture/ handloom weaving had become loss-making proposition.
Plantation-related	Working as tea plantation worker on tea estates, working for plantation on forest land and private land.	Plantation work provided additional opportunities for wage labour.	There was the problem of getting regular wage with falling tea prices. Plantation work was seasonal and often one-off activity.
Construction activities	Working as labour for construction of roads, bridges, culverts, buildings etc., doing earthwork, working in brick kilns, cleaning water bodies and digging them for deepening.	Construction labour got higher wages as compared to agriculture labour.	Limited opportunities were available.
Other activities	Working as house maid, making haria and brewing local alcohol and selling.	Provided an avenue of employment.	Low return.

Note: Collated from field notes on different study villages.

- In case of degraded forests, the forest dependent communities were forced to migrate during the off-farm seasons. Some households were dependent on plantation and horticulture, whose strength depended on local markets and cost of cultivation. Such sources of livelihoods were vulnerable such as those dependent on *aman* paddy, tea, jute and sericulture produce whose prices were unstable and also un-remunerative.
- Those poor households, which had access to natural resources such as thick Sal forest, fish pond/s or reasonable water for cultivation of crop/s, were in a better position to compose their livelihoods along with their human asset, i.e. physical labour. Those households had better options, which were endowed in terms of skills in sericulture, bamboo craft, weaving, *beedi* rolling, tailoring and other income generating activities. However, those persons who were physically weak and aged or handicapped had very limited options and found it difficult to cope with chronic poverty, especially during the off-seasons.

5.4.4 Poverty and Livelihoods' Outcomes

Livelihoods' outcomes varied depending on asset structure of poor households, vulnerabilities faced, policy and institutional framework and strategies adopted. Poor people's livelihoods were far from being sustainable. Many poor households undertook migration to cities and other states as a strategy. Some field results indicating broad patterns of livelihoods' outcomes are as follows:

- Any single source of livelihood was not sustainable so the poor households were combining diverse sources of livelihoods. Such sources of livelihoods differed seasonally and there were considerable variations in using assets for composing livelihoods on a seasonal basis. This was true, both at the inter-household level and at the intra-household level across villages, also amongst women, men and children and between young and old. The returns from livelihood-related activities vary widely across activities and localities as shown in Table 5.10. Bartering and exchange of labour were also prevalent.

- The economics of rice cultivation in terms of financial returns turned out to be negative. Though agriculture was a critical livelihood, cultivation of aman paddy and jute was no longer profitable. The economics of paddy cultivation showed that per bigha of land a farmer could make a surplus of about INR 200, 230 without adding the imputed cost of his/her family labour and the cost of "enterprise". On an average, there was a net loss of INR 300 to INR 330, of which INR 100 could be recovered from the sale of straw.
- The situation was more complex in case of growing crops other than rice. Cultivation of alternative crops required a much higher outlay and hence credit needs were considerably high. This also helped explain as to why farmers cultivated paddy despite poor returns.
- There was rapid fall in land productivity. Land was not laid fallow and there was excessive use of fertilizers and insecticides. To cope with such a problem, people had started developing compost pits. Due to the absence of extension support these were not always done in the best manner.
- A noticeable trend was towards rapid conversion of agricultural land into non-agricultural land as pointed out by some local villagers, which adversely impacted on sustainability of agriculture-related activities.
- Many owners leased their lands to others for cultivation. Many irrigated lands grew 3 crops, e.g. rice, jute, wheat/ pulses/vegetables depending on agro-climatic conditions and facilities available.

Table 5.10: Earnings/Wage from Selected Livelihoods Pursued by Poor Groups

Livelihood related Activities	*Wage Rate/Selling Price*
Wage labour for agriculture	INR 30 + food or INR 40 without food ('terai' district), INR 15 plus one meal ('flood plain' district or district no. 3), harvesting paddy – 5 kg of paddy ('flood plain' district).
Wage labour-non-Agriculture	INR 62 per day for un-skilled labour; carrying bricks—INR 55 (for women) per 1000 bricks ('rice bowl' district) INR 80 to INR 120 per day for skilled labour (e.g. panchayat work for road construction, culvert etc.).

(*Contd.*)

(*Contd.*)

Livelihood related Activities	*Wage Rate/Selling Price*
Selling paddy and other items	Selling haria (local brew) for INR 20 to INR 25 per day ('terai' district).
Beedi rolling	For 1000 beedis INR 37 is the rate, output per day is around 700 beedis, thus wage per day is approx. INR 25 ('flood plain' district).
Work as maid in household	For adult—INR 200 per month + left over food; for child—INR 100 per month + left over food ('flood plain' district)
Harvesting and selling homestead products	Papaya—INR 8/kg, bottle gourd—INR 3/kg, Pumpkin—INR 3/kg and beans— INR5-INR 6/kg ('forest-based' district), Betel nut—INR 3.50/kg ('flood plain' district).
Harvesting (NTFP) from forest etc.	For Sal leaf plate-making the rates vary. For 500 Sal leaves they get INR 20 (for each plate they use at least 6 to 7 leaves). They can prepare 80 leaf plates with 500 Sal leaves. ('forest-based' district); For 1000 Sal leaves made into plates they receive INR 30 to INR 50 ('rice bowl' district). Sal leaf plate making and selling @ INR 80 per 1000 plates ('rice bowl' district)—price in good season; Leaf plate making @ INR 50 per 1000 plates ('rice bowl' district); Selling wood—INR10 to INR15 ('flood plain' district) Babui rope sold at INR 5 to INR 10 per kg; *babui* grass sold at INR 2/INR 3 per kg. Around 500 grams of *barha* gum can be sold at INR 18/kg. *Kachra* fruits can be sold at INR 5/kg. Eggs of an ant Kurkut is sold at INR 20/25 per kg. Mahul flowers—INR 20 kg. Ledachhal collection at INR 5 kg.
Livestock rearing	Pigs reared for one year is 20 kg at INR 16 per kg. one goat reared sells for INR 300.
Catching fish	A day's toil yields INR 250 to INR 300 grams of fresh fish ('flood plain' district).
Exchange of labour	The households mutually help each other in daily work. They also exchange labour or pay in terms of paddy or INR 30 per day.
Traditional art and craft	*Kula* (made of bamboo) is INR 10 in season and INR 7 in off-season; *Jhuri* (made of bamboo) is INR 14 in season and INR 10 in off-season ('flood plain' district);
Mining and quarrying	Sand quarry work with daily wages between INR 50 to INR 120 ('rice bowl' district);
Tea plantation	Casual labourer—INR 45 per day paid bimonthly; permanent workers get additional support in terms of rice, wheat, kerosene oil, tea, umbrella, medicine, slippers etc. ('terai' district)

Note: Collated from field notes on different study villages.

- Contract cultivation was on the rise. Though agriculture was an important source of livelihood, the owners did not always cultivate their own lands. There was contract cultivation, i.e. those who owned the land leased out the land on fixed rent. The rent varied from location to location. For instance, in a village in the 'flood plain' district nearly 40 per cent of land was cultivated on "contract" basis. In the same village, contract cultivation was on the rise as migration was increasing. Around 50 per cent of local households were migrants working outside the state and had contracted their land on lease.
- Mixed forest, e.g. Sal forest provided a range of livelihoods especially for the ultra poor groups residing near forests. However, the poor groups expressed difficulties in harvesting NTFPs due to constraints posed by forest department and there was also a declining trend noticeable in forest produce.
- Marketing opportunities/linkages were difficult for cooperatives, textiles and crafts-related products.

5.4.5 Preferred Sources of Livelihoods

Given a chance, the poor groups' preferred sources of livelihoods are as shown in Table 5.11. The preference rankings indicated a combination of access to one's own land for cultivation supplemented by different types of livestock-rearing activities. However, in absence of one's own land such preference in study villages of both district No. 4 (3rd rank) and district No. 3 (2nd rank) was in favour of increased days of wage labour (tea garden labourer), especially for agriculture/plantation-related work. In the study villages of district 1 or the 'forest-based' district, income generating activities (2nd rank) were equally preferred as much as Sal leaf plate making through machine (2nd Rank) and also making bamboo items with value added through upgraded skills (2nd Rank).

Tea cultivation on one's land (4th rank) was preferred in district No. 4. In case of district No. 2, this included making puffed rice (2nd rank), Sal leaf plate making through machine (3rd rank) and fishery activities in re-excavated ponds (4th rank) since they appeared to be promising and yielded quick returns. In both district No. 4 and district No. 3, skill-based IGAs were 5th in preference especially for women who perceived the importance of skill training in food processing. In district No. 3, making items of bamboo craft was 3rd in preference as compared to silk thread weaving (5th rank) due to falling prices of silk reels. In district No. 4, selling country liquor came last in priority due to limited market whereas for district No. 3, maid's work was least preferred due to heavy workload and often bad treatment meted out by employers.

Table 5.11: Preference Ranking of Livelihoods

Activities	*'Terai' District or District No. 4*	*'Flood plain' District or District No. 3*	*'Forest-based' District or District No. 1*	*'Rice bowl' District or District No. 2*
Cultivation of one's own land	1		2	
Livestock rearing	2	1	1	1
Increase in days of wage labour	3	2		
Tea cultivation	4			
Skill-based IGA	5	5	2	
Selling Haria	6			
Weaving		4		
Silk thread making	6			
Bamboo craft		3	2	
Working as maid		7		
Making Sal leaf plates by machine			2	3
Making "*muri*" (puffed rice)			4	2
Fishery through pond excavation			6	4
Plantation			6	

Wage labour, whether in agriculture, plantation, construction and mining, a dominant mode of livelihood was least preferred by the poor, because it meant strenuous work, high uncertainty and discrimination against the weak and the disabled. Similarly, migration outside was much low in preference for both poor women and men due to inconvenience and uncertainty of finding jobs.

5.4.6 Gender and Livelihoods

There were separate domains of livelihood-related activities for women and men although some activities were common to both as shown in Table 5.12. Even when women were sharing work with men, their roles were defined either by tradition, social construction and societal pressure. In some villages, it was pointed out that in difficult seasons when men had no work, it was generally the responsibility of women to procure food and feed the family. Women from poor households were over-loaded with work and had little or no recreation time as compared to men. Children from poor households including school dropouts were engaged in many of the above activities.

Table 5.12: Livelihoods-related activities—Women and Men

Livelihood-related activities	*Women*	*Men*
Collecting Sal leaf from forest	*	*
Making Sal-leaf plates	*	
Selling Sal plates in the market	* (Women-headed HH)	*
Collecting fire wood	*	*
Selling fire wood	*	*
Growing homestead vegetable	*	
Rearing back yard poultry	*	
Agriculture work	*	*
Agriculture labour	*	*
Collecting bidi leaves, other NTFP	*	*
Nabal (migration) to distant places for earning livelihood	Sometimes women accompanying men	*
Making *muri* (puffed rice) and selling	*	
Making Talai and selling	*	*
Fishing		*
Rearing cattle	*	*
Making rice from paddy	*	
Selling eggs	*	
Rearing goats/sheep	* (often taken care of by children and elderly)	*
Selling goats/sheep	* (Women-headed HH)	*
Work in brick field, sand/morrom querry	*	*
Work in tea plantation	*	*

Note: HH stands for households; * Stands for who does it—women, men or both.

Table 5.12 lists some common livelihoods and provides an indicative picture of the gender aspects of who did what. Gendered division of livelihood-related activities had some local variations.

5.4.6.1 Assets—During the field inquiry, it was stated by women groups in selected study villages of the 'forest-based' district that poor women's asset in terms of social capital, awareness and skills had increased over time through self-help group (SHG) formation under a government programme. As expressed by two women groups that though the men were supportive of such women's SHGs, they were not that hard working to improve their own lot. It was also found that women were relatively more active than men and had inculcated thrift habit on a regular basis. The men were found to be indifferent to thrift and local women were of the view that men had a tendency to spend more and shoulder less responsibility. Even in deficit households, when men had cash in their hands they spent it on liquor and merry making. The women thought that cash in hands of women was more useful for the family. Though literacy was higher among men, the women, mostly illiterate, were becoming conscious of the significance of education for their children. However, many poor households were forced to make their children work due to poverty.

5.4.6.2 Power, Status and Exclusion—Gender bias was pronounced in most study villages in terms of men wielding social and political power in the sphere of governance, institutions and processes. The social status of women as compared to men was low in general and abysmally low for widows, deserted, divorced and mentally and physically challenged women. Women-headed households, whether ultra poor or destitute, were socially invisible and were excluded. Many men died young and the young widows had added social problem due to their age. In case of elderly women, the participants mentioned that the trend was that of neglect of elderly parents by children.

5.4.6.3 Decision-Making—In the study villages, men made the major decisions except for a few women SHGs under SGSY, which were spearheading certain village-level decisions and were raising issues not normally done by women. In most cases, decentralized village-level planning including those of Forest Protection Committees were dominated by men, and the women were generally neither vocal nor visible. Women functionaries in panchayat mostly belonged to the better off households. Amongst the four districts studied, it may be said that women groups from poor households were relatively more progressive and performing better in selected blocks of district No. 1. As regards the study villages of district Nos. 2, 3 and 4, there was a social bottleneck in terms of conservative attitude towards women's roles. Women from poor households faced socio/cultural inhibitions in terms of work opportunities, e.g. women working as construction labour found it difficult to get their daughters married.

5.4.6.4 Access and Responsibility—For many poor households, including *adivasi* households, a woman had access to cash available from her own earnings and what her husband gave her. Though the women had the responsibility of rearing livestock the men sold them in the market.

5.4.6.5 Livelihoods Preferences—Common preferences of groups of poor women were those related to skill training and self-employment opportunities in activities such as sewing-cutting-tailoring, making of spices, bamboo craft, embroidery, etc. while men preferred to continue with their existing activities.

Table 5.13 provides an illustration of preferred ranking of livelihoods by women and men groups in a village in the 'flood plain'-prone district. It shows how agriculture on one's land was the best opportunity and undertaking migration was the least preferred activity

Table 5.13: Livelihoods Preferences of Women and Men, a Village in 'Flood Plain' District

Livelihood-related Activity (Men)	*Current Significance of Activity (Men)*	*Ranking showing Preference of Men*	*Current Significance of Activity (Women)*	*Ranking showing Preference of Women*
1. Agriculture—growing paddy, mustard, vegetable, pulses, jute	8/16	1	1/10	5
2. Agriculture labour	5/16	2	9/10	2
3. Non-agriculture labour	1/16	3	—	—
4. Migrant worker	0.5/16	6	—	—
5. Petty trade	0.5/16	5	—	—
6. Traditional bamboo work	1/16	4	9/10	2
7. Goat-rearing	—	—	5/10	3
8. Cow-rearing	—	—	2/10	4
9. Pig-rearing	—	—	5/10	3
10. Duck-rearing	—	—	10/10	1
11. Chicken-rearing	—	—	1/10	5

Note: Collated from field notes. The local groups of women and men indicated current significance of an activity in terms of scoring individual activity out of a total score of 16 (resembling 16 anna of a Rupee) by men group and a total score of 10 used by women group.

by men. For women, duck rearing was the most significant activity followed by agriculture labour and traditional bamboo work like *kula* and *jhuri*, which were used for cleaning and transporting paddy. Their preference for raising chickens and selling their eggs was lower as they are more susceptible to diseases. In one village in the 'forest-based' district, a women group pointed out that chicken rearing was risky due to the high mortality rate and that vaccines were not available in small quantum, hence were not economic.

5.4.7 Assets Poor Access and Use

The village exercises indicated that in general there was a positive trend associated with asset holdings of poor groups. With development activities, there was general progress in different rural assets. With increased assets and more choices, the quality of life had improved over time. However, there were crucial aspects of asset holding, which indicated that though this was a good start, there were major issues in asset status and access, both in case of poor households and also in case of poor villages, especially those which were relatively interior-located. It became difficult for poor households to cope with loss in asset/s without having any fallback position in terms of government support, compensation or insurance.

Table 5.14 provides a generic picture of the different kinds of assets used by poor households from the study villages and their status in terms of improvement or degradation. It is important to mention that though different assets were locally available in a village their access and ownership issues were critical in terms of composing livelihoods by poor households. Some field findings in this context were as follows:

Though the process was ongoing, not enough assets had been created for the poor. Such assets creation was disproportionately small in size with regard to the scale required and much more was needed to be done. The ultra poor groups remained relatively deprived and did not experience any increase in assets except a few households supported under Government schemes such as Indira Awas Yojana and widow/old age pensions and food transfers. There was absence of critical threshold of physical assets in many study villages and the quality of existing physical assets/services was low, e.g. tube-well for drinking water, quality of embankment constructed, functioning of health centres etc.

Table 5.14: Assets Status—Accessed by Poor Households

Type of Assets	*Illustrations of Assets from study villages*	*Illustrations of Improvement/s in Asset*	*Illustrations of Degradation of Asset*
Natural assets	Land—high land, low land, laterite soil, alluvial soil, silt traps, irrigated field, un-irrigated field, ponds, doba, water pools, lake, trees, Sal forest, other forest, river, mines, quarry, bamboo groves, plantation of tea, eucalyptus, acacia, hedges, home garden.	Growth in area under forests, growth in social forestry, rise in availability of fuel wood, increase in crop cultivation, increase in NTFP	Polluted pond, doba and rivers, silting of rivers, decline in soil fertility, late and erratic rainfall, acute water shortage, degraded Sal forest, deforestation, decline in fish population, decline in wild food and other NTFPs from forest, depleting ground water level, problem of arsenic in drinking water, high population growth.
Physical assets	Village roads, feeder roads, school buildings, primary health center, tube well, dug well, hospital, school, electric pump, sanitary latrines, cow shelter, compost pit.	More hand pumps and wells, increase in irrigation facilities, improved conditions of housing, construction of village roads, increase in number of utensils	Defunct tube wells, polluted well, broken river embankments, broken dams and irrigation channels, village roads not maintained, no transportation facilities for interior villages, poor functioning of health centres and schools, no middle/high school in the vicinity, theft of cattle.
Human assets	Literacy, training, skill building, good health, honesty and confidence	Expansion of knowledge, children attending school, increase in technical know-how, more exposure, more communication, higher political awareness, increase in confidence	Rise in dishonesty, theft, corrupt minds, reluctance in taking initiative, having high expectations of government, dis-empowering process for ultra poor with falling access to resources and support, prevalence of child labour, falling health, difficulties in accessing medical facilities, rising cost of medical treatment, rising number of quacks, difficulties in accessing quality education, lack of opportunities for increasing skills, poor quality of training and follow up.

(Contd.)

(Contd.)

Type of Assets	*Illustrations of Assets from study villages*	*Illustrations of Improvement/s in Asset*	*Illustrations of Degradation of Asset*
Social assets	Decentralized local governance, self-help group formation and functioning, watershed groups, cooperative societies, access to patta land, decentralized village planning, youth club, peace and harmony	Group formation such as self-help groups, watershed groups were on the rise, cooperatives were being formed, credit societies were functioning, Anganwadi centre were functioning	Traditional social bonds breaking down, people becoming selfish, discriminatory attitude of local governance towards their party supporters, increase in dowry payment, adult children neglecting parents, desertion, lack of organized wage labour, reduced access to government services for poor groups.
Financial assets	Bank loans, savings, barter, exchange of labour, livestock	Rise in thrift habit, rise in sources of borrowing, increase in primary credit societies and bank branches	Rise in indebtedness, rise in cost of capital, banks' inflexibility towards pro-poor, inability of poor households to repay loans due to poverty

Note: Collated from field notes on study villages.

Many natural assets such as ponds and rivers had degraded over the years thus leading to diminishing structure of asset portfolio for the poor and limited options for livelihoods.

Assets created in the public domain differed from the perspectives of poor people's livelihoods. For example, in many areas, species for forest regeneration had been decided by the 'top' authority without attention to issues important to those groups, which were dependent on such forest.

5.4.8 What Made Poor People Vulnerable?

The vulnerability of the poor relates to particular sensitivity to an event or occurrence that poses a threat to health and social and/or economic well-being. It is important to learn about the vulnerability context in which the asset exists. The factors determining such context have been grouped under trend, shock, seasonality and local cultural practices, which affect livelihoods of poor households. In the villages studied such factors were identified as follows:

5.4.8.1 Trends

There were clear trends in adoption of agriculture-related practices, in diversification of opportunities, in strengthening/deterioration of resource-base (such as forests) and access to resources, in social exclusion/inclusion, which impacted on the vulnerability context thus affecting livelihoods of the poor households. Box 5.1 illustrates some of the trends, both positive and negative, shared by poor groups though they are not universally applicable to all poor groups in the study villages.

Box 5.1: Selected Trends

Regular incidence of flood over the years
Gradual erosion of riverbank
Gradual silting of river/pond/water bodies
Increase in agriculture production
Movement from traditional farming towards more chemical-based agriculture
Regular pest attacks on crops cultivated
Animal attacks on crops

(Contd.)

(Contd.)

Changing trend of livelihoods from food crop to cash crop cultivation
Non-diversified economy with little diversification towards cottage/ village industries
Increased dependence of majority people on agriculture
Increased dependence on markets for both acquiring inputs and selling outputs
Falling prices of commodities such as tea
Rising inputs prices (fertilizers, seeds, pesticides)
Rise in public theft and corruption
Increased social exclusion of ultra poor and destitute households
Increase in dowry payment for daughter's marriage
Rise in incidence of homelessness and residing on other's land/ home, especially for women-headed households
Location of village still interior due to low growth of rural road network

5.4.8.2 Shocks and Vulnerability

In the study villages, the shocks have been such that their impacts have been devastating for poor households, with their assets getting depleted, damaged or wiped out.

5.4.8.3 Market Uncertainties

In one village fall in market prices of silk due to imports from abroad affected livelihoods in sericulture. If this shock became a trend then those in sericulture may have to close down and migrate. Similarly, poor labourers in tea gardens in the 'terai' district were affected by fluctuations in tea prices.

5.4.8.4 Seasonality and Vulnerability

Vulnerability of assets was made acute by seasonal forces, which were pronounced in case of poor households. The rainy season was especially difficult when the incidence of disease of both humans and cattle/birds increased. Typhoid/jaundice was quite common in areas using water from shallow and indigenous wells. Fever was a common occurrence. The cattle and poultry suffered from different diseases. The non-availability of health centre and veterinarians made life difficult during the rainy season. Flood was a seasonal occurrence in many areas in the province and incidence of drought in different areas was also a common occurrence.

The prices of agriculture inputs and outputs and selling price of NTFPs differed depending on the seasons. Many poor and ultra poor groups undertook seasonal migration during the off-seasons. Workload between women and men was influenced by seasons, for instance Table 5.15 shows that in the village under reference, the women did all the work in the months of *Magh-Phalgun-Chaitra-Baisakh-Jyaistha*, while men did not have much to do. The impact of seasonality on livelihoods is illustrated in Table 5.15.

5.4.8.5 Cultural Practice

Cultural practice was a factor to reckon with in livelihood composition of the poor and tended to influence seasonality. For instance, in case of a Muslim study village in the forest-based district, the men worked harder than women in the months *of Asadh, Sraban, Poush* and *Magh*.

5.5 Policies, Institutions and Processes and Poor People's Livelihoods

Policies, institutions and processes are critical in determining who gains access to which type/s of assets, which in turn determine feasibility of livelihoods' strategies. Markets and legal restrictions impacting on asset conversion and livelihoods strategies are also significant variables. In the SLA study as above, some groups remained socially excluded from policies and institutions and it was important to identify the processes through which such exclusion occurred and what could make for an inclusive process. Based on fieldwork certain common factors were identified, which made for social exclusion (partial/total) of the poor groups as briefly mentioned below.

Exclusionary processes and impacts on livelihoods—Attitude and behaviour was a major factor leading to social exclusion of poor households. For specific poor groups such as ethnic tribes attitude and behaviour engrained in local governance, was a major issue. The attitude of different government departments, police, banking institutions and others were seen as problematic. Also attitudes/ cultural beliefs/social practices were loaded against women-headed

Table 5.15: "Our Seasonal Coping Strategies" —Village Women's Perspective

Period 1—Difficult	*Period 2—Medium*	*Period 3—Most Difficult*	*Period 4—Medium*
Months—Magh—Phalgun—Chaitra—Baisakh—Jyaistha	*Months—Asar—Sraban*	*Months—Bhadra—Aswin*	*Months—Kartick—Aghrayan—Poush*
We (women) went to collect different types of wild food/sak (Jhunjhunu, Silunda, Pitan, Khantashar, Ulli, Dengu, Palka, Garundi). We (women) made Sal leaf plate and fed the family. There was no work available for our men except for a few days *Magh*. When our men worked there was not much benefit to us for they spent the money in drinking or going to cinema and enjoying. We drank palm juice during *Baisakh-Jaisthya*. We also took loans at a monthly rate of INR 10 in INR 100. Then we had to buy straw for thatching our house. In Magh some of us had bronchitis, pneumonia and children suffered from intestinal worms.	Work was available for both women and men and households could repay their debts based on that. We (women) went to catch snail, crab, fish, snake etc. from the field and sold it and ate some of it.	Very little work was available. Rice stock at home was negligible and there was dearth of cash. We ate little and there were not enough clothes to wear. We collected wild food from the forest such as different types of sak (Chonga, Tak, Thuin). With rain water receding, we caught crab, fish and snake etc. from the rice field and other water bodies. We also ate palm from the trees. Our debts rose and we were forced to borrow from the grocer. The incidence of water-borne diseases also increased in this season.	In absence of irrigation there was rain fed farming where we, both women and men found work.

Source: From the field notes of Neela Mukherjee and Vivekananda Satpathy.

households, where people treat such households as "invisible" in their own localities. The local/state administration was generally aware of such issues as indicated in the meetings held.

Lack of resources and livelihoods impacts—Many landless and homeless lacked a minimum threshold level of asset structure for constructing livelihoods. Many poor households lacked access to basic physical and financial capital and institutional linkages. In many study villages, road, health centre, functioning wells and tube wells were not available.

Decentralized governance—The policy of decentralization helped the local government to support local people and its role was crucial in lending support to poor groups. The local government functionaries had done good work in a few villages though not in all the study villages. In some villages where their performance was below mark in terms of asset creation, they had at least developed good communication with local community. Poor groups performed better in those villages where such functionaries had taken interest and had created enabling conditions. By and large, in most study villages, the ultra poor and destitute households were mostly excluded from the local development process.

Lack of transparency and accountability—For development schemes especially on the part of functionaries of local governance hindered information dissemination and awareness building of poor groups including the ethnic groups. As perceived by many poor households, corruption and dishonesty was rampant in governance. This resulted in inefficient and low quality asset creation at local level, which in turn impacted on livelihoods of the poor. Similarly, in many study villages, villagers remarked that official exercise for identifying households below poverty line led to the inclusion of many better-off households and exclusion of poor.

Lack of an effective and well-implemented state policy on literacy/ education—Posed a constraint for poor groups from participating in the local development process.

Lack of access to health services—(both in terms of facility and quality) by the poor was another problem area. With high incidence of diseases including malaria, fever and diarrhoea-related diseases, on a yearly and seasonal basis this was all the more serious.

Availability of drinking water—Was a problem in many tribal villages. The tube wells were mostly out of order and/or provided low quality water. Maintenance was not routinely carried out.

Agriculture policy—The agriculture policy of promoting agriculture through usage of chemical fertilisers and pesticides without checks and balances had adversely affected land productivity in many study villages. As expressed by farmers during field study, the HYV crops required higher doses of chemical inputs over time, which led to rapid deterioration in soil conditions and productivity. For the ultra poor, this affected availability of their traditional wild food from the crop fields. The policy of minimum support price of agriculture produce did not work in the villages studied. The farmers got between INR 420 to INR 450 per quintal of paddy against the support price of INR 530 per quintal The farmers are aware of the minimum support price of the government but in practice received much less.

Forest policy—Forest policy affected livelihoods. Forest department's decision to grow Acacia or Sal or some other species lent differential impacts on poor people's livelihoods, especially the ultra poor. The richer the local forest (e.g. a Sal forest) and its access, the easier it was to cope with difficult seasons.

Banking policy—Banking facilities for BPL families formed into SHGs under SGSY programme were generally constrained. For some banks such SHGs were a low priority and they refused/delayed giving loans to them. Bank workers, in remote branches often considered transfers to rural/remote areas as a punishment posting. They viewed recovery of loans to SHGs as problematic since they did not perceive them as credit-worthy.

Marketing linkages—The poor groups of weavers, both women and men in the handloom sector were adversely affected as a result of poor management of government institutions, purchasing their products for marketing. Marketing linkages were weak and competition from the power-loom sector further affected their livelihoods and increased uncertainties.

5.6 Selected Policy Recommendations

Some recommendations[12] flowing from the livelihoods study are listed below:

- Linking-up governance to poor people's livelihoods.
- Strengthening social capital by strengthening local group solidarity and movements.
- Building sustained capacity of local governance.
- Adopting ways for supporting ultra poor groups/destitute women for overcoming exclusionary processes.

- Developing human resource by supporting education.
- Promoting primary health care.
- Adopting policy/practice for enhancing natural resource base.
- Strengthening agriculture as mainstay of rural livelihoods.
- Exploring opportunities in rural non-farm sector.
- Developing livestock wealth.
- Adopting different ways for facilitating rural marketing.
- Building and nurturing partnerships with civil society.
- Supporting right to information for poor households.
- Setting up livelihood resource centre at block level.

NOTES

1. This part of the chapter has been adapted from Sustainable Livelihood Guidance Sheets, www.livelihoods.org; for details see the different files in the same web site.
2. Both material and social resources
3. Also see Chambers and Conway (1992)
4. Sumita Roy and Shanti Mardi
5. 1 Bigha = 1/3 Acre (0.1338 Hectare or 0.3306 Acre); 7.5 Bigha = 1 Hectare; and 100 Decimal = 1 Acre
6. See footnote 5
7. 1 Bigha = 1/3 Acre (0.1338 Hectare or 0.3306 Acre); 7.5 Bigha = 1 Hectare; and 100 Decimal = 1 Acre
8. See footnote 7
9. See footnote 7
10. See footnote 7
11. See footnote 7
12. These recommendations have been listed in this Chapter for illustration purposes so to indicate how there could flow a series of recommendations from any SLA study. In any SLA study recommendations are to be specific and need to be treated at proper length.

REFERENCES

Chambers, R. and G. Conway: (1992), *Sustainable rural livelihoods: Practical concepts for the 21st century*, IDS Discussion Paper 296. Brighton: IDS (pp.7-8).

www.livelihoods.org

6

Integrated Participatory Poverty Assessment

In this chapter, we discuss Integrated Participatory Poverty Assessment (IPPA) where different dimensions of human poverty and their proximate causes and solutions are captured through IPPA. We explain how IPPA is a tool to map poverty assessment and changes at the local level and their integration at higher levels to produce a synthesis picture of poverty as mapped by local stakeholders.

6.1 Setting up the 'Larger Picture'

Going to scale or up-scaling participation is very much an 'in' thing with many governments and non-governmental organizations. Recent approaches around the world have shown that there are both positive and negative aspects, especially institutional issues for up-scaling participation (Kar and Backhaus: 1994; Samaranayake: 1994; Backhaus and Wagachchi: 1995; Guijit: 1995; Thompson: 1995). Though in many countries there have been active engagement of key stakeholders for participatory approaches/tools such as PPA (Narayan, *et al.*: 2000, Chambers: 2005, Yves: www.google.com), participatory budgeting or Citizen Report Card, such attempts have been mostly *ad hoc* in absence of any regular mechanisms for institutionalization. For establishing a mechanism for up-scaling, it is important to seek answers to the following questions:

- How to up-scale and institutionalize the 'larger picture'?
- How to build capacity and good team work?
- Who participates in the participatory assessment process?
- Who decides on the indicators?
- Who uses the data and whose indicators drive such process? and

- For whom is the participatory assessment mechanism being set up?

One initial step is team building, understanding the objectives, the methods and process, the criteria and the total task involved. A proper appreciation of the type of task involved is important for carrying out the field work required for PPA and the follow up for collating data and constructing such assessment. Towards attaining such objectives, some initial requirements could be spelled out such as:

- a team with commitment,
- having listening skills,
- team with clarity of thought,
- having appropriate attitude and behaviour,
- knowledge of participatory skills,
- ability to manage people's expectations, and
- code of ethics as practitioners for facilitating groups/ individuals.

Though forming a team with commitment is crucial, there are many other aspects in up-scaling PPA. The important aspects are explained below.

6.2 Integrated Participatory Poverty Assessment (IPPA)

Integrated Participatory Poverty Assessment is a tool for situational assessment of poverty mainly from the perspectives of the poor and the disadvantaged to arrive at an integrated picture of poverty assessment and its reduction. It is a tool to map poverty assessment and changes at the local level and their integration at higher levels to produce a synthesis picture of poverty as mapped by local stakeholders. One important purpose of IPPA is to improve the effectiveness of actions aimed at poverty reduction. There could be multiple topics/components assessed through IPPA as listed below.

Components of IPPA

(i) Component A — Social Group/Well-Being Assessment
(ii) Component B—Asset/Resource Assessment

(iii) Component C— Vulnerability and Risk Assessment
(iv) Component D—Livelihoods Assessment
(v) Component E—Problem-Opportunity Assessment
(vi) Component F—Gender Assessment
(vii) Component G—Institutional Assessment
(viii) Component H—Social Opportunity Assessment

The IPPA components and their contributions are described below:

6.2.1 *Social Group (Well-Being) Assessment* is component A of IPPA, related to human poverty/well-being assessment through local perspectives. While generating and constructing component 'A', it is useful to generate separate clusters of information at the field level on different group/s, excluded group/s and women-headed households as and when required. This will also provide human poverty/well being dimensions of socially excluded groups in addition to other social groups. Component 'A' of IPPA can have two sub-components:

Sub-Component A.1 is on human poverty (well-being) dimensions of households within social groups (with marginalized, disadvantaged and women-headed households as separate groups for identifying ways for social inclusion).

Sub-Component A.2 is on the proportions of households within different social groups.

6.2.1a *Sub-component A.1* relates to an assessment of the dimensions on human poverty (well-being) of different social groups (with marginalized, disadvantaged and women-headed households as separate focus groups). The Sub-component A.1 will help focus on the status of human poverty indicators of different social groups from local perspectives (as baseline data) and with repeat IPPAs over time, sub-component A.1 will help indicate changes in human poverty (well-being) dimensions (mostly in qualitative terms) of different social/poor groups. For data generation, collation and up-scaling, sub-component A.1 will be based on qualitative scoring. Changes in the sub-component A.1, over time, will help reflect changes in human poverty dimensions of different social groups.

6.2.1.2 *Sub-component A.2* will provide information on the proportions of households within the social groups—both poor and non-poor groups. Changes in sub-component A.2, over time, will help capture both inter- and intra-shifts in proportions of households across poor and non-poor groups.

With base line data constructed on this IPPA component 'A' related to human poverty (well-being), further updating of information would reflect the following:

- Comparative changes in human poverty (well-being) dimensions;
- Shifts of households within social groups meaning, thereby, changes in the proportions of poor and non-poor households over time.

The Social Group (well-being) Assessment could be up scaled unto the meso level and the macro/national level in order to gain larger macro pictures of human poverty and well-being and also the proportions of households falling under different social groups.

6.2.2 *Asset/Resource Assessment* is PPA component B related to status and access of assets by different social groups as assessed locally. Such assessment help indicate the status of local resources and the status of access of the poor to at least 6 types of assets/resources—natural, physical, human, financial, socio-cultural and political assets/ resources. Such assessment can have two sub-components.

Sub-component B.1 will help assess the local status/conditions of assets/resources, and

Sub-component B.2 will help assess the status of access to assets/ resources by poor groups.

With construction of baseline data on IPPA component B, sub-components B.1 and B.2 will help indicate changes in two major variables—local asset status/condition and access to assets/resources by poor groups.

6.2.3 *Vulnerability and Risk Assessment* is IPPA component C. It helps provide the status of vulnerability over years and over seasons and helps monitor the status of vulnerability of poor groups, both over time and on a seasonal basis. First, there is a need to understand the vulnerability context in which assets related to the poor groups exist. These are the trends, shocks, seasonality and local cultural practices, which affect poverty status and process. Trends, for example, in natural resource stock, population density, technology, political representation and economic trends affect poverty and well-being. Shocks, e.g., in the form of climate disasters, conflicts, etc. undermine asset base. On a seasonal basis, deficit months in a year affect people's well-being. Cultural practices can make assets vulnerable and impact on livelihoods. For purposes of the IPPA being developed, such vulnerability assessment will have two sub-components. In case of IPPA, both trend and seasonality could be assessed through local perspectives so as to capture the vulnerability context related to human poverty. The two subcomponents C.1 and C.2 can be on 'trend' and 'seasonality', respectively.

Sub-component C.1 will help assess data on trends of selected variables through time.

Sub-component C.2 will help explore seasonality factors faced by the poor groups.

Sub-component C.1 on trend can help cover food security, literacy and education, health and sanitation, migration, peace and conflict over a period of past 5-10 years.

Sub-component C.2 on seasonality faced by poor groups can help capture seasonal movements over one year in food, drinking water, work opportunities, wages, migration, illness and livestock disease.

6.2.4 *Livelihoods Assessment* or IPPA component D is entirely focused on assessments of livelihoods of poor. "Livelihood" is how people compose their means of living from their asset-base (6 Assets—natural, physical, socio-cultural, human, financial and political), capability and activities. A livelihood is sustainable both in the present and future by recovering from shocks (e.g. drought, flood), maintaining assets and capabilities and without undermining natural resource base (DFID: www.livelihoods.org). Livelihoods Assessment D will have 3 sub-components and all of them will be gendered for further use at the VDC/DDC level.

Sub-component D.1 relates to the list of existing livelihoods and related opportunities/constraints.

Sub-component D.2 relates to the indicative preferences of the poor for existing livelihoods and aspired livelihoods.

Sub-component D.3 relates to the earning/wages/remuneration of the poor groups from different sources of livelihoods.

6.2.5 *Problem-Opportunity Assessment* is IPPA component E and is an integral part of IPPA's contribution to people's planning process.

The problem-opportunity assessment under IPPA component E is considered more effective as a planning tool than a monitoring tool. It helps bring out people's problems and opportunities as perceived by them. In IPPA, the problems are listed, prioritized and analyzed by the local groups and communities, whether rural or urban. The problems that emerge in different areas often have many generic similarities though tend to differ widely due to local context. Thus the main problem domain may be similar but some of the sub-criteria can emphasize local features. The problems and opportunities revealed by the poor could then be clustered by analysts under different sectors for up-scaling to micro level, meso level, regional level and macro level for future action at appropriate levels. Such problems and opportunities then constitute a prime basis for micro/meso/regional/national planning and also provide inputs/feedback at the sectoral level.

Problems-Opportunity Assessment or IPPA component E can have 2 sub-components, which are gendered.

Sub-component E.1 will be the problems prioritized by groups of poor women and men along with the opportunities, and

Sub-component E.2 will relate to the problem-opportunity domains up-scaled at the local, meso, regional and national level.

6.2.6 *Gender Assessment* is IPPA component F and relates to various dimensions of gender at the local level. Gender assessment can have sub-components F.1 and F.2.

Sub-component F.1 revolves around short queries, which are gender-based and qualitative.

Sub-component F.2 reflects qualitative scores on the following gendered parameters:

- Type of work, workload and responsibility.
- Having knowledge/skills.
- Taking part in household decision-making.
- Having Access and Control over resources.
- Having Power and Status.
- Victim of alcoholism/domestic violence.

6.2.7 *Institutional Assessment* is IPPA component G and plays an important role in people's lives. It is important to understand the role and effectiveness of institution/organization such as Government, NGO, community based organization, private sector, etc. and

Table 6.1: Relevance of Sub-Components of IPPA Tools for Different Levels

IPPA Tool						
Component	*Sub-Component/s*	*Type of data*	*Relevance at National Level (whether relevant to MDG)*	*Relevance at Sectoral Level*	*Relevance at Regional Level*	*Relevance at Local Level*
Component A Social Group/Well-Being Assessment	**A.1** is on human poverty (well-being) dimensions of households within social groups	Mostly qualitative data related to multiple indicators of human poverty and clustered across social groups	For monitoring human poverty indicators (Relevant to MDG 1— Eradicate extreme poverty and hunger)	Only a few sectors, e.g. health, education, infrastructure	The sub-national picture provide regional insight	It helps identify poverty indicators for different social groups and help to target better.
	A.2 is on the proportions of households within different social groups	Numerical data (in proportion/ percentage)	Can help monitor proportions of poor (Relevant to MDG 1— Eradicate extreme poverty and hunger)	Not directly relevant	It can indicate proportions of poor and help identify shifts in poverty amongst social groups	It can indicate proportions of poor and help to identify shifts in poverty amongst social groups.

(*Contd.*)

(*Contd.*)

IPPA Tool						
Component B Asset/ Resource Assessment	**B.1** will help to assess the local status/conditions of assets/resources	Qualitative data clustered across criteria and social groups	Can help monitor asset status; (Also relevant to MDG 7—Ensure environmental sustainability)	Can help monitor changes in specific assets at the sectoral level, e.g. education, health, drinking water, nutrition, local governance	Can help study impact monitoring of status/ conditions related to group assets/ resources at the regional level	Can help study impact monitoring of status/conditions related to group assets/ resources at the local level.
	B.2 will be on the status of access to assets/resources by poor groups	Data based on judgemental scoring on different degrees of asset accessibility	Can help in impact monitoring of social inclusion related to access to assets/ resources by the poor at the national level	Can help in impact monitoring of social inclusion for selected sectors only	Can help in assessing impact monitoring of social inclusion related to access to assets/ resources by the poor at the regional level	Can help in impact monitoring of social inclusion related to access to assets/ resources by the poor at the local level.
Component C Vulnerability and Risk Assessment	**C.1** will help to assess data on trends of selected variables through time	Qualitative data over long period of 7 to 10 years	Would help indicate policy impacts on vulnerability aspects at the national level	Not directly relevant	Would help indicate differential policy impacts on vulnerability with regard to regions	Would help indicate policy impacts on vulnerability aspects at the local level.

(*Contd.*)

(*Contd.*)

IPPA Tool						
	C.2 will help to explore seasonality factors faced by the poor groups	Seasonal data over one year showing 3 periods—bad, normal and good. In addition, qualitative data clustered as per coping strategies.	Would help indicate policy impacts on vulnerability aspects at the national level	Not directly relevant	Would help indicate differential policy impacts on vulnerability with regard to regions	Would help indicate policy/ programme impacts on vulnerability aspects at the local level.
Component D Livelihoods Assessment	**D.1** on list of existing livelihoods and related opportunities/ constraints	Qualitative data clustered criteria-wise related to specific livelihoods	If scaled up to the national level, it will help show policy impacts on different local livelihoods and provide policy inputs for appropr ate changes.	If opportunities and constraints to specific livelihoods are scaled up sectorally then it would help to show sectoral policy impacts on different local livelihoods and provide sectoral policy inputs for appropriate changes.	Need not be scaled up to the regional level	Would help to indicate policy/programme impacts on livelihoods at the local level—can also help to highlight key opportunities and constraints at local level.

(*Contd.*)

(*Contd.*)

IPPA Tool						
	D.2 on preferences of existing livelihoods and aspired livelihoods	Ranked and indexed data on types of livelihoods, existing and preferred	Preferences for livelihoods scaled up to the national level would provide inputs for appropriate policy-making	No direct relevance	No direct relevance	Shows preferences for livelihoods at local level.
	D.3 on earning/wages/ remuneration of the poor groups from different sources of livelihoods	Numerical data on wages/remuneration from different livelihoods—related activities	—	—	—	Provides a micro picture of the local level.
Component E Problem-Opportunity Assessment	**E.1** will be the problems prioritized by groups of poor women and men along with the opportunities	Ranked and indexed data on problems corresponding to qualitative data on opportunities clustered as per criteria	Ranked and indexed data on problems corresponding to qualitative data on opportunities clustered as per criteria for the national level	Ranked and indexed data on problems corresponding to qualitative data on opportunities clustered as per criteria for the sectoral level	Ranked and indexed data on problems corresponding to qualitative data on opportunities clustered as per criteria at the regional level	Ranked and indexed data on problems at the local level. corresponding to qualitative data on opportunities clustered as per criteria.

(*Contd.*)

(*Contd.*)

IPPA Tool						
	E.2 will be on the problem—opportunity domains up scaled for local, district, regional and national level	Ranked and indexed data on problems projected at higher levels. Qualitative data on opportunities clustered as per criteria	Problem—opportunity domains projected at national level	Problem—opportunity domains projected at sectoral level	Problem—opportunity domains projected at a regional level	Ranked and indexed data on problem domains projected at local levels. Qualitative data on opportunities clustered as per criteria.
Component F Gender Assessment	**F.1** revolves around workload, knowledge/skills, household decision-making, access and control, power and status and alcoholism/domestic violence	Qualitative data on the actual position with regard to the gendered aspects	For monitoring impact related to social inclusion of women, access and control and power and status (Relevant to MDG 3—Promote gender equality and empower women)	Relevant as an impact monitoring tool for Women's Development	—	Relevant as an impact monitoring tool for women's development at local level.
	F.2 reflects qualitative scores on the above gendered parameters	Judgmental data based on qualitative scoring as per gendered criteria				

(*Contd.*)

(*Contd.*)

IPPA Tool						
Component G Institutional Assessment	**G.1** will relate to people's rating of delivery of different services	Numerical data in terms of proportion (percentage) through judgmental scoring based on multiple criteria for assessment	For monitoring implementation related to service delivery organizations	Relevant for all sectors involved in providing public services	If collated on a regional basis it would help indicate the degree of institutional impact at the regional level	Would help indicate the degree of institutional impact at the local level.
	G.2 will be on the constraints and possible opportunities	Qualitative data clustered as per criteria related to improvement of public service delivery	For monitoring implementation and actions related to service delivery organizations	Relevant for all sectors involved in providing public services	If collated on a regional basis it would help indicate the type of changes in institutional performance required at a regional level	Would indicate required changes in institutional performance at local level.
Component H Social Opportunity Assessment	**H.1** will be an assessment of social capital based on a set of criteria	Numerical data in terms of proportion (percentage) through judgemental scoring based on 4 criteria of social capital	Would help provide assessment of social opportunities at national level based on a set of criteria	Would help provide assessment of social opportunities at local level based on a set of criteria	Would help provide assessment of social opportunities at regional level based on a set of criteria	Would help provide assessment of social opportunities based on a set of criteria.

Processes (policies, laws, incentives etc.), which define people's opportunities and options for living. Institutional assessment can have 2 sub-components as given below.

(This IPPA component G is similar to the Community Voice Card and for further details see next chapter of the book).

Sub-component G.1 relates to people's assessment of delivery of different services.

Sub-component G.2 relates to possible opportunities related to different services.

6.2.8 *Social Opportunity Assessment* is IPPA component H and is essentially centred on social opportunity and capability. Experience shows that mere setting up establishment or organization does not guarantee social opportunity and human development. The instrument of social opportunity, so critical to develop human freedom, will be determined by a range of criteria related to productivity, equity, sustainability and empowerment, which in turn, would influence the collective achievement of common goals/objectives by the community/group involved in the social development. Social Opportunity Assessment has one sub-component H.1 which is an assessment of social opportunities based on a set of criteria as above. For further details see Chapter 3, Section 3.2.6 of the book.

6.2.9 *Relevance of Sub-Components of IPPA*—After a discussion of the sub-components of IPPA, Table 6.1 presents an indicative relevance of the different sub-components.

6.3 Social Group (Well-Being) Assessment

To begin with, it is important for any IPPA exercise to be informed of the social groups, who they are with what background, what is their poverty level, what are their dimensions of human poverty, who is excluded and who participates and which group/s they represent. It is for this purpose that social group assessment is undertaken (*see* Box 6.1), which helps learn about group-related human poverty dimensions, well-being/ill-being, access-related issues, status of social and political capital etc. The first round of such assessment provides a baseline upon which future rounds could show changes over time in poverty trends. Added to this is the approximate proportion of households in each social group, which then provides a basis for up scaling data at the village/block/meso levels and even higher levels. Such data over time when compared to the baseline could provide signals with regard to shifts in percentage households in and out of poverty and also intra-group and inter-group shifts. So both qualitative and numerical aspects of poverty status would emerge through social group assessment. The qualitative aspect helps understand the numerical aspects and both are important and complement each other. Data on both the aspects could be generated through focus group discussions and application of social grouping technique (*see* Box 6.1).

Box 6.1: Method for Social Grouping

Social Grouping is a PRA method for arriving at types of social groups in a community/village. There are other ways of doing social grouping. In order to keep matters simple only one method is suggested here. (For other methods see Mukherjee: 2002). In this method the participants discuss and identify different social categories of households based on local criteria. Once the social categories emerge through group discussion, they place them on ground/chart paper with the help of symbols and/or in writing. Then the participants are facilitated to arrive at proportion of households in each social category by using "fixed" or "free" scoring. In fixed scoring there is a fixed number of nuts/seeds/leaves etc., representing total number of households in their village. The participants arrive at estimated proportions and accordingly apportion nuts/seeds/leaves amongst different social categories, in their locality. (In case of representing fraction/s, nuts/seeds/leaves are broken into pieces and then placed against the social group/s concerned). In case of "free" scoring the participants use a certain amount of seeds/stones, whether large or small to indicate "more" or "less" number of households in each social category. The proportion of each social category is broadly drawn upon based on relative quantities of seeds/stones used. This is then cross-checked and recorded generally by the participants and any error and omission is taken care of.

6.3.1 *Social Group (Well-Being) Assessment* is PPA component A, related to human poverty/well-being assessment through local perspectives. While generating and constructing component 'A', it is useful to generate separate clusters of information at the field level on the poor and the marginalized group/s and women-headed households as and when required. This will also provide human poverty/well-being dimensions of socially excluded groups in addition to other social groups. Component 'A' of IPPA will have 2 sub-components:

Sub-Component A.1 is on human poverty (well-being) dimensions of households within social groups (with poor, marginalized and women-headed households as separate groups for assessing social inclusion).

Sub-Component A.2 is on the proportions of households within different social groups.

6.3.1.1 *Sub-component A.1* relates to an assessment of the dimensions on human poverty (well-being) of different social groups (with poor, marginalized and women-headed households as separate groups). The Sub-component will help focus on the status of human poverty indicators (*see* Box 6.2) of different social groups from local perspectives (as baseline data) and with repeat IPPAs over time. Sub-component A.1 will help indicate changes in human poverty (well-being) dimensions (mostly in qualitative terms) of different social/poor groups (including poor, marginalized and women-headed households as separate groups). For data generation, collation and up-scaling, Sub-component A.1 will be based on qualitative scoring. Changes in the Sub-component A.1, over time, will help reflect changes in human poverty dimensions of different social groups.

6.3.1.2 *Sub-component A.2* will provide information on the proportions of households within the social groups, both poor and non-poor groups. Changes in sub-component A.2, over time, will help capture both inter- and intra-shifts in proportions of households across poor and non-poor groups.

With base line data constructed (see Table 6.1 and Box 6.3) on this IPPA component 'A' related to Human Poverty (Well-Being) further updating of information would reflect the following:

- Comparative changes in human poverty (well-being) dimensions; and
- Shifts of households within social groups meaning thereby, changes in the proportions of poor and non-poor households over time.

Table 6.2: Sample Way of Data Collation: PPA Component 'A'

Social Group	*Type of dwelling and land holding*	*Food Security*	*Education and Schooling*	*Health*	*Drinking Water*	*Skills*	*Responsive governance and social status*	*Dependents*	*Access to Micro-credit*	*State of mind-peaceful/worrying*
Social group 1										
Social group 2										
Social group 3										
Social group 4										
Social group 5										
Social group n										

Note: The groups will include poor and marginalized as separate categories in the study villages.

Box 6.2: Selected Dimensions of Human Poverty

Some aspects of discussion on human poverty dimensions could include the following checklist for PPA component A. These are broadly—economic, human, socio-cultural, protective and political aspects of human poverty. More items can be added to this list.

Economic—income, capability to afford children to school, agricultural asset, living standard, food quality, non-agricultural assets.

Human (health, education, nutrition, water, housing)—housing, drinking water, sanitation, health, quality of school, teaching, agricultural skills.

Socio-cultural—respect in community, markets.

Protective—access to micro credit, village security, local ecological condition.

Political (voice, influence, power)—group decision, grassroots organization, process of decision making, social relationships.

The Social Group (Well-Being) Assessment could be up-scaled upto the meso level and the macro/national level in order to gain larger macro pictures of human poverty and well-being and also the proportions of households falling under different social groups.

Box 6.3: Clustering Sub-components of Human Poverty Dimensions

Sub-component could be based on participants' key indicators of human poverty such as health, sanitation, education, food security, water and housing skills, state of mind. This is a starting point only and needs to be developed through group discussions.

Type of dwelling—thatched hut; live in others' houses; homeless; homestead with hut; big house with tinned roof; tiled roof

Land holding—possess no land; IDP; have 1 or 2 hectares of upland; more than 2 hectares of upland; or less land etc.

Food security—2-3 months of food self sufficiency; 4-5 months; 6-8 months; food available round the year; surplus food available;

Children's schooling—children cannot attend school, school drop-out, children irregular to school; children regular to school; children passed out from school.

Health—To be developed.

(Contd.)

(Contd.)

> *Drinking water*—To be developed;
> *Skills*—Agriculture-related; non-agriculture-related; no skills for IGA;
> *Respect in Community*—
> *Dependents*—large number of dependents; no dependents; children as dependents; elderly only;
> *Access to Micro credit*—no knowledge of credit, cannot access credit outreach at a distance, tried but failed;
> *State of mind* — peaceful, less peaceful, sometimes worried, intense anxiety.

6.4 Local Resource Assessment

A localized resource assessment could be up-scaled to have a broader picture of resources from the perspectives of the poor. There are 6 different types of assets upon which individual/group/community draw to build their livelihoods.

These are :

(i) *Natural Capital*—Natural resource stocks from which flows are useful to livelihood such as land, water, wildlife, biodiversity etc.
(ii) *Social Capital*—Social resources such as networks, membership of groups, trusts.
(iii) *Human Capital*—Skill, knowledge, ability to work, good health.
(iv) *Physical Capital*—Basic infrastructure—transport, shelter, water, energy and communications.
(v) *Financial Capital*—Financial resources available to people whether savings, credit, remittances etc.

The framework suggests that there is a close correlation between people's overall asset status, the resources that they can draw upon and their robustness. Building up assets is considered a core component of empowerment. The under-pinning fact is the multi-dimensional approach of poverty and well-being. The social analysis for distinguishing particular groups is followed by analysis of capital assets for different social groups.

Table 6.3: Sample Way of Data Collation—Status of Local Assets—Component B.1

Type of Assets	*Main Assets from Sampled Villages*	*Asset Improvement (Positive changes)*	*Proximate reasons**	*Asset Degradation (negative changes)*	*Proximate reasons**
Natural Asset			(a) Environment-related (b) Finance-related (c) Rule of law-related (d) Policy/administration/ governance-related (e) Social issue-related (f) Human asset-related (g) Migration-related (h) Conflict-related (i) Others		(a) Environment-related (b) Finance-related (c) Rule of law-related (d) Policy/administration/ governance-related (e) Social issue-related (f) Human asset-related (g) Migration-related (h) Conflict-related (i) Others
Physical Asset			(a) Environment-related (b) Finance-related (c) Rule of law-related (d) Policy/administration/ governance-related (e) Social issue-related (f) Human asset-related (g) Migration-related (h) Conflict-related (i) Others		(a) Environment-related (b) Finance-related (c) Rule of law-related (d) Policy/administration/ governance-related (e) Social issue-related (f) Human asset-related (g) Migration-related (h) Conflict-related (i) Others
Human Asset			(a) Environment-related (b) Finance-related (c) Rule of law-related		(a) Environment-related (b) Finance-related (c) Rule of law-related

(Contd.)

(*Contd.*)

Type of Assets	*Main Assets from Sampled Villages*	*Asset Improvement (Positive changes)*	*Proximate reasons**	*Asset Degradation (negative changes)*	*Proximate reasons**
			(d) Policy/administration/ governance-related (e) Social issue-related (f) Human asset-related (g) Migration-related (h) Conflict-related (i) Others		(d) Policy/administration/ governance-related (e) Social issue-related (f) Human asset-related (g) Migration-related (h) Conflict-related (i) Others
Social Asset			(a) Environment-related (b) Finance-related (c) Rule of law-related (d) Policy/administration/ governance-related (e) Social issue-related (f) Human asset-related (g) Migration-related (h) Conflict-related (i) Others		(a) Environment-related (b) Finance-related (c) Rule of law-related (d) Policy/administration/ governance-related (e) Social issue-related (f) Human asset-related (g) Migration-related (h) Conflict-related (i) Others

(*Contd.*)

(Contd.)

Type of Assets	*Main Assets from Sampled Villages*	*Asset Improvement (Positive changes)*	*Proximate reasons**	*Asset Degradation (negative changes)*	*Proximate reasons**
Financial Asset			(a) Environment-related (b) Finance-related (c) Rule of law-related (d) Policy/administration/ governance-related (e) Social issue-related (f) Human asset-related (g) Migration-related (h) Conflict-related (i) Others		(a) Environment-related (b) Finance-related (c) Rule of law-related (d) Policy/administration/ governance-related (e) Social issue-related (f) Human asset-related (g) Migration-related (h) Conflict-related (i) Others
Political Asset			(a) Environment-related (b) Finance-related (c) Rule of law-related (d) Policy/administration/ governance-related (e) Social issue-related (f) Human asset-related (g) Migration-related (h) Conflict-related (i) Others		(a) Environment-related (b) Finance-related (c) Rule of law-related (d) Policy/administration/ governance-related (e) Social issue-related (f) Human asset-related (g) Migration-related (h) Conflict-related (i) Others

Note: * Proximate reasons are approximate and qualitative.

Some relevant questions are as follows:

- How has asset status been changing over time?
- Have there been upward or downward changes in the assets?
- What are the root causes of changes and how do they vary between different social groups?

Who could be approached?—Key informants from different groups.

Asset/Resource Assessment is IPPA component B related to status and access of assets by different social groups as assessed locally. Such assessment will provide the status on local resources and the access of the poor to at least 6 types of assets/resources—natural, physical, human, financial, socio-cultural and political assets/ resources. Such assessment will have 2 sub-components.

Sub-component B.1 will help assess the local status/conditions of assets/resources; and

Sub-component B.2 will help assess the status of access to assets/ resources by poor groups.

With construction of baseline data on PPA component B, sub-components B.1 and B.2 will help indicate changes in 2 major variables—local asset status/condition and access to assets/resources by poor groups.

Methods Suggested

(ii) *Warming up*—Types of Assets and Status of Assets Aocessed by Poor Households.

(iii) *Asset Mapping circle*—Where the centre point would be the ultimate maximum in terms of access to assets and 6 lines from the radius would reflect positive changes and the continuation of the 6 lines outside the radius would indicate negative changes.

Asset Mapping Circle—As shown in Chart 6.1, the asset mapping circle has 6 assets to be mapped on it. The 6 assets are—natural assets, physical assets, human assets, social assets (including local security), financial assets and political assets. Poverty is heightened by lack of access to assets. Each asset is represented by a straight line, which runs from the centre of the circle to its radius and then a part of it lies outside the circle.

Chart 6.1: Asset Mapping Circle

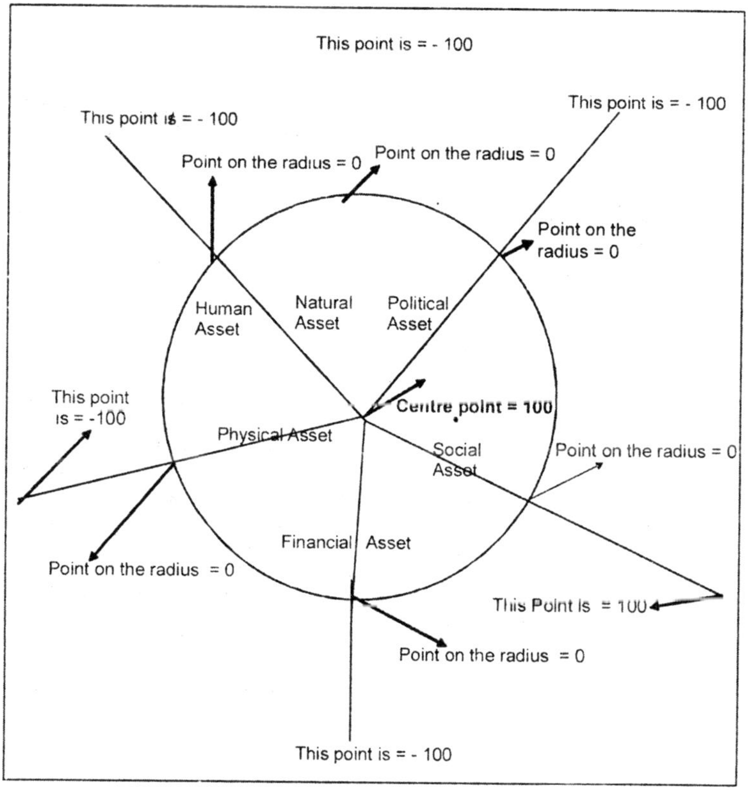

The centrepoint of the asset mapping circle in Chart 6.1 is the ultimate final point for status of the asset in question and is measured as (+) 100; the point touching the radius of the circle is the zero point and that part of the straightline lying outside the circle shows lack of access to assets whose end-point is measured as (–) 100. One major objective of this asset mapping is to capture the status of local assets and its change over time. This asset mapping could be done by a few key informants who have enough credibility at the local level and would provide a unbiased picture of which way the assets of poor groups are moving in the locality. If the status of the asset is positive and increasing then it could be shown anywhere between the zero point in the radius and the centre point of the circle. In case such status is deteriorating and negative then it could be shown anywhere between the zero point in the radius and the point at the end of the straight line which falls outside the circle and is measured as –100. In order to capture the change/magnitude of the status of the asset this method can prove handy.

Table 6.4: Access to Assets—Sample Way of Data Collation—Component B.2

Social Group/Asset	*Natural Asset*	*Physical Asset*	*Human Asset*	*Social Asset*	*Financial Asset*	*Political Asset*
Social group 1	High	High	High	High	High	High
	Medium	Medium	Medium	Medium	Medium	Medium
	Low	Low	Low	Low	Low	Low
	None	None	None	None	None	None
Social group 2	High	High	High	High	High	High
	Medium	Medium	Medium	Medium	Medium	Medium
	Low	Low	Low	Low	Low	Low
	None	None	None	None	None	None
Social group 3	High	High	High	High	High	High
	Medium	Medium	Medium	Medium	Medium	Medium
	Low	Low	Low	Low	Low	Low
	None	None	None	None	None	None
Social group 4	High	High	High	High	High	High
	Medium	Medium	Medium	Medium	Medium	Medium
	Low	Low	Low	Low	Low	Low
	None	None	None	None	None	None
Social group 5	High	High	High	High	High	High
	Medium	Medium	Medium	Medium	Medium	Medium
	Low	Low	Low	Low	Low	Low
	None	None	None	None	None	None

Note: Based on notes prepared by Neela Mukherjee for assessing access to assets by social groups for Doon Valley Watershed evaluation study.

6.5 Vulnerability and Risk Assessment

First, there is a need to understand the vulnerability context in which assets exist. These are the trends, shocks, seasonality and local cultural practices, which affect livelihoods (www.livelihoods.org). Some key issues related to the vulnerability context are indicated below. Trends in natural resource stock, population density, technology, political representation and economic trends, affect livelihoods. Shocks in the form of climate disasters, conflicts, etc. undermine asset base. Seasonality such as deficit months in a year affects people's well-being. Cultural practices can make assets vulnerable and impact on livelihoods. Two most important factors considered in the present study are trends and seasonality.

Trend will be covering food security, literacy and education, health and sanitation, peace and conflict over a period of at least 7 years (*see* Table 6.5—Sample for data collation).

Seasonality Assessment

To factor in the seasonality forces faced by poor groups, the 12 months in a year are clustered into normal months and hardship months. Such impact of seasonal forces could be captured through 8 aspects such as food, drinking water, work opportunities, wages, migration, illness and health, livestock disease and expenses compared over normal months and hardship months. Seasonality assessment when repeated for each year would show the changes in impact of seasonal forces from year to year (*see* Table 6.6—Sample for data collation).

6.6 Livelihoods Assessment

What is "livelihood"?—"Livelihood" is how people compose their means of living from their asset-base (6 Assets—natural asset, physical asset, social asset, human asset and financial asset, political asset), capability and activities. As regarding sustainability of livelihoods, a livelihood is sustainable both in the present and future by recovering from shocks (e.g. drought, flood), maintaining assets and capabilities and without undermining natural resource base.

Livelihoods Assessment is IPPA component D and is entirely focused on assessments of livelihoods of poor. "Livelihood" is how people compose their means of living from their asset-base (6 Assets—natural, physical, socio-cultural, human, financial and political), capability and activities. A livelihood is sustainable both in the present and future by recovering from shocks (e.g. drought, flood), maintaining assets and capabilities and without undermining natural resource base (DFID: www.livelihoods.org). Livelihoods Assessment D will have 3 sub-components and all of them will be gendered for further use at the village/block/meso level. There are 3 tables under livelihoods assessment relating to:

(i) Listing of Livelihoods
(ii) Preferences—Ranking of Livelihoods—Women and Men
(iii) Earnings/Wages from Livelihoods

Table 6.5: Trend Assessment—Sample Way of Data Collation—Component C.1

Criteria	*Food security*	*Drinking water*	*Education*	*Health and Sanitation*	*Work availability*	*Migration*	*Conflict*	*Ecological degradation*
Current year	Increasing No change Decreasing	Increasing No change Decreasing	Increasing No change Decreasing	Increasing No change Decreasing	Increasing No change Decreasing	Increasing No change Decreasing	Increasing No change Decreasing	
5 years back (compared to last 5 years)	Increasing No change Decreasing	Increasing No change Decreasing	Increasing No change Decreasing	Increasing No change Decreasing	Increasing No change Decreasing	Increasing No change Decreasing	Increasing No change Decreasing	
5 years back (compared to last 5 years)	Increasing No change Decreasing	Increasing No change Decreasing	Increasing No change Decreasing	Increasing No change Decreasing	Increasing No change Decreasing	Increasing No change Decreasing	Increasing No change Decreasing	

Table 6.6: Seasonality Assessment—Sample Way of Data Collation—Component C.2

Criteria	*Food insecurity*	*Lack of drinking water*	*Lack of work availability*	*Low wages*	*Migration*	*Illness and bad health*	*Livestock disease*	
Normal months	Increasing No change Decreasing	Increasing No change Decreasing	Increasing No change Decreasing	Increasing No change Decreasing	Increasing No change Decreasing	Increasing No change Decreasing	Increasing No change Decreasing	Increasing No change Decreasing
Hardship months	Increasing No change Decreasing	Increasing No change Decreasing	Increasing No change Decreasing	Increasing No change Decreasing	Increasing No change Decreasing	Increasing No change Decreasing	Increasing No change Decreasing	Increasing No change Decreasing
Coping Strategies to overcome hardship								

Note 1 = Increasing = 1, No change = 0, Decreasing = -1.
Note 2 = Coping Strategies can be grouped into (i) going without the item and tightening the belt, (ii) selling assets, (iii) making additional effort such as undertaking more work, (iv) borrowing or (v) others.

Table 6.7: Livelihoods Assessment–Sample Way of Data Collation

Livelihoods—Key Constraints and Opportunities			
Main Categories of Livelihoods	*Livelihood-related Activities—Illustrations*	*Key Constraints*	*Key Opportunities*
(i) Forest/Micro Environment-related	Leasehold forestry and homestead gardening	(a) Environment-related (b) Finance-related (c) Rule of law-related (d) Policy/administration/governance-related (e) Social issue-related (f) Human asset-related (g) Migration-related (h) Conflict-related (i) Others	(a) Environment-related (b) Finance-related (c) Rule of law-related (d) Policy/administration/governance-related (e) Social issue-related (f) Human asset-related (g) Migration-related (h) Conflict-related (i) Others
(ii) Community forest-related	Harvesting of fodder, fuel wood and timber	(a) Environment-related (b) Finance-related (c) Rule of law-related (d) Policy/administration/governance-related (e) Social issue-related (f) Human asset-related (g) Migration-related (h) Conflict-related (i) Others	(a) Environment-related (b) Finance-related (c) Rule of law-related (d) Policy/administration/governance-related (e) Social issue-related (f) Human asset-related (g) Migration-related (h) Conflict-related (i) Others
(iii) Agriculture-related	Land preparation, plantation of crops, e.g. rice, maize, pulses, millet,	(a) Environment-related (b) Finance-related (c) Rule of law-related	(a) Environment-related (b) Finance-related (c) Rule of law-related

(*Contd.*)

(*Contd.*)

Livelihoods—Key Constraints and Opportunities			
Main Categories of Livelihoods	*Livelihood-related Activities—Illustrations*	*Key Constraints*	*Key Opportunities*
	soya bean, vegetables; watering fields; weeding; harvesting of crops; selling produce	(d) Policy/administration/ governance-related (e) Social issue-related (f) Human asset-related (g) Migration-related (h) Conflict-related (i) Others	(d) Policy/administration/ governance-related (e) Social issue-related (f) Human asset-related (g) Migration-related (h) Conflict-related (i) Others
(iv) Livestock rearing	Goat-rearing, cow/ox-rearing, buffalo-rearing, pig-rearing, chicken-rearing, rabbit-rearing and other types of livestock-rearing	(a) Environment-related (b) Finance-related (c) Rule of law-related (d olicy/administration/ governance-related (e) Social issue-related (f) Human asset-related (g) Migration-related (h) Conflict-related (i) Others	(a) Environment-related (b) Finance-related (c) Rule of law-related (d) Policy/administration/ governance-related (e) Social issue-related (f) Human asset-related (g) Migration-related (h) Conflict-related (i) Others
(v) Non-agriculture and Construction-related	Working as labour/coolie for construction activities such as construction of roads, culverts, buildings, working in brick kilns	(a) Environment-related (b) Finance-related (c) Rule of law-related (d) Policy/administration/ governance-related (e) Social issue-related	(a) Environment-related (b) Finance-related (c) Rule of law-related (d) Policy/administration/ governance-related (e) Social issue-related

(*Contd.*)

(*Contd.*)

Livelihoods—Key Constraints and Opportunities

Main Categories of Livelihoods	*Livelihood-related Activities—Illustrations*	*Key Constraints*	*Key Opportunities*
		(f) Human asset-related (g) Migration-related (h) Conflict-related (i) Others	(f) Human asset-related (g) Migration-related (h) Conflict-related (i) Others
(vi) Crafts/Artisan-related	Making bamboo craft, weaving cloth, baskets, mats, beads, ropes; tailoring, carpentry, blacksmith, selling grocery and others	(a) Environment-related (b) Finance-related (c) Rule of law-related (d) Policy/administration/ governance-related (e) Social issue-related (f) Human asset-related (g) Migration-related (h) Conflict-related (i) Others	(a) Environment-related (b) Finance-related (c) Rule of law-related (d) Policy/administration/ governance-related (e) Social issue-related (f) Human asset-related (g) Migration-related (h) Conflict-related (i) Others
(vii) Other activities	Brewing/selling alcohol in the locality	(a) Environment-related (b) Finance-related (c) Rule of law-related (d) Policy/administration/ governance-related (e) Social issue-related (f) Human asset-related (g) Migration-related (h) Conflict-related (i) Others	(a) Environment-related (b) Finance-related (c) Rule of law-related (d) Policy/administration/ governance-related (e) Social issue-related (f) Human asset-related (g) Migration-related (h) Conflict-related (i) Others

Note 1: The constraints and opportunities will need to be clustered under different categories as indicated above. They will be clustered at different levels.

Sub-component D.1 is on the list of existing livelihoods and related opportunities/constraints (*see* Table 6.6).

Sub-component D.2 is on the preferences of existing livelihoods and aspired livelihoods (*see* Table 6.7).

Sub-component D.3 relates to the earning/wages/remuneration of the poor groups from different sources of livelihoods (*see* Table 6.8).

The key Opportunities/Constraints in Table 6.6 are categorized as follows:

- Environment-related,
- Finance-related,
- Rule of law-related,
- Policy-related,
- Social issue-related,
- Human asset-related,
- Migration-related, and
- Conflict-related.

Table 6.8: Existing and Preferred Sources of Livelihoods in Study Villages

Sources/Activities	*Women – Existing Sources of Livelihoods: Rank*	*Men – Existing Sources of Livelihoods: Rank*	*Women – Preferred Ranking of Livelihoods*	*Men – Preferred Ranking of Livelihoods*
Livelihood Activity 1				
Livelihood Activity 2				
Livelihood Activity 3				
......				
Livelihood Activity n				

Table 6.9: Earnings/Wages from Selected Livelihoods Pursued by Poor Groups

Livelihood-related Activities	*Wage rate/Selling price/Earnings*
Livelihood Activity 1	
Livelihood Activity 2	
Livelihood Activity 3	

6.7 Problem Prioritization—Solution Assessment

Problem-Opportunity Assessment is IPPA component E and is an integral part of IPPA's contribution to people's planning process. The problem-opportunity assessment under IPPA component E is considered more effective as a planning tool than a monitoring tool. It helps bring out people problems and opportunities as perceived by them. In IPPA, the problems are listed, prioritized and analyzed by the local groups and communities, whether rural or urban. The problems that emerge in different areas often have many generic similarities though could differ widely due to local context. Thus the main problem domain may be similar but some of the sub-criteria would emphasize local features. The problems and opportunities revealed by the poor could then be clustered by analysts under different sectors for scaling up to the village level, block/district level, regional level and the national level for future action at appropriate levels. Such problems and opportunities will then constitute a prime basis for village/district /regional planning and also provide inputs/feedback at the sectoral level.

Problems-Opportunity Assessment or PPA component E will have 2 sub-components, which are gendered.

Sub-component E.1 will relate to the problems prioritized by groups of poor women and men along with the opportunities, and

Sub-component E.2 will relate to the problem-opportunity domains up-scaled at local, district, regional and national level.

6.8 Gender Assessment

Gender Assessment is IPPA component F and relates to various dimensions of gender at the local level. Gender assessment has sub-components F.1 and F.2.

Sub-component F.1 revolves around short queries, which are gender-based and qualitative.

Sub-component F.2 reflects qualitative scores on the following gendered parameters:

- Type of work, workload and responsibility.
- Having knowledge/skills.

- Taking part in household decision-making.
- Having access and control over resources.
- Having power and status.
- Victim of alcoholism/domestic violence.

6.10: Gender Assessment

Gender Aspects		*Men*	*Women*	*Both Women and Men*	*Remarks*
(1) Type of work, workload and responsibility	(i) Household (ii) Agri-related (iii) Non-agri-related (iv) Others				
(2) Knowledge and Skills	(iv) Food (v) IGA (vi) Agri (vii) Public services				
(3) Decision Making	(viii) Food (ix) Health (x) Children (xi) Income				
(4) Access and Control	(xii) Food (xiii) Health (xiv) Income				
(5) Power and Status	(xv) Home (xvi) Social (xvii) Legal				

Note 1: Qualitative Scoring: Measurement of gender dimensions are based on scoring on 5 main criteria and 17 sub-criteria, as follows None = 1 negligible = 2, low = 3, medium = 4 and high = 5.

Note 2: There are 17 criteria for measurement of gender dimensions. Each criterion with the highest score of 5, leads to a total score of 85. Any group or people's committee, which scores "high" on all criteria has a total score of 85 (5 multiplied by 17) while that, which scores "none" on all criteria has a total score of 17 (1 multiplied by 17).

6.9 Institutional Assessment

It is important to understand the Structures (Institutions/organizations such as government, NGOs, community based organizations, private sector etc.) and processes (policies, laws, incentives etc.), which define people's livelihood options.

There are three main ways in how institutions impact:

- They are critical in determining who gains access to which type of asset and what the effective value of such asset is.
- Along with people's asset status they help define which livelihood strategies or activities are feasible and attractive.
- Again, markets and legal restrictions also determine the extent of which one asset can be converted into another type of asset (e.g. natural capital into financial capital).

Institutional Assessment is IPPA component G and plays an important role in people's lives. It is important to understand the role and effectiveness of institution/organization such as Government, NGO, community based organization, private sector etc. and processes (policies, laws, incentives etc.), which define people's opportunities and options for living. There are at least 3 ways in how such institutions/organizations, their policies and processes impact on people's well-being, lives and livelihoods.

Institutional assessment can have 2 Sub-components:

Sub-component G.1 will relate to people's assessment of delivery of different services, and

Sub-component G.2 will be on the possible opportunities related to different services.

For details see Chapter 7 on community voice tool/card.

6.10 Social Opportunity Assessment

Mere setting up establishment or an organization does not guarantee social opportunity and human development. It does not indicate automatic human development or choice that localized natural resources will be managed in a sustainable manner. The instrument of *social opportunity*, so critical to develop human freedom, will be determined by a range of criteria, as indicated below, which in turn, would influence the collective achievement of common goals/ objectives by the community/group involved.

Social Opportunity Assessment is IPPA component H and is essentially centred on social opportunity and capability. Experience shows that mere setting up establishment or organization does not guarantee social opportunity and human development. Changes in social opportunity over time are important for tracking purposes. The instrument of social opportunity, so critical to develop human freedom, is generally determined by a range of criteria, as indicated below, which in turn, tend to influence the collective achievement of common goals/objectives by the community/group involved in social development. Tables 6.11 and 6.12 provide a list of the measures of *social opportunity* under consideration.

Table 6.11: Criteria for measuring Threshold Level of Social Opportunity and Its Changes

Criteria for Productivity	*Criteria for Equity*	*Criteria for Sustainability*	*Criteria of Empowerment*
1. Group membership, keenness, leadership and sense of responsibility 2. Group capacity and level of confidence 3. Status of financial capital base 4. External linkages, both vertical and horizontal 5. Technologies and improvement	1. Broad-based understanding of group activities and worldview 2. Group participation in decision-making 3. Equity in benefit-flows 4. Livelihood impacts and reduction in vulnerability	1. Vision/Ideas for future 2. Group-based resource regeneration/ conservation 3. Internal norms, mutual trust and role clarity 4. Group attachment/ ownership 5. Ability to raise issues and resolve conflict 6. Maintenance of asset	1. Social inclusion and emotional well-being 2. Freedom to function as a group and power to influence decision-making 3. Power "within" and power "with" 4. Access to information and responsive governance 5. Transparent decision-making from 'above'

Source: Derived from Mukherjee (2002), Forest Protection Committees of West Bengal: *Measuring Social Capital* in Joint Forest Management, (*see* www.livelihoods.org).

Table 6.12: Illustration—Measurement of Social Opportunity of Self-Help Groups/Communities

Criteria of Social Opportunity	*FPC 1 – Village X (Baseline: Year: 2005)*	*FPC 2 – Village Y (Baseline Year: 2005)*	*SHG 1– Village X (Baseline Year: 2005)*	*SHG 2 – Village Y (Baseline Year: 2005)*
Productivity				
1. Group membership, keenness, leadership and sense of responsibility	1	1	3	4
2. Group capacity and level of confidence	1	1	3	4
3. Status of growth in financial capital	1	1	1	2
4. External linkages – vertical and horizontal	1	1	2	2
5. Technologies and improvement	1	1	1	1
Equity				
6. Broad-based understanding of group activities and worldview	1	2	3	4
7. Group participation in decision-making	1	1	2	2
8. Equity in benefit-flows	1	1	4	4
9. Livelihood impacts and reduction in vulnerabilities	1	1	5	2
Sustainability				
10. Vision/Ideas for future	1	1	3	4
11. Group-based natural resource regeneration/ conservation	1	1	4	4
12. Internal norms, mutual trust and role clarity	1	1	3	3
13. Group attachment/ ownership	1	1	2	3
14. Ability to raise issues and resolving conflict	1	1	2	2
15. Maintenance of asset/s	1	1	3	4
Empowerment				
16. Social inclusion and emotional well-being	1	2	6	4
17. Freedom to function as a groups and power to influence decision-making	1	1	4	4

(Contd.)

(Contd.)

Criteria of Social Opportunity	*FPC 1 – Village X (Baseline: Year: 2005)*	*FPC 2 – Village Y (Baseline Year: 2005)*	*SHG 1– Village X (Baseline Year: 2005)*	*SHG 2 – Village Y (Baseline Year: 2005)*
18. Power "within" and power "with"	1	1	3	3
19. Access to information and responsive governance	1	1		
20. Transparent decision-making from 'above'	1	1	3	3
Total score	20/120	22/120	57/120	63/120
Total score on 100	16.7	22.5	47.5	52.5

Note 1: Qualitative Scoring: Measurement of social opportunity are based on scoring on 20 criteria, as follows: 1 = Negligible; 2 = Low; 3 = Medium; 4 = High; 5 = Very High; 6 = Excellent.

Note 2: There are 20 criteria for measurement of social opportunity. Each criterion with the highest score of 6, leads to a total score of 120. Any group or people's committee, which scores "excellent" on all criteria has a total score of 120 (6 multiplied by 20) while that, which scores "negligible" on all criteria has a total score of 20 (1 multiplied by 20).

After a discussion on different aspects of IPPA, the following chapter presents a voice tool for assessment of governance for social accountability.

7

Voice Tool for Assessing Governance

The present chapter describes a voice tool for assessing governance for social accountability purposes. Such assessment could relate to any public or private service area, e.g. in the area of providing child care, drinking water, primary schooling or any other aspect. The tool described in this chapter is mainly based on qualitative responses though validated by semi-structured questionnaire and a mechanism for up-scaling it. Community Voice Tool (CVT) for assessing service delivery is mainly a tool for social accountability purposes. However, it can be combined with participatory assessments as and when required.

7.1 Tool for Participatory Assessment of Governance

Participatory assessment of governance (PAG) is a way in which the communities/citizens/groups provide their views, opinions, scores on selected aspects, e.g. performance of government related to 'quality', 'coverage of services', 'efficiency', 'cost', 'responsiveness' in the area of providing different types of services to the community. The tool could be based on a structured questionnaire with a set of closed questions, or it could be based on a set of relatively open questions, qualitative in nature. The tool could be a combination of both closed and open questions. The tool described in this section is mainly based on interactive sessions with local communities though validated by semi-structured questionnaire and up-scaled at different levels.

7.2 Flexibility and Openness

In the tool for assessing governance as described in this section relatively open questions and group interactions allow space for people to participate and to express their views with greater degree of freedom. Open questions help elicit people's views and opinions from different quarters and people are asked to score different services based on selected criteria. Such information is then analyzed, aggregated, converted to percentages or made into indices to provide the 'larger picture' of public service delivery (or even private service delivery as required) of those services being assessed. It helps indicate the areas of progress and problematic areas of the services concerned from local perspective and possible ways for better delivery of such services.

7.3 Significance of Tool for Assessment of Governance

A qualitative tool for participatory assessment of services delivered by public (or private) bodies is widely applicable though has special significance for those countries and regions/areas where there is a large proportion of social exclusion in context of delivering services. Such a tool based on interactive meetings with local communities tends to reduce investigator's bias so abundantly present in questionnaire and other similar tools applied for assessing delivery of services. It enables excluded and weaker segments of the population to participate and express their views and to have better grasp of the issues being openly discussed in small group meetings. The tool also helps convey better the objectives of a participatory assessment especially to weaker and marginalized sections of the society, provides them space to participate and flexibility in scoring of criteria related to provision of services by different service delivery organizations.

7.3.1 How the Tool helps?

The tool for Participatory Assessment of Governance (PAG) has a special utility to make people think and assess the services delivered and arrive at a score for rating such services. Few other merits of the tool are mentioned below:

- It is a tool to reach 'voices', especially of the poor to the service provider. It helps flag areas of concern and related issues in service delivery for future action. It helps make sense of what works and what doesn't—the strengths and weaknesses of the services delivered and the agencies, which deliver them.

- It helps get connected with people to get public feedback and ideas of different aspects of service delivery. It helps empower public to provide their opinion. It creates space for accountability of the service provider. It can be used as a strategic tool for the service provider who cares.
- Regular use of the tool helps establish regular communication with people and creates a channel from the 'down' (people) to the 'top' (service provider) for people's assessment. This, in essence, then becomes a tool for participatory monitoring of public services. It could constitute a part of participatory poverty monitoring when poor people are involved in assessing public services on a systematic basis.

A comparative picture of assessment of service delivery through questionnaire survey, generally utilized for Citizen Report Card *vis-a-vis* Participatory Qualitative Tool as in PAG is given in Table 7.1.

Table 7.1: Comparative Assessment of Service Delivery through Questionnaire Survey and PAG Tool

Citizen Report Card (CRC) based on Questionnaire Survey with closed questions	*PAG—a Participatory Qualitative Tool based on open questions*
(i) It is more appropriate for literate population–has an in-built literacy bias	(i) It is more appropriate for facilitating population, which are semi-literate and literate one main objective is to facilitate interactive participation for getting feedback on service delivery.
(ii) The questionnaire is to be mainly canvassed to individuals.	(ii) The qualitative tool is flexible based on group interactions and mainly emerge as group output. There can be separate groups of women and men participating, which can yield gendered results. Interactive process tend to help in consensus building towards a group output though there can be voices of dissent.
(iii) The questionnaire when canvassed at a quick space helps to save time but can also result in loss of information and lack of well thought out responses.	(iii) It has a warming-up process to help the participants relate to criteria for assessment of services based on their knowledge and experience of service delivery.

(*Contd.*)

(*Contd.*)

Citizen Report Card (CRC) based on Questionnaire Survey with closed questions	*PAG—a Participatory Qualitative Tool based on open questions*
(iv) The questionnaire has a strict standard of sampling and core elements of 'representativeness'.	(iv) Purposive sampling goes well with PAG and it is mainly indicative. However, by and large, it can also be made representative. With a warming up process it may need relatively more time and the participants' assessment is more trustworthy and realistic with group discussion and group analysis.
(v) Data is relatively machine-efficient and smart though the degree of participation is low. The questionnaire is based mostly on closed questions though a few open questions can be included.	(v) Data being qualitative is relatively less sleek though the degree of participation is much higher and open-ended questions help participants to exercise their choice. There is also lower incidence of 'diplomacy' bias.
(vi) The enumerator is in control of the process of canvassing questionnaire.	(vi) "Ownership" element in PAG can increase if participants can suggest criteria for assessment.
(vii) All criteria can be rated low if people are in a negative mood due to some reason. Questionnaires are difficult to canvass when people are in a negative mood.	(vii) It is possible to counter negative mood of people through facilitating participation and creating positive environment. However, it is important to manage the participatory process.

7.4 Criteria for Assessing Service Delivery

For a relatively open and participatory PAG, there could be a range of criteria to consider. Some of the criteria, which could be considered, are as Box 7.1:

Criteria for PAG:

Box 7.1

(i) Awareness
(ii) Access and Inclusion
(iii) Attitude and Behaviour
(iv) Quality, Timeliness and Efficiency
(v) Responsiveness
(vi) Infrastructure
(vii) Cost (including hidden cost)
(viii) Sustainability
(ix) Suggestions for Improvement

The above criteria are important for assessing any quality of governance. 'Awareness' implies awareness of service consumers whether they have been made aware of availability of certain service and the terms and conditions of provision of such service. As a criterion 'access and inclusion' help determine whether certain groups are socially included into the service and whether there are enabling conditions for them to access the service concerned. It is important to have customer-friendly 'attitude and behaviour' of the service providers without which the poor and marginalized groups may be discouraged to approach the former. About 'quality, timeliness and efficiency' the service providers have to be vigilant to provide service in time and effectively. 'Infrastructure' signifies whether the service providers have necessary base for providing the service. 'Cost' is another important criterion, which would determine the demand for any particular service. The higher the cost of indispensable services such as health service, the greater would be the burden on the consumer. The criterion on 'sustainability' shows whether services provided are regular and sustainable on a long-term basis. The last point is regarding suggestions for improvement of service delivery.

7.4.1 PAG and its 4 Parts—Application of PAG could be looked into as a combination of 4 parts as described below:

(i) The first part of PAG relates to small group discussions in open forums and scoring of services based on a basket of criteria, which include: 'awareness', 'access and inclusion', 'attitude' and 'behaviour', 'quality, timeliness and efficiency', 'responsiveness', 'infrastructure', 'cost' (including hidden cost) and 'sustainability'. Such small groups of participants discuss and arrive at 'group' assessment and scores based on different criteria related to service provision. Each group assessment and score is examined by the groups before finalizing it. There can also be participants who do not agree with group score and their note of dissent is taken care of.

(ii) The second part of PAG relates to suggestions by participants for bringing about improvements in the standard and quality of relevant services provided.

(iii) The third part of the PAG relates to validation of the group analysis and scores by means of semi-structured interviews of local persons/key informants.

(iv) In the fourth part, the results from the group discussions are then presented in summarized forms to groups of local service providers[1] who respond to local people's assessment and also help validate. The data and information generated are then processed and analyzed for gaining the 'larger picture' on service delivery whether at micro, meso and macro levels as required.

7.5 Suggested Steps for PAG

Some steps in PAG can be illustrated through discussions which emerged during a training workshop in Moldova as indicated below:

(a) Select a team of 12 experienced facilitators who have good skills in interacting with poor groups. For conducting facilitation, they could be in pairs of 2, which imply a total of 6 pairs. Also select at least 2 field coordinators from the 12 facilitators to collate information and to maintain quality of field interaction.

(b) Decide a list of government/public/private services on which the consumers' voice and assessment is to be made. Each interactive session could be of 2 to 3 hours. Experience shows that in any one interactive session not more than 4 services, are possible to be assessed efficiently. In case there are more than 4 services separate sessions could be held.

(c) Going by Box 7.1, selected criteria for assessment by consumer group/s can be clustered together as follows:

(i) Awareness, access and inclusion to services,
(ii) Attitude and behaviour of service providers,
(iii) Quality, responsiveness and efficiency of service providers,
(iv) Quality and adequacy of infrastructure for services,
(v) Cost of services,
(vi) Sustainability of services.

For each criterion as above, they need to be first defined in the local context and then a list of 4 or 5 open questions with few closed questions can be prepared to explore the criterion in different aspects depending on the service delivery to be assessed. So there will emerge a list of open

Table 7.2: Compact PAG Scores—Part 1

Assessment by Focus Group/Individual/s

Location/Village Name: County:

Name of the Participant/s: ; Age = ; Male/Female = ;

Whether Poor/Very Poor = ; Other Criteria = ; Ethnicity:

Illustrations of Public Services Delivery/Criteria	*Col. (i)* *Awareness, Access and Inclusion*	*Col. (ii)* *Attitude and Behaviour*	*Col. (iii)* *Quality, Timeliness and Efficiency, Responsiveness*	*Col. (iv)* *Quality and Adequacy of Infrastructure for Services*	*Col. (v)* *Costing*	*Col. (vi)* *Sustainability*
Local Health Post	Very Poor Poor Average Good Very good	Very Poor Poor Average Good Very good	Very Poor Poor Average Good Very good	Very Poor Poor Average Good Very good	Very high High Average Low Lowest	Very Poor Poor Average Good Very good
Primary School	Very Poor Poor Average Good Very good	Very Poor Poor Average Good Very good	Very Poor Poor Average Good Very good	Very Poor Poor Average Good Very good	Very high High Average Low Lowest	Very Poor Poor Average Good Very good
Drinking Water	Very Poor Poor Average Good Very good	Very Poor Poor Average Good Very good	Very Poor Poor Average Good Very good	Very Poor Poor Average Good Very good	Very high High Average Low Lowest	Very Poor Poor Average Good Very good

(Contd.)

(Contd.)

Illustrations of Public Services Delivery/Criteria	*Col. (i)* *Awareness, Access and Inclusion*	*Col. (ii)* *Attitude and Behaviour*	*Col. (iii)* *Quality, Timeliness and Efficiency, Responsiveness*	*Col. (iv)* *Quality and Adequacy of Infrastructure for Services*	*Col. (v)* *Costing*	*Col. (vi)* *Sustainability*
Forest Office Services	Very Poor Poor Average Good Very good	Very Poor Poor Average Good Very good	Very Poor Poor Average Good Very good	Very Poor Poor Average Good Very good	Very high High Average Low Lowest	Very Poor Poor Average Good Very good
Farm-related Services	Very Poor Poor Average Good Very good	Very Poor Poor Average Good Very good	Very Poor Poor Average Good Very good	Very Poor Poor Average Good Very good	Very high High Average Low Lowest	Very Poor Poor Average Good Very good
Livestock rearing Services	Very Poor Poor Average Good Very good	Very Poor Poor Average Good Very good	Very Poor Poor Average Good Very good	Very Poor Poor Average Good Very good	Very high High Average Low Lowest	Very Poor Poor Average Good Very good

(Contd.)

(Contd.)

Illustrations of Public Services Delivery/Criteria	*Col. (i) Awareness, Access and Inclusion*	*Col. (ii) Attitude and Behaviour*	*Col. (iii) Quality, Timeliness and Efficiency, Responsiveness*	*Col. (iv) Quality and Adequacy of Infrastructure for Services*	*Col. (v) Costing*	*Col. (vi) Sustainability*
Micro Credit Delivery Services	Very Poor Poor Average Good Very good	Very Poor Poor Average Good Very good	Very Poor Poor Average Good Very good	Very Poor Poor Average Good Very good	Very high High Average Low Lowest	Very Poor Poor Average Good Very good
Police Station	Very Poor Poor Average Good Very good	Very Poor Poor Average Good Very good	Very Poor Poor Average Good Very good	Very Poor Poor Average Good Very good	Very high High Average Low Lowest	Very Poor Poor Average Good Very good
Local Raiyon Services	Very Poor Poor Average Good Very good	Very Poor Poor Average Good Very good	Very Poor Poor Average Good Very good	Very Poor Poor Average Good Very good	Very high High Average Low Lowest	Very Poor Poor Average Good Very good
Local NGO Services	Very Poor Poor Average Good Very good	Very Poor Poor Average Good Very good	Very Poor Poor Average Good Very good	Very Poor Poor Average Good Very good	Very high High Average Low Lowest	Very Poor Poor Average Good Very good

(Contd.)

(*Contd.*)

Illustrations of Public Services Delivery/Criteria	*Col. (i)* *Awareness, Access and Inclusion*	*Col. (ii)* *Attitude and Behaviour*	*Col. (iii)* *Quality, Timeliness and Efficiency, Responsiveness*	*Col. (iv)* *Quality and Adequacy of Infrastructure for Services*	*Col. (v)* *Costing*	*Col. (vi)* *Sustainability*
Any other locally important services	Very Poor Poor Average Good Very good	Very Poor Poor Average Good Very good	Very Poor Poor Average Good Very good	Very Poor Poor Average Good Very good	Very high High Average Low Lowest	Very Poor Poor Average Good Very good

Note 1: Qualitative Scoring: For all Criteria except "Cost" the scores are as follows: Very Poor = 1; Poor = 2; Average =3; Good = 4; Very Good = 5.
For Criteria on "Cost" the scores are as follows: Very High = 1; High = 2; Average =3; Low = 4; and Very Low = 5.

Note 2: There could be at least 8 criteria for assessing delivery of public services. These have been combined into 6 criteria as above. Each criterion with the highest score of 5, leads to a total highest score of 30. Any service delivery agency, which scores "Very Good" on all criteria has a total score of 30 (5 multiplied by 6 as per the combined criteria as above) while that, which scores "negligible" on all criteria has a total score of 6 only (1 multiplied by 6). The scores can be changed to percentage in the final analysis.

Note 3: Scores allotted by different client groups can be collated to arrive at compact PAG for different agencies. Putting the different scores on one card would indicate a comparative performance on service delivery.

Source: Tool first applied to participatory sessions held at villages of Quang Binh Province, Vietnam with small groups of local women and men from the local communities.

questions (semi-structured questionnaire) for each service delivery based on the above set of criteria.

(d) While assessing criteria as above by local communities/ groups, both social groups and gender could be mainstreamed so also age and ethnic factors can be considered through multi-stage sampling of groups under consideration. One illustration from Moldova can further highlight selection of focus groups as follows. For assessment of 2 types of services, such as 'education' and 'health' small groups were interacted within the following composition:

- *Poor groups*—2 groups—one women group and one men group of 10-15 participants, each.
- *Middle class groups*—2 groups—one women group and one men group of 10-15 participants, each.
- *Better off groups*—2 groups—one women group and one men group of 10-15 participants, each.

(e) Parallel to small group interactions, it is also important to field open and semi-structured questionnaire to selected individuals on different criteria for assessment as in Box 7.1. This has objectives in terms of validating and cross-checking group responses, scores and those who dissent. This also helps understand better the basis of scoring by groups and individuals. The set of semi-structured and open questionnaire is to be fielded separately to those individuals, who may be key informants or who are dominating personalities and hence could influence group opinions, or who are generally quiet and shy to participate in group discussions. Use of questionnaire on an individual basis has 3 objectives:

- To cross-check group views and group scores;
- To have more individual analysis supplement group discussion; and
- To engage opinion-makers and dominant person in separate questionnaire exercise.

(f) Of the 10-15 participants from each group, 10 of them could sit for group discussion and group scoring, while 5 (including women, men, dominant persons and opinion makers) could be fielded questionnaire separately preferably in separate locations so as to reduce the bias. The group discussion could be facilitated with the help of a big poster paper on which the scores could be written down either by the participants or by the facilitators so that it is visible to all participants, for discussion and change, if required.

(g) When the group discussion and group scoring are over, the 2 field coordinators are expected to meet up with the facilitators and collate key information from group scoring and individual questionnaire and hold a meeting at the local level of service delivery organizations and share such local community's views with them. The facilitators and other citizens can be present at this meeting and clarify issues as and when required.

(h) Group scoring should be facilitated taking a range of 1 to 10 or 1 to 20 or 1 to 100. Any criterion for assessing each service delivery could be scored on a range of 1 to 10 or 1 to 20 or 1 to 100. It is important to keep in mind that the criterion of 'cost' will have reverse scores (very high, high, average, low, very low) as shown in Table 7.2, column (v).

(i) The data could be collated in SPSS/Excel package and PAG will be presented in the following format for each village/ town or at other levels such as the meso level.

This exercise could be on an annual basis and the first exercise forms some kind of a base line data.

7.5.1 PAG and Country Experience

In a field report entitled "Report on piloting the CVT (PAG) in Zubresti and Galesti villages, Straseni rayon"[2] in Moldova, an ex-Soviet country, the field application and research in 2006 comprised several stages: (i) working out small group discussion and interview guide and semi-structured questionnaires, (ii) activity in the field, which included group discussions with local participants and also groups of service delivery officials, (iii) submission of preliminary data to local public authorities and public services providers that were evaluated, (iv) data processing through computer software and, (v) working out the report. The group discussions helped arrive at group scores for local services related to education and health and both women and men participated with much enthusiasm. The participants had indicated both strengths and weaknesses of local services. The group scores and people's suggestions under different criteria helped enlighten the service providers and they thought that it was rather a useful way of understanding how people perceived their services and what more could be done.

In Nepal, the CVT (PAG) was piloted[3] in 2006 to monitor government services in 10 areas including schools, health, agriculture, livestock, drinking water, electricity, vital registration, land revenue collection etc. Through the application of CVT (PAG), the services delivered by line agencies in the districts were assessed by the users at the grassroots under different criteria such as 'awareness', 'access', 'use', 'satisfaction', 'inclusion', 'quality', 'sustainability' etc. All criteria were treated with equal importance if the services were to be offered in the best possible manner. Based on their perceptions, the users rated the services. The ratings were on a 5 point scale ranging from 1 to 5, 1 being very poor and 5 being excellent.

Nepal's study covered two districts, viz. Saptari in the terai and Gorkha in the hills where both household survey and focused group discussion were held. The sample size covered a total of 406 households with 24 focus group discussions together with a gender balance. Amongst many results, one important finding was that there is considerable variation in the size of service users of different services. Of the sample households, the service users were higher in education (96.6%) and health (77.8%). The percentages of service users were low at 45.3 per cent for land tax and registration, 44.3 per cent in electricity and 30 per cent in drinking water. The corresponding figures were quite low for instance, 12.6 per cent for livestock services and 7.1 per cent for agriculture services.

7.5.2 Some Lessons from the field

People are ready to assess local service delivery since it impinges on their daily lives. Depending on the time that local communities can spare, they like sitting in small groups to discuss and assess local delivery of services based on different criteria. They are wise and also capable of arriving at group consensus and ways of improving the services concerned. They are looking for opportunities to do so. If people can provide a balanced view then service providers can be encouraged to learn about people's assessment. Much depends on the facilitators of such community voice tool. They are required to be flexible, patient and create enabling conditions for people to participate. They need to find ways to avoid domination of group discussions by local elites. It is desirable that the facilitators also have some conflict management skills since local people are willing to speak their minds and it is generally not possible for the local service delivery to resolve issues instantaneously. The latter are often not that empowered to even answer many of the queries sought by local people. Hence, it is advisable to have some decision makers from service providing agencies to be present at such feedback sessions. In case of Moldova, the local governors were present to validate the issues raised by local participants.

PAG could provide a channel to mainstream marginal/excluded 'voices', to provide people's feedback and ways of improving quality of public services/infrastructure at the grassroots. PAG can help improve governance in terms of service delivery, efficiency, accountability and transparency. It can evolve to provide a "larger picture", for example, of MDG-based initiatives and performance at the macro level by constructing smaller 'pictures' from the grassroots. It can also help explore resources for policy/programme/project, which emerge out of group discussions and hence are demand-led. It can throw up innovative and practical ways for people's involvement and reduce corruption, which hurts the poor, the most. PAG can help cross-verify conventional indicators and to know whether participants are actually benefiting from, for example, MDG-related programmes.

Some constraints faced for application of PAG include lack of institutional space for people's assessment of service delivery. In most countries, there is lack of institutional space and appropriate mechanism for eliciting people's feedback for both higher and local levels. There can be one-off exercises, which are of limited use. Many countries have some kind of umbrella assessment and monitoring system from the 'top', which is useful for reporting on the physical targets though not for non-physical targets or those related to people's satisfaction, which could be assessed only by the people concerned. Performance-based results from PAG can help bridge the low awareness levels of top political leaders *vis-à-vis* the expectations of the ordinary people. Only when people's voices find institutional space in decentralized policy frameworks of the countries' concerned will the real picture of progress made towards effective service delivery get resolved at the grassroots. There is need to encourage public participation for assessment of service delivery and to organize appropriate institutional space for community voices.

Table 7.3: Compact PAG—Part 2

Suggestions by Focus Group/Individual/s
Location/Village Name:
Name of the Participant/s: ; Age = ; Male/Female = ;
Whether Poor/Very Poor = ; Other Criteria = ; Ethnicity:

Illustration of Public Services Delivery/ Criteria	Col. (i) Awareness, Access and Inclusion	Col. (ii) Attitude and Behaviour	Col. (iii) Quality, Timeliness and Efficiency, Responsiveness	Col. (iv) Quality and Adequacy of Infrastructure for Services	Col. (v) Costing
Local Health Post					
Primary School					
Drinking Water					
Forest Office					
Micro Credit Agency					
Police Station					
Local County					
Local NGO					

Apart from compact PAG, there could be topical PAG for focused inquiry on selected services. Based on the set of criteria developed as above, such scores could relate to any theme of public interest such as public service delivery. As illustrated in Chart 6.4, relatively semi-structured—open questionnaire are to be fielded with individuals on different services—one illustrated below is that on primary education. This exercise could be on an annual basis and the first exercise could form some kind of a base line.

7.5.3 One initial step is team building, understanding the objectives, the methods and process, the criteria and the total task involved. A proper appreciation of the type of task involved is important for carrying out the fieldwork required for the PAG and the follow up for collating data and constructing such card. Towards attaining such objectives, some initial requirements are:

- a team with commitment,
- having listening skills,
- team with clarity of thought,
- having appropriate attitude and behaviour,
- knowledge of participatory skills,
- ability to manage people's expectations,
- code of ethics as practitioners for facilitating groups/ individuals.

7.6 Challenges for PAG

In terms of undertaking a PAG exercise, there are certain challenges and one can find ways to overcome such challenges. Some of the key challenges are listed below:

(a) Economists/technical experts tend to show *less flexibility* to voices of the poor. This could be partly overcome by experiential field learning.
(b) Not all government bodies prepared to listen to people's assessment. Some governments can do without listening to such voices. Hence as a strategy, it is important for people to start with listing the strengths of the agency and also look for opportunities to include senior officials/decision makers while sharing.
(c) Lack of good facilitators for small group discussions—combined good facilitators with inexperienced ones.
(d) Rising community expectations from service providers—inquired about contributions by the public.
(e) Keep list of criteria flexible so as to be able to add new criteria as required (all countries).
(f) No Institutional Space—people's voices.

Lessons Learned

From attempts at mainstreaming, piloting

(a) Have country experience and case studies ready for sharing with key institutions and key people (CIS countries).

(b) Demonstrate and publicize significance of CVT to policy makers/service delivery organizations so that they do not feel threatened (all countries).
(c) Prepare teams of good facilitators to convey and advocate CVT findings at policy and practice level (CIS countries).
(d) Field team find ways to manage people's expectations on service delivery (all countries).
(e) Have data processors ready at CVT workshops and after field visits, preferably with SPSS package for scaling up (all countries).

Potential for cross-border tailoring, replication

- CVT—easy to use, easy to tailor—amply applicable across services and countries.
- Participants easily understand its objective/s.
- Can produce neat picture of people's assessment of service delivery.
- Experiential lessons in CVT are still emerging.
- Explorations and innovations as strategic tool continue.

7.7 Complementary Usage of Tools—PPA and PAG

Two of the citizen voice tools, which could complement and be mutually supportive, are PPA and PAG. PPA is a much broader participatory tool unlike PAG, which is generally more focused and specific with snap-shot view/s. PPA is a qualitative tool unlike PAG which is based on participatory methods and also based on selected use of questionnaire for validation. In a comparative framework, PPA would provide in-depth assessment while PAG would provide a quick assessment. PPA can cover a much broader canvass based on people's analysis and has greater flexibility than the PAG, which is more focused on service delivery. Different dimensions of human poverty and their proximate causes could be captured through PPA. PPA as a monitoring tool could help track changes in key social variables depending on the way the segments of PPA are constructed *in situ*.

PPA helps emerge people's priorities and preferences in the macro/meso/micro planning process and also supports people's feedback on the effectiveness of policies, programmes, service delivery and many other aspects. Sometimes, PAG[4] as a constituent of PPA (UNDP: 1996) supports and adds value to the latter. Different dimensions of human poverty and their proximate causes are easily captured through PPA. It has a broad server for tracking poverty

Table 7.4: An Illustrative PAG Voice Card
For Service Delivery
Scale of Scoring: between 1 and 5

Criteria scoring: VB=Very Bad; B=Bad; A=Average; G=Good; and VG=Very Good Criterion scoring for "Cost": VH=Very High; H=High; A=Average; L=Low; and VL= Very Low

Location: ; Sample: ; No. of women and men: ;
No. of Ethnic Minority : etc.

Criteria Scored		Education		Health Services	
How much Aware?		Poor = Middle = Upper =	Women = Men =	Poor = Middle = Upper =	Women = Men =
How much can we Access?		Poor = Middle = Upper =	Women = Men =	Poor = Middle = Upper =	Women = Men =
What Behaviour we face?		Poor = Middle = Upper =	Women = Men =	Poor = Middle = Upper =	Women = Men =
What Quality and Efficiency?		Poor = Middle = Upper =	Women = Men =	Poor = Middle = Upper =	Women = Men =
How is Infrastructure?		Poor = Middle = Upper =	Women = Men =	Poor = Middle = Upper =	Women = Men =
Service at what Cost?		Poor = Middle = Upper =	Women = Men =	Poor = Middle = Upper =	Women = Men =
How Sustainable?		Poor = Middle = Upper =	Women = Men =	Poor = Middle = Upper =	Women = Men =
Overall Score	Health = Education =	Poor = Middle = Upper =	Women = Men =	Poor = Middle = Upper =	Women = Men =

Note: Sampling Areas described.

changes and helps to gain both overviews and in-depth analysis. This is a main strength of PPA, as compared to the PAG, which has a relatively narrow ambit though in certain instances the latter can help to enrich the checklist for PPA's field inquiry, especially in those cases where PPA inquiry is sequenced after canvassing of PAG. For the purpose of this study, PAG has been considered as an integral component of PPA for institutional analysis. However, PAG can be undertaken both separately and also as a constituent of PPA.

Problems/Constraints	*Strengths/Progress*	*Ways to Improve*
Education	Education	Education What Government can do? What Local Communities can do?
Health	Health	Health What Government can do? What Local Communities can do?

Notes: Sampling, areas covered etc.

Excerpts from Community Voice

Provide selected excerpts on what the citizens had to say

Apart from PAG voice card, there could be topical score cards for focused inquiry. Based on the set of criteria developed as above, such a score card could relate to any type of public service delivery. As shown in Charts 6.1 to 6.4, there are illustration for relatively open-type questionnaires to be used for PAG.

7.8 Semi-Structured Interviews for PAG

Semi-structured Interviews for PAG help cross-check community scoring. For this purpose, appropriate questionnaires would need to be devised for which few illustrations in Charts 6.1 to 6.4 are given below. Such questionnaires are flexible and can be changed depending on local requirements. Additional points/criteria may be added as and when necessary to reflect local conditions. Data analysis based on semi-structured interviews, illustrations of which are indicated below will provide the pattern of assessment on different types of service delivery.

Semi-structured Interview outlines illustrated below relate to following types of service delivery.

(i) Education (see Chart 6.1)
(ii) Citizenship Certificate (see Chart 6.2)
(iii) Agriculture Extension (see Chart 6.3)
(iv) Health Post (see Chart 6.4)

Chart 7.1: Illustrative Questionnaire for Primary Education (Focus Group—Those families who have small children—girl and boy—of school going age)

---

1. Name (Female/Male/Adult/Child) —
2. Father's and Mother's Name— 2 (a) Ethnicity =
3. Temporary/Permanent Residential Address —

Age = *Male/Female =* *Whether Disabled/Others =*

---

4. Awareness, Access and Inclusion

4.1 Does any one attend primary school from your family?

Response—Yes/No/Sometimes/Dropped out

If the response is 'No'/'Sometimes'/ 'Drop-out', then list the reason/s:

4.1.1 Not aware/No information that such a service exists in the locality (TO BE RECORDED SEPARATELY)
4.1.2 Difficult to get entry to the school
4.1.3 Attitude and behaviour of school authority is problematic (TO BE RECORDED SEPARATELY)
4.1.4 School is located far (Approximate km)
4.1.5 Do not have time for school
4.1.6 Problems at home in attending school
4.1.7 Cannot pay for schooling, e.g. uniform/fees/books/hidden cost
4.1.8 Not sending girl child to school (To be RECORDED SEPARATELY)
4.1.9 Any other reason

---

5. Quality, Timeliness and Efficiency of Services

5.1 Quality of Schooling (including efficiency and timeliness)

5.1.1 Do the teachers teach well?
5.1.2 Are there enough teachers available to teach children?
5.1.3 Do they hold the classes/exams in time?
5.1.4 Is the school open on school days?
5.1.5 How is the school building?
5.1.6 Is the parent-teacher committee active?

(Contd.)

(Contd.)

6. Responsiveness

6.1 Responsiveness of the teachers, school committee and authority

6.1.1 Do they listen to the parents as required?

6.1.2 Is the parent teacher committee active and taking feedback?

7. Cost of Services

7.1 Is the education costly? Yes/No/Sometimes

If the answer is 'Yes'/ 'Sometimes', then what are the reasons?

7.1.1 Pay for fees—how much amount?

7.1.2 Pay for uniform/textbooks—how much amount?

7.1.3 Pay for other charges—how much amount?

7.1.4 Pay for bribes—how much amount?

8. Sustainability

8.1 Do you think your child will complete primary schooling? Yes/No

If the answer is 'No', then what are the reasons?

8.1.1 Home conditions

8.1.2 School conditions

8.1.3 Locality conditions

8.1.4 Other factors, if any

9. Any 3 Key Suggestions for Improving Services

9.1

9.2

9.3

Remarks of Facilitator

Chart 7.2 Illustrative Questionnaire for Citizenship Certificate (Focus Group— Those families who have applied, who have received and those who were denied Citizenship card)

District— ; Village— ; Location – ;

1. Name (Female/Male) —
2. Father's and Mother's Name— 2 (a) Caste/Ethnicity =
3. Temporary/Permanent Residential Address – ;

Age = Male/Female = Whether disabled =

4. Awareness, Access and Inclusion

4.1 Have you a citizenship certificate or applied/planning to apply for one? Response—Yes/No/Could Not

If the response is 'No' or 'Could not', then list the reason/s:

4.1.1 Not aware/lack of information that such a certificate needs to be made

4.1.2 Not aware that such a service exists in the locality

(Contd.)

(Contd.)

4.1.3 Difficult to procure citizenship certificate from the office
4.1.4 Attitude and behaviour of citizenship certificate authority problematic—tend to harass
4.1.5 Discriminatory behaviour
4.1.6 Office is located far (Approximate km)
4.1.7 Office remains mostly closed
4.1.8 Do not have time for approaching office
4.1.9 Cannot pay the cost for procuring citizenship certificate
4.1.10 Any other reason

---

5. Quality, Timeliness and Efficiency of Services

5.1 Quality of Issuance of Certificate (including efficiency and timeliness)

5.1.1 Is the citizenship certificate issued in time?
5.1.2 Are there enough officials available for helping to get the citizenship certificate?
5.1.3 Is the office asking for too many documents and proof? Do you think they are relevant?
5.1.4 Is the office open regularly on office days?
5.1.5 How good is the quality of the certificate issued?

---

6. Responsiveness

6.1 Responsiveness of the officials and the concerned authority

6.1.3 Does the office listen to grievances and take action?
6.1.4 Does the office tell the applicant how to proceed?
6.1.5 Does the office help the applicant to complete the procedure?
6.1.6 Does the office process the whole exercise and issues certificate in 1 day, 2 day, or a reasonable time or take a long time.
6.1.7 Is the receiver told after how many days the certificate would be delivered?
6.1.8 Does the office respond to the government charter on service delivery?

---

7. Cost of Services

7.1 Is procuring the card costly? Yes/No/Sometimes

If the answer is 'Yes'/ 'Sometimes', then what are the reasons?

7.1.5 Payment for fees—how much amount?
7.1.6 Payment for transport—how much amount?
7.1.7 Payment for other charges—how much amount?
7.1.8 Payment for bribes—how much amount?

---

8. Sustainability

8.1 Do you think the quality of service delivery has deteriorated from earlier years? Yes/No

If the answer is 'No', then what are the reasons?

---

9. Any 3 Key Suggestions for Improving Service Delivery of Citizenship Certificate

9.1

(Contd.)

(*Contd.*)

9.2
9.3
Remarks of Facilitator

Chart 7.3 Illustrative Questionnaire for Agriculture Extension (Focus Group— Those families who have received, not received and who were denied agriculture extension services)

District— Village— Location—
1. Name (Female/Male) —
2. Father's and Mother's Name— 2 (a) Caste/Ethnicity—
3. Temporary/Permanent Residential Address— ;

Age = Male/Female =

---

4. Awareness, Access and Inclusion

4.1 Do you get agriculture extension services? Or have you approached or planning to approach the extension department for their services?
Response—Yes/No/Could Not
If the response is 'No' or 'Could not', then list the reason/s:

4.1.1 Not aware/lack of information that such agriculture extension services exist
4.1.2 Not aware of the place to go to find such a service
4.1.3 Difficult to get such extension services from the office—teacher not-in-residence/staff generally not available for service
4.1.4 Attitude and behaviour of the extension staff is problematic—tend to harass
4.1.5 Discriminatory behaviour
4.1.6 Office located far (Approximate km)
4.1.7 Office remains mostly closed
4.1.8 Do not have time to approach extension office
4.1.9 Cannot pay for procuring extension service
4.1.10 Any other reason

---

5. Quality, Timeliness and Efficiency of Services

5.1 Quality of Issuance of card (including efficiency and timeliness)

5.1.1 Is the extension service delivered in time?
5.1.2 Are there enough officials available for helping to get the extension service?
5.1.3 Is the office asking for too many documents and proof?
5.1.4 Is the office open on office days?
5.1.5 How good is the quality of service provided?

---

6. Responsiveness

6.1 Responsiveness of the officials and the concerned authority

6.1.1 Does the office listen to grievances and take action?

(*Contd.*)

(Contd.)

6.1.2 Does the office tell the applicant how to procure extension services?
6.1.3 Does the office help the applicant to complete the procedure for getting such services?
6.1.4 Does the office take a long time to respond? If 'yes', how long?
6.1.5. Is the receiver informed after how many days she/he can get the service?
6.1.6 Does the office respond to the government charter on service delivery?

---

7. Cost of Services
7.1 Is procuring the service costly? Yes/No/Sometimes
If the answer is 'Yes'/'Sometimes', then what are the reasons?
7.1.1 Payment for fees—how much amount?
7.1.2 Payment for transport—how much amount?
7.1.3 Payment for other charges—how much amount?
7.1.4 Payment for bribes—how much amount?

---

8. Sustainability
8.1 Do you think this service has deteriorated from earlier years and was better earlier? Yes/No
If the answer is 'No', then what are the reasons?

---

9. Any 3 Key Suggestions for Improving Service Delivery of Citizenship Card
9.1
9.2
9.3
Remarks of Facilitator

Chart 7.4: Illustrative Questionnaire for Health Post

District— Village— Location—
1. Name (Female/Male) —
2. Father's and Mother's Name— 2 (a) Caste/Ethnicity —
3. Temporary/Permanent Residential Address — ;

Age — Male/Female — Disabled —

---

4. Awareness, Access and Inclusion
4.1. When you or your family members are sick, are you able to access health services?
Response—Yes/No/Cannot
If the response is 'No' or 'Cannot', then list the reason/s:
4.1.1 Not aware/lack of information that such health services exist locally.
4.1.2 Not aware of the location to go to find such a service.

(Contd.)

(*Contd.*)

4.1.3 Difficult to access health services from the office—health personnel not-in-residence/health staff not generally available for service.
4.1.4 Attitude and behaviour of the health staff is problematic—insensitive/tends to harass.
4.1.5 Behaviour of health staff discriminatory.
4.1.6 Health post located far (Approximate km).
4.1.7 Health post mostly closed.
4.1.8 Do not have time for approaching the health post?
4.1.9 Cannot pay for procuring health services?
4.1.10 Visit a traditional healer.
4.1.10 Visit a private practitioner.
4.1.11 Visit others.
4.1.12 Any other reason.

---

5. Quality, Timeliness and Efficiency of Services

5.1 Quality of health services (including efficiency and timeliness)

5.1.1 Is the health service delivered in time?
5.1.2 Are there enough health staff available for providing health services?
5.1.3 Is the government health worker available regularly?
5.1.4 Is the health post open on all office days?
5.1.5 How good is the quality of health service delivered?

---

6. Responsiveness

6.1 Responsiveness of the health post officials and the concerned authority

6.1.1 Does the health post listen to grievances and take action?
6.1.2 Does the health post tell how to proceed for follow up, check up and referrals?
6.1.3 Does the health post help the patient to complete the formalities for health check-up?
6.1.4 Is there a long waiting period for health check up?
6.1.5 Is the treatment effective?
6.1.6 Is the behaviour of health staff discriminatory?

---

7. Cost of Services

7.1 Is procuring health services costly? Yes/No/Sometimes
If the answer is 'Yes'/ 'Sometimes', then what are the reasons?

7.1.1 Payment for fees—how much amount?
7.1.2 Payment for transport—how much amount?
7.1.3 Payment for other charges—how much amount?
7.1.4 Payment for bribes—how much amount?

---

8. Sustainability

8.1 Do you think health services have deteriorated as compared to the past years? Yes/No. If the answer is 'Yes' then what could be the reasons?

(*Contd.*)

(*Contd.*)

8.1.1 Deterioration in the quality of treatment.
8.1.2 Deterioration in the behaviour of health staff.
8.1.3 Rise in cost of treatment.
8.1.4 Difficulty in availability of medicines.
8.1.5 Absenteeism of health staff.
8.1.6 Difficult to cover distances.
8.1.7 Rise in Discriminatory behaviour.

9. Any 3 Key Suggestions for Improving Service Delivery of Citizenship Card

9.1
9.2
9.3
Remarks of Facilitator

7.9 Selected Methods to Facilitate PAG

In addition to semi-structured interviews and focus group discussion, institutional diagramming and communication linkage matrix can be applied for facilitating assessment of service delivery under Citizen Score/Report Card. Both institutional diagramming and communication linkage matrix are described below in general terms.

7.9.1 Institutional Diagramming

Institutional listing is listing of major institutions that affect the participants' life. Institutional diagramming, also known as '*Chapati*' (Venn) diagrams, are visual methods to represent the role of individuals/institutions and the degree of their importance in decision-making. In such diagrams, circles of different size represent an individual or an institution, whose size shows its degree of importance in decision-making in a local community and the overlapping of circles indicate overlapping in decision making. Overlapping of circles arise due to one institution/individual interacting with another institution or individual in which case the circles overlap on one another. Such overlaps may be large or small depending on the extent of interaction. If the circles are separate, the institutions have no contact and if they touch each other there is information passing between institutions. Strong/weak linkages between two institutions represented by two circles can also be shown by steady/broken lines/arrows.

Venn diagrams can be useful in study of relationships of institutions/individuals with local communities. For local community members, Venn diagrams would reflect the kind of communication between the local community and different organizations including governmental organizations and NGOs. Different aspects of local life can be taken up to see their interaction and their role in decision making involving local level planning, in running of projects, in distribution of land, credit, water and other assets, in construction of roads, school building, dams etc.

7.9.2 Communication Linkage Matrix

Communication linkage matrix indicates the level of communication between different individuals/institutions assessed on the basis of different criteria. Venn diagram can be extended and analyzed through communication linkage matrix as shown below in Table 7.5. In the Venn diagram, those village households raising livestock were placed at the centre while their relationships with different service providing institutions were shown through circular-shaped papers of different size and distance, either kept on the ground or pasted on the paper. These institutions are shown in the matrix given in Table 7.5. Through the communication linkage matrix the village groups further analyzed aspects of communication with the institutions against selected criteria such as "behaviour", "timeliness", "information exchange" and suggestions for improving communication. This matrix given in Table 7.5 was done by a village group through group discussion upon completion of the Venn diagram.

7.9.3 Community Interactions and PAG

PAG would also mean conducting interactive sessions with different poor groups and communities. In case of conflict situations, it may be said that conducting PPA under the present circumstances is not at all an easy task. This would depend on the locations in question, the reach of CBOs and NGOs (given the limited reach of the Government machinery) and the mood of the local groups and communities, whether they would consider it and be able to participate freely and interact in their own way for revealing their perspectives on poverty. This is especially true for those socially excluded communities and remote areas where the intensity of the conflict is relatively high. So what could be a way out? It is important to identify CBOs and NGOs which have better access to such areas and can

Table 7.5: A Simplified Illustration of *Communication Linkage Matrix*

Institutions	*Behaviour*	*Timeliness of Service*	*Information Exchange*	*Suggestions*
HH-Extension Service	Strong bond	Regular	Receive Information from Villagers	More training courses required.
HH-Veterinary Service	Good linkage	Frequent	Fast, punctual	Provision of medicine should be in time
HH-People's Committee of Village	Strong bond	Regular	Fast	can provide information on good techniques, disease and its treatment, marketing
HH-People's Committee of Commune	Good linkage	Irregular	Fast	Officials must visit HH more often on a regular basis.
HH-Commune Farmers' Association	Strong bond	Regular	Fast, punctual	Can provide regular information on economic benefit of farmers.
HH-Village Farmers' Association	Strong, cooperative bond	Regular	Good linkage	—
HH-Women's Association	Good linkage	Regular	Fast	Awareness creation on ways of livestock raising and application of new techniques required.
HH-District Agriculture Unit	Weak bond	Irregular	Slow	Livestock raising programme inputs should be provided in time.

Note: HH stands for households raising livestock in village Thon Trung in Vo Ninh Commune, Quang Ninh District, Vietnam. The above matrix was done by women group from the village on 19th December, 1997 after completion of a Venn diagram showing relationship of different institutions with households raising livestock.

undertake such a task. For purposes of making the citizen voice tools meaningful and operational over time, it is important to develop an organizational data base for grassroots organization engaged in listening to community voices. Developing a strategic plan for approaching remote areas and excluded communities will help make such larger picture more meaningful. Such a strategic plan must also consider ways of creating environment of trust and faith amongst the participants engaged in evolving the larger picture.

PPA raises people's expectations. The more people talk about their poverty the more they feel expectant that some good things are going to happen. So it is important to find out ways to manage expectations arising out of PPA. One way would be to mainstream their problems and opportunities (emerging from PPA) into the national planning process and allocate resources and implement. This would also imply sharing findings of PPA with the people and disseminating the follow up actions taken up by the government. For any PAG, the people would like to see many of their suggestions turned into action. One way would be that the relevant authority consider as many suggestions as possible, implement them and feed them back with the news of implementation disseminated to the public. This would emphasize the accountability part of PAG and make people motivated to do further assessment of service delivery organizations. Any lethargy or delay in not taking action based on people's suggestions and recommendations would mean that people would be less enthusiastic to participate in repeat PPAs and PAGs. Similar consequences could be expected for situations where actions are taken based on people's recommendations but not disseminated to the public. For both PPAs and PAGs, advocacy and wide dissemination and communication with the public could be considered as essential aspects whether through public announcements, informal group meetings, public meetings, door-to-door meetings, distributing leaflets, making shows, announcements through media, announcements through hoardings, announcements through notice boards of local government offices, schools, dispensaries, hospitals, ration shops etc. Such steps help sustain the process of participation and motivate people to actively engage in assessing their own conditions and come up with ideas for improvement. All such monitoring tools are not that effective if people are generally in a negative mood for different reasons or have little or no hope in their local institutions and the government at large. Such participatory assessment tools and social accountability tools are best applied in normal environment for helping to get tangible results.

After a discussion on voice tool for assessment of governance, the next chapter presents an overview on gaps and weaknesses in conventional frameworks, aspects of institutionalizing community voices, methodological notes and lessons learnt.

NOTES

1. In the presence of local people.
2. Supported by Participation Council, Moldova, Government of Moldova/ UNDP Moldova.
3. Supported by National Planning Commission/UNDP, Nepal and Development Vision, Nepal. Field study was undertaken by Development Vision, Nepal.
4. A form of participatory assessment was used in UNDP: 1996 for assessing service delivery of different organizations. This was a part of PPA in 10 districts of Bangladesh.

REFERENCES

Development Tracks, RTC (2005), *Participatory Poverty Assessment,* West Bengal, Draft Report submitted to Asian Development Bank, Manila, June.

Gloppen, Siri L. Rakner, A. Tostensen, "Responsiveness to the Concerns of the Poor and Accountability to the Commitment to Poverty Reduction" (WP 2003:9, Chr. Michelsen Institute, Development Studies and Human Rights, Bergen, Norway.

Mukherjee, Neela (2002), *Participatory Learning and Action with 100 Field Methods*, Concept Publishing Co., New Delhi.

8

Institutionalizing Community Voice

This chapter contains selected aspects of institutionalizing community voices including major gaps and weaknesses of the conventional policy framework, aspects of institutional mechanism and limitations of 'Voice' mechanisms.

8.1 Institutionalizing Community Voice

Mechanisms for weaving community voice in the conventional policy framework lie in almost a vacuum where such system is essentially built around a quantitative framework based on the classical survey method. Some major gaps and weaknesses related to the existing system include the following:

- The classical system does not portray a balanced picture, i.e. a mix of quantitative data (through classical surveys) and qualitative aspects of poverty (through community's own voice). It is mainly based on the direction and indicators of experts and planners from the 'top' or macro level. It is naïve to assume that conventional questionnaire surveys with pre-determined and structured questionnaires, which require simple 'yes'—'no' answers or some numerical figures can prove effective to find out how policies and programmes actually perform on the ground. If the people of the land are to participate in expressing their own situation, then they should be given opportunities to speak their own language and highlight aspects/indicators which they think are important. It is important to ask people about what policy aspects should be considered for any realistic assessment of poverty situation. It is in this context that participatory assessments of different types (as described in this study) become important.

- There is little or no mechanism in the conventional survey-based system to capture integral aspects of human capability, access and exclusion, social opportunity, vulnerability, risk, protective security, etc., which are important to the poor. Many aspects tend to remain under-emphasized or get overlooked in the process of inquiry through the conventional framework. It is important to find out how people's voice tools can add value or supplement conventional surveys. Combining people's voices with conventional surveys can help the best from both the worlds. For such a purpose, one needs to look for areas/sectors where participatory assessments can yield meaningful results, enrich the existing system and add value. It is also important to look for aspects which are systematically overlooked or under-emphasized due to flaws in the current conventional system.
- Another issue is that the present conventional system is mostly 'top down' and activity-oriented and targets outputs in terms of numerical figures and physical quantities. The challenge is how to mainstream qualitative milestones of human poverty reduction and include indicators from the voices of the poor and those from the grassroots. The indicators for the conventional system need to accommodate much more than mere emphasis on activity/implementation, emphasis on meeting numerical/physical targets and/or changes in income levels of poverty.
- The conventional framework is rather weak in capturing nuances of policies and processes. More thinking is required on mainstreaming those policy aspects and indicators for the poor which tend to remain overlooked in conventional policy framework. For example, what is happening to poor people's livelihoods, food security, threshold level of basic needs, social opportunity, protective capability, etc.? What is the status of social protection for the poor? Are poor people being helped by macro/meso policies and processes to organize their livelihoods and/or to gain social protection? What is happening to their resource base, coping strategies and their well-being? Such and many other related questions have assumed far greater importance in today's context which the conventional framework is finding difficult to handle.

- The conventional data system is not adaptable enough to imbibe the principles and types of outputs emerging from the participatory framework. Hence, one related issue is how to construct and institutionalize a participatory data system, which could then be utilized for future planning, outcome and impact monitoring and poverty assessments, as required from time to time. Such participatory data system can complement, supplement and enrich the conventional data system and help interpret some of the quantitative data in new light. It can help solve some of the puzzles on human poverty and help connect economic policies with their impacts on the ground. Such data system can help link the micro with the meso and the macro level and support better policy choices apart from tracking impacts at the grassroots.

8.1.1 Mechanisms for Institutionalization of Community Voice

If people's voice and feedback are to be considered as a regular part of the system then the 'larger picture' needs to be institutionalized in a manner so that it evolves on a regular basis for providing continuous feedback to public policy making. Given the objective of institutionalizing 'the larger picture' form people's voices, it is desirable to involve different stakeholders and build long-term partnership between public policy-making bodies and other stakeholders such as community-based organizations, groups, civil society and other relevant organizations. In this direction, it is important that the organizational structure meant for evolving the 'larger picture' has the following desirable criteria:

- It reflects honesty of purpose and credibility;
- It helps generate inclusive data;
- It is efficient and provides timely data;
- It helps provide quality and dependable data;
- It helps provide regular and timely feedback; and
- It is based on user-friendly ways of communicating data to different stakeholders/channels.

For institutionalizing 'larger pictures' of community voices, there needs to be a joint effort/collaboration between communities and different levels/tiers of public policy making. There are at least

6 levels—village/ward, district, province, sector/region, national and the international.

8.1.1.1 *Autonomous Organization*: For purposes of conducting field inquiry, ideally, an independent field research organization with a large network of civil society organizations at the grassroots is desirable. Amongst some desirable features of such an organization, it may be mentioned that it should be people-friendly, field-based, working hands-on, action-research based, experienced, efficient, dependable and credible enough. Such an organization with a wide network can be made responsible and put in charge of generating, managing and advocating participatory and inclusive data at the national, sectoral, district and the local levels. As regards evolving of 'larger picture' process and system, it is not only a regular and periodic feedback that needs to be institutionalized but its inclusiveness; credibility, efficiency, quality and power of communication are equally important criteria to be considered within the framework of such institutionalization. With regard to the objectives of such institutional mechanism the following could be considered:

(i) To have regular and periodic updates,
(ii) To institutionalize an inclusive, broad-based and credible mechanism,
(iii) To create institutional space for voices of the poor at the national level,
(iv) To connect people's voices with public policy-making bodies at different levels.

8.1.1.2 *Well Networked*: Such an organization/network will have many levels of interactions with different committees to facilitate and oversee its timely and efficient management of generating participatory and inclusive data. There could be at least two parallel and interlinked processes of institutionalizing the evolving process of the 'larger picture' of community voices.

(a) One process is that of generating, managing and advocating participatory and inclusive data through regular/periodic applications of methods and tools such as PPA, PAG, SLA and other voice tools.

(b) The other process is of over-seeing the data generation and facilitating use of it for monitoring and action. At the level of data generation, an independent and well networked field research organization of a national stature could actually facilitate such task by involving many grassroots organizations across the length and breadth of the country as desired. Inclusive data should be made a mandatory part of the whole process. The primary aim of this data generation is to bring on board the voices of the poor, the marginalized and the socially excluded.

8.1.1.3 *Local Outreach:* The field research organization at the village level or the municipality level will constitute hubs for local participatory exercises and data synthesis with a clear pro-poor focus. It will require capacity building for its role and performance along with a coordinator. A local implementation committee of village-based facilitators can be constituted, which will lead from the front with social commitments, socio-technical skills in participatory data generation and management and in-depth understanding of local issues. The local outreach's primary engagement will be with different poor/ultra poor/excluded groups in different localities. The local committee will have capacity to negotiate local issues relevant to the poor with other stakeholders. The local outreach will be responsible for validating and negotiating with other local stakeholders. A pro-poor vision, values and appropriate attitude and behaviour towards poor/excluded groups will form integral part of such task force and the local outreach.

8.1.1.4 *Learning Organization*: It will be important to build and nurture local outreach as a learning organization. This will help sustain its capacity for supporting poor households/groups and motivating them to do their own poverty analysis and monitoring and flag changes over time. It is desirable that the outreach at the village/ward and municipality level is in a position to access knowledge networks, update skills, establish linkages with different organizations, review and revise its strategies and in the ultimate contribute towards participatory and inclusive data for poverty monitoring. Such a network of local organization needs to be adequately engaged with local groups and communities, equipped to provide basic support to poor groups/households on home economics, business economics, ways to overcome vulnerabilities, facilitate funds/technology flows, establish linkages, provide marketing support and other support as required.

8.1.1.5 *Apex Committee at National Level*: Apart from the task force at the district/province, level there can be a Steering Committee at the national level. The task force at district level is expected to support, facilitate and monitor local outreach at the village/ward level. The district level task force can attend to issues raised by the local outreach and will also monitor the latter. Its reporting to the Steering Committee at the national level can be periodic and systematic. The national level Steering Committee, in turn, would be in charge of overall monitoring and disseminate decisions and feedback to sectoral agencies and the local level. The national-level Steering Committee can be the highest decision-making body and the highest working body for an integrated and holistic approach to participatory data management policy. It can constitute different sub-committees for effective functioning. The district/province level task force will pass those issues to the national level Steering Committee, which relate to regional, sectoral and national level. The Implementation Committee at the village/ward and municipality level needs to have enough autonomy to act and need to be backed by the Steering Committee and its sub-committees from the top. Decisions will need to be broad-based and less bureaucratic. The Federations of civil societies at different levels will act as pressure points.

8.1.1.6 *Broad-Based Representation in the Process*: To synchronize the dynamics of these two parallel processes for the purpose of institutionalization, it may be suggested that representatives of different kinds of community-based organizations including self-help groups, poor women, forestry groups and other groups may be inducted as members of respective monitoring committees at the local, district, sectoral and national levels. New members could be inducted every 2 years on a rotational basis, though there needs to be proper representation of grassroots organizations belonging to those districts with relatively low level of human development. This will have two fold effects—on one hand, the interest of civil society organizations can find a voice in the participatory and inclusive data system. On the other hand, the village and district level committees can utilize the services of such organizations for data generation and other activities and raise awareness about the role and functions of the local governance and their service delivery. In the long run, as local civil society organizations get more mature they can act as advocacy channels for the local poor. It is envisaged that for advocacy purposes at appropriate levels, it may be important to have a large minimum critical mass of coalition of poor groups, which any single organization may not have by themselves. In absence of federated structures of local groups, it may be desirable in the long run to encourage formation of federated structures at local levels and eventually at district and national levels to act as pressure points for people's data generation, poverty monitoring and policy change.

8.1.2 Managing the Process

In order to best manage the process of institutionalizing 'community voices', it requires the system to be flexible and responsive. Generally, it is not easily manageable through typical government bureaucratic system due to inherent inflexibility of the system, rule-based procedures and 'top-down' style of functioning of government machinery. Since participatory approaches and inclusive data generation involve flexible learning processes, which are iterative and evolve through facilitation and embracing errors, the structured rule-based, target-oriented command system does not easily fit into the ways of people's participation. The attitude and behaviour of the government personnel are generally not conducive to institutionalizing voices. However, active and purposive involvement of the government machinery at different stages is crucial for at least three reasons:

- Institutionalizing and mainstreaming people's feedback mechanism—their 'voice'.
- Creating systematic space to improve governance and delivery system.
- Informing conventional data system for planning, implementation and monitoring.

8.1.2.1 *Aspects of Management*: The task of setting up an appropriate system for institutionalizing voices, running the process with regularity and having a check on quality would involve the following aspects:

- Setting up an appropriate framework for institutionalizing voices through stakeholders' consultation process.
- Setting up institutional mechanism for planning and action.

- Capacity building of the team and "Handing over the Stick".
- Decision making on aims, objectives, process, checklist and indicators.
- Mainstreaming social exclusion.
- Working together with stakeholders—synergy creation and flexibility.

The factors mentioned above are important for institutionalizing community voices based on different tools and mechanisms. However, some limitations of voice tool are mentioned in the following section.

8.2 Some Limitations of 'Voice Tool' Mechanism

There are some limitations of participatory mechanisms, which are normally faced. A few of them are flagged below:

- With heterogeneous communities living in different areas and under different conditions, community views may be widely divergent. Data sources would tend to vary in size and coverage and hence it will not always be easy to synthesize. In heterogeneous communities, dangers of generalization from locality-specific trends always lurk round the corner. The mechanism for organizing and recording community voices would need to include purpose, area, level, institutional mechanism, criteria, formats, periodicity, frequency and list of tools.
- Social exclusion is another practical issue to overcome. Approaching socially excluded groups and socially excluded areas in far-flung and remote areas could be a difficult proposition. Those whom we want to reach may not be easy to reach. Ways will need to be devised whether through civil society organizations and others local groups to explore opportunities to listen to the perspectives of the socially excluded groups and to have in-depth engagement with socially excluded areas.
- Size and composition of participants in the field cannot be predicted beforehand. Field inquiry is open-ended and demands good skills in facilitation for clarity and focus provided the facilitators do not feel intimidated. Fieldwork for people's participation is not expected to be problem-free,

especially when participants' motivation to participate under difficult conditions could often turn out to be low.

- Problem of raised expectations is almost always present amongst the participants (Mukherjee: 1993). There could also be high degree of under reporting about sensitive information for obvious reasons. It is not always easy to report what the poor don't say, i.e. their hidden transcripts.
- There is trade-off between 'breadth' of data and 'depth' of data. To strike the balance between the two is critical since the 'breadth' of listening to community voice is as important as its 'depth'. However, spending enough time with communities for the depth of data may sometimes may not be easy.
- Fieldwork for community voices to emerge is not always problem-free, especially when participants' motivation to participate is important. There could be different de-motivating factors such as lack of trust in the official machinery, lack of time, lack of interest, lack of good health, etc.
- Generalization of locality-specific data from community voice makes it indicative and not representative.
- Problem of raised expectations is almost always present amongst the participants.
- There can be under reporting about sensitive information for different reasons. This is especially true of conflict areas and topics which the participant may consider sensitive.
- Adequate resources to conduct participatory exercises could be an issue. There is also the point of getting skilled facilitators and analysts of qualitative data.
- Participatory process for providing larger picture is still evolving. No blueprint for participatory monitoring, no quick formula. Any approach or framework will need to be consulted, discussed, disseminated, piloted, tested, validated, negotiated and improved. Synthesizing and integrating people's perspectives/data could be done in more than one way. Creation of baseline data in this regard is important.
- Participatory indicators emerge mainly from the bottom, in a process-oriented manner. However, there is always a rushed process by development agencies where everything becomes time-bound. It is easy and simple to start with manageable

size of data and indicators. The data would need to be linked from micro and meso level to the macro level.

- Both qualitative and numerical data could emerge from participatory exercises. Some important question to answer—Whose participation? Who decides the indicators? Who uses the data and the indicators and for whom?
- It is important to present the qualitative data in a user-friendly manner. People are not aware whether or not government will use the information/data. So one point to consider is who all are going to be the consumers of this information and in what form. It is also important to build capacity and identify topics where qualitative indicators provide realistic pictures, help bridge gaps and are more useful for policy-making.

Annexes 'A' and 'B' for IPPA

Annex A

Annex 'A'— Table of Content

Integrated Participatory Poverty Assessment (IPPA) voice tool in this book is based on recent field research from different developing countries such as India, China, Bangladesh, Nepal and other countries where PPA-type studies have been undertaken in different States and Provinces. The purpose of Annexes 'A' and 'B' is to evolve suitable methodological design, objectives, and the scope for issue-based assessment of poverty from the perspectives of the poor.

A.1 PRA, PRRA: Principles and Methods

PRA/PLA is a widely used methodology for an interactive process of social development throughout the world. It is a way of learning from the people, with the people and by the people. It is quite different from RRA, which is quicker with information gathered from one or two members of a local community, which are then interpreted by external experts in their own way.

Though the principles of PRA/PLA (*see* Chapter 2 of this book for explanation of participatory principles) are foremost in deciding the basis of field research in IPPA, the approach adopted can be that of Participatory Rapid Rural Appraisal (PRRA). "PRRA is a variation of PRA, which is widely used where information is required by external agencies but must be expressed by the communities themselves in their way and with their own emphasis" (UNDP: 1996).

Based on PRA's principle of 'optimum ignorance' (see Chambers: 1997; Mukherjee: 1993; and Chapter 2 of this book), PRRA aims to acquire as much information as is necessary from people's own knowledge and experience by creating an enabling environment for a participatory analysis of the situation under consideration. Similar to RRA, it is generally a "one off" and extractive exercise but differs in its emphasis on the process of participation and ensures that people themselves define their preferences and priorities. PRRA is often used to provide illustrative views of community for future use in development activities. It can also provide an entry point for more intensive community participation (UNDP: 1996). It is important to recognize that PRRA similar to PRA is neither exhaustive nor conclusive. It is rather indicative and seeks to embrace the diversity of situations and diversity of people's own experience and perspectives.

A.2 Field Inquiry

It may be suggested that the field exercises for IPPA would be through PRRA based on the methodology and the principles of PRA/PLA. Field inquiry for IPPA would include some generic steps as listed below and there lies scope for enough flexibility in the steps and, hence, deviations from the steps are to be expected to be normal in the course of related fieldwork as per local situation at hand. It is not being proposed that each step listed below would get covered for all social groups interacted with. Coverage of the steps in each village/ locality would depend on the best judgement of the facilitators/ motivators and the local circumstances. Following review of the secondary data, literature and discussion with the official agencies and government, the generic steps for participatory interactive sessions at the local level could be as follows:

(i) Rapport building, warming up.

(ii) Exploratory interactions with local women and men "those who matter" (the poor and the disadvantaged groups) and other primary stakeholders including the non-poor.

(iii) Exploratory overviews.
(iv) Topical probing.
(v) Probing for gap filling.
(vi) Validation of findings.
(vii) Sharing with different stakeholders.
(viii) Scaling up at appropriate levels—micro, meso and macro.
(ix) Documentation and dissemination/advocacy.

A.2.1 Tracks for Field Inquiry

The fieldwork for IPPA could be based on 4 tracks of field inquiry through participatory methods, as listed below. Each track will have a generic/topical checklist for field inquiry.

- *Track 1*—at the level of social/gender groups mainly probed through group discussions, word pictures, social/asset/ institutional mapping/analysis, poverty grouping and criteria scoring, which are explained below.
- *Track 2*—at the area/sectoral level mainly probed by interacting and holding semi-structured interviews and social/ asset mapping with key informants.
- *Track 3*—at the household level/individual level based on constructing profiles/participatory case studies/word pictures/ institutional analysis by poorer households/individuals/ groups socially excluded.
- *Track 4*—at the level of development agencies done through interfacing with local development workers/other agencies, whether government, non-government or private.

A.2.2 Rationale for adopting the 4 tracks of field inquiry is as follows:

- To learn from the knowledge, wisdom and experience of the poor and the disadvantaged and also from different people/ sources, social/gender groups/communities, households, key informants and development workers;
- To generate wider participation and views for broad-basing results;
- To have both exploratory and topical probing including differential analysis;

- To focus on poverty analysis, disempowerment, social exclusion, livelihoods analysis, vulnerabilities and institutional relationships; and
- To crosscheck, validate and share findings.

A.2.3 Different Participatory methods, tools and techniques proposed for IPPA are as follows: (See below for a brief description of the methods/tools)

- semi-structured interviews
- focus group discussions
- criteria listing and scoring
- word picture
- poverty grouping/mapping
- joint walk and observation
- livelihood timeline
- listing
- oral livelihood analysis
- livelihood matrix
- social/resource/institutional/facility mapping
- trend analysis
- criteria scoring
- matrix scoring
- institutional (Venn) diagramming
- empowerment/ownership diagram
- relationship/linkage matrix
- linkage diagramming
- seasonality analysis
- historical transect
- others

The different PRA tools/techniques will need to be sequenced in ways to achieve the objectives of the field study and to portray the realities of the poor and the disadvantaged.

A.3 Exploratory and Topical Probing for Field Inquiry

Here are some PRA tools proposed, which could be sequenced for IPPA. Field inquiry will be both exploratory and topical in line with the purpose of IPPA as desired.

To start with some general steps are as follows:

(i) Rapport building and warming up.
(ii) Identification of different groups and social exclusion—types of groups/households ("those living alone/isolated from social networks"; those partially excluded, those totally excluded, those discriminated and isolated).
(iii) Face-to-face interactive PRA/PLA sessions with selected groups/communities/individuals—women and men.
(iv) Sharing of lessons learnt.

A.3.1 Exploratory Probing

Once the groups/communities/households are identified through poverty mapping/grouping as poor and disadvantaged, the following sequencing of PRA/PLA tools is proposed though at the field level there needs to be enough flexibility to move around the tools or to adopt alternative ways of sequencing. Hence the suggested sequencing of tools is at best a starting point.

(i) Poverty grouping, mapping and listing of assets/resource (natural resource, physical resource, human resource, social resource, financial resource and others)—access and use through asset mapping and group discussion, assessment of livelihoods and related copies strategies, process of disempowerment, seasonality analysis and time line.
(ii) For initiating discussion/exploring constraints/issues and power relations at the local level—the "power" circle [a variant of "ownership"/"empowerment" applied for project impact assessment (Mukherjee *et al.* : 2002a and Mukherjee:1996), see PRA tools and methods below] can be applied. In this "power" circle the ideal conditions for reduction of poverty is thought to lie at the centre of the circle, which is the most desirable position. Contribution of each resource/capital towards poverty reduction can be shown on a separate axis of the circle. Discussion on each axis is focused on the position of the group/household/s regarding different capitals/resources, their access and use, the constraints, problems faced, the vulnerability factors, coping strategies and other related issues.

(iii) Once the constraints/problems/issues have been identified with regard to different capitals, they can be prioritized by the group/households through 'scoring' method. Depending on local situation such 'scoring' can be done for all the constraints/problems faced by groups/households and/or separately for each capital and gender-wise.

(iv) Mapping and discussions of institutions/agencies and other power centres at different levels—local/meso/sub-national—provide a basis for juxtaposing the "power" circle with the role/s, rules, practices, 'influences' and policies of the listed institutions and other power centres/structures.

(v) The above can lead to both institutional diagramming and/or relationship-linkage matrix in terms of different criteria/processes for analyzing stakeholder relationships. Drawing from this (Meyers: 2001): "Power Tools", (www.iied.org), such relationships may be categorised by functions (criteria: service, legal/contractual, market, information exchange, interpersonal links, power building etc.) and quality (criteria: awareness, relevance, frequency, timeliness, accessibility, communication, attitude, control etc.).

(vi) The relationship matrix can help in listing of the "do-ables" suggested by the poor and the disadvantaged and the scope for changes as per their perspectives.

(vii) The criteria scoring method would also enable the poor to list out their priorities and preferences with regard to service delivery, support for livelihoods and other institutional changes envisaged in the exercise.

A.3.2 Topical Probing

For topical probing, there will be focused application of PRA/PLA methods to farming, off-farming, forestry, social aspects such as education, health, nutrition, women's empowerment, financial aspects—such as micro credit and banking, specific sources of livelihoods—such as forestry, livestock-raising, fish ponds, capacity building, empowerment, technology, etc.

(viii) Depending on the situation, any relevant topic, e.g. 'household indebtedness', either identified through exploratory sessions or independently, will be taken up for probing with the help of 7 helpers— "what", "who", "why", "how", "how much", "when", and "where" based on any combination of PRA/PLA methods.

(ix) Poverty and disempowerment processes can be discussed related to livelihood activities' flowchart in terms of backward and forward linkages, horizontal linkages to other sources of livelihoods, vulnerabilities, constraints, problems, coping strategies, viability-issues, priorities and prospects, and the do-ables.

(x) Discussion on relationship/linkage matrix on institutional and processes-criteria scoring and the do-ables are also important.

(xi) People's analysis for identifying different forces/ mechanisms (Bradley-type) impacting on the means for poverty reduction or gaining livelihoods including geography, entry barriers, corruption, intimidation and physical violence and ways of mitigating them, if any will also be useful.

(xii) Case study method can be woven around some mechanisms for social exclusion geography, entry barriers, corruption, intimidation and physical violence and ways of mitigating them, if any.

Validation and gap filling are important aspects of any methodology. See Chart A.1. Fieldwork on IPPA studies is best done in terms of iterative sessions and field experience and lessons need to be documented and shared. Considerable broadening and narrowing of field inquiry help build reasonable flexibility given the contours of the field study. Chart A.1 shows some of the aspects of field inquiry where exploratory probing is important for gaining overviews and for the process of seeking diversity. Topical probing focuses on selected topics for in-depth inquiry. Gap filling is an important exercise followed by validation and sharing with different stakeholders (Mukherjee: 2002, ITAD: 2004).

A.4 Area Selection

In this sub-section, the different criteria proposed for village selection are indicated based on poverty criteria. This section also contains a code of conduct for field facilitators/researchers together with some

Chart A.1

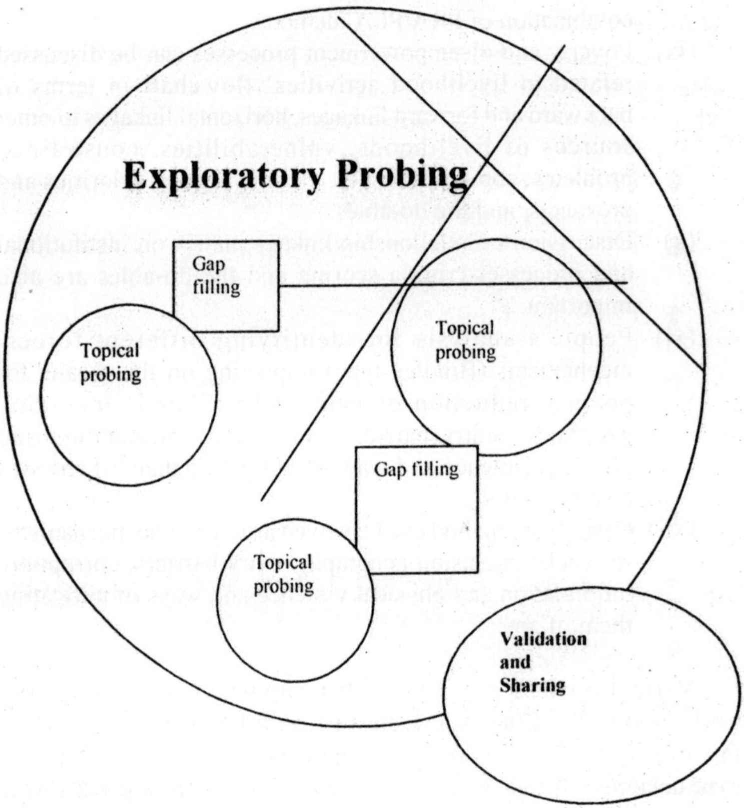

Note: The above diagram has been adapted from Note on Social Exclusion prepared for UN-IFAD, Rome by Neela Mukherjee (2002).

essential characteristics, which would help in facilitating quality field research in participation.

A.4.1 Selection of Study Areas/Districts/Blocks/Villages

An appropriate field design and sampling frame for IPPA needs to be adopted based on reasonable coverage of districts/provinces, villages, towns and other localities where poverty is concentrated and poor people reside (the sampling frame also needs to be representative of socially, culturally and ecologically vulnerable groups). Selection of districts needs to consider agro-ecological and social diversities and the incidence of human poverty as well.

Some generic criteria are being proposed as illustrations for selection of villages/hamlets, based on multiple stages of sampling. Other criteria can be added depending on specific objectives.

- Coverage of villages, with remote location and some located near roadside/headquarters.
- Coverage of villages with concentration of poverty and those without (control villages).
- Coverage of villages of different size—large, medium and small.
- Selection of villages for broad coverage of socio-ecological-physical features/agro-ecological zones.
- Coverage of villages having different communities/minority groups and those without.
- Coverage of villages/hamlets with concentration of different livelihoods.
- Coverage of villages with different development agencies, both government/NGO.
- Both with success stories and not so successful ones.

A.4.2 Reducing "Extractiveness" of IPPA

With regard to IPPA not becoming "extractive" for poor communities/ groups, it is important to make attempts to reduce such "extractiveness". Some steps are suggested below while others may be added:

- Clarification of objectives and roles of outside facilitators,
- Asking communities/groups for suggesting ways to reduce "extractiveness",
- Not trying to impose one's agenda and time on local groups,
- Sharing results/findings amongst groups on a daily basis, and
- Making contributions, if required towards any local development activity and also covering cost of snacks, food taken with participants.

A.5 Code of Conduct for Field Researchers

In PPA, since the process of inquiry is equally important as the output, a code of conduct based on participatory principles (also *see* Chapter 2) is proposed for the field.

- Listening, learning and respecting—having enough patience,
- Clarifying objectives and mutual roles,
- Having team spirit—positive approach,
- Not raising expectations—clarifying objectives,
- Creating space for disadvantaged groups/households/ individuals to offer views,
- Adhering to 'optimal ignorance',
- Maintaining 'appropriate imprecision',
- Cross-checking and noting,
- Recognizing/minimizing biases of rural development tourism—gender, time, road-side, professional, diplomacy, people's biases, and
- Embracing errors.

A.5.1 Desirable Characteristics: Field Researchers

Because in PPA, the process of research inquiry is considered as an equally important output, it is important to ensure that the field researchers have at least the following characteristics:

- They appreciate and respect local culture, and are able to understand/preferably speak local language and interact with the community directly.
- They have empathy for the poor and the disadvantaged, socially excluded groups/women/others.
- They have experience in conducting fieldwork.
- They have sufficient experience in conducting participatory field-based research on issue relating to poverty and poverty reduction.
- They have the ability to observe, listen, analyze, infer and embrace errors.

A.5.2 Risks and Assumptions

Since the field inquiry is *in situ*, open and inclusive, it is difficult to influence many variables, which tend to influence the process. Some risks and assumptions are mentioned below:

(i) Location-specific variations in size, quality and depth of data and coverage,
(ii) Location-specific variations in composition of participants,
(iii) Non-predictability of size of participants,
(iv) Possibility of non-cooperation/conflict from participants,
(v) Problem of aggregating qualitative information and scaling them up,
(vi) Tendency of under/over-reporting by participants for different aspects
(vii) Facilitator's bias,
(viii) Low level skills of facilitators' in understanding and interpreting body language and hidden transcripts,
(ix) Problem in maintaining both breadth and depth of data, and
(x) 'Noise' factor from other parallel events and process during field inquiry.

A.5.3 Organization and Management

About organization and management of IPPA this section deals with coordination and quality control.

IPPA Management and Coordination

There needs to be a team of field researchers/facilitators who are expected to perform different tasks for IPPA and the coordination and liaison of IPPA team with other stakeholders would rest with the team leader. Each researcher/facilitator is responsible for their part of the reporting. For organizing and managing facilitation of local communities/groups in rural/urban areas, exploratory and topical sessions can be held at different levels preceded by social analysis of poverty groups.

- At the level of poor households –through selected case studies at household level.
- At the level of social/gender groups—through focus group discussion, semi-structured interview, social grouping and

scoring. Such sessions would be exploratory and topical and catering towards differential impact study.

- At the level of key informants within social groups—there could be more of topical probing and analysis through poverty mapping and diagramming.
- At the level of local development agencies/workers—it could be mainly through semi-structured interviews and time line.
- At the village, district/province, regional and national levels, scaling up exercises could be undertaken through data collation, processing, review by key stakeholders and a series of consultations and reporting.

A.5.4 Quality Control

The quality of IPPA study at the field level can be assessed in the following manner:

(i) Peer group reviews on a daily basis,
(ii) Emphasis on obtaining depth of data,
(iii) Emphasis on validation and cross-checking,
(iv) Increasing the sample size and reducing the scope for biases and errors,
(v) Improving the application of tools and checklist on an iterative basis, and
(vi) Continuous learning by exploring new aspects/issues from the field.

A.6 Selected Steps in IPPA

The following could be the steps in the course of the IPPA:

- Secondary literature and data survey,
- Holding training courses/workshops in IPPA,
- Preparing checklist etc. for piloting and field inquiry,
- Conducting piloting exercise in the field,
- Collation and processing of data from piloting,
- Presentation/Interaction with key stakeholders,
- Review of field IPPA design for wider coverage,
- Conducting field inquiry on a wider scale in sampled locations/areas,

- Exploring selected issues for better coverage,
- Checking on quality of data,
- Gap-filling,
- Validating and broad-basing field results,
- Collation and processing of data from field inquiry,
- Presentation/interaction with key stakeholders,
- Scaling up at village level,
- Preparation and sharing of study reports and data,
- Scaling up at district/province level,
- Preparation and sharing of study reports and data,
- Scaling up at regional/sector level,
- Preparation and sharing of study reports and data,
- Scaling up at national level, and
- Preparation and sharing of study reports and data.

A.7 Generic/Topical Checklist for IPPA Field Inquiry (preliminary)

The following preliminary checklist is proposed for track 1 concerning social/gender groups (women and men). This checklist is at best preliminary and indicative where other issues need to be added as required.

- The differentiation by groups/communities in terms of socio-economic, ethnic and well-being groups; income and human poverty indicators; poverty of dalits, ethnic groups, minorities, other disadvantaged groups; poverty dynamics and vulnerability of women-headed households;
- Asset holding—access and use by the poor and the disadvantaged groups—strengths, problems, constraints and opportunities; vulnerabilities—shocks, seasonal issues, trends, culture, population and coping strategies;
- Livelihood patterns in terms of asset (capital) profiles, activities, seasonality etc.; dominant livelihoods and those not dominant—historical, present and future perspective – related to rural sector—agriculture, forestry, livestock, poultry, fisheries and natural resource sector;
- Gender relations in the household and the community (issues that will cross-cut other aspects of the livelihood analysis):

- Social, political and economic relations of association and inequality (local elite, patronage, share-cropping, group organisation, informal credit etc.), which influence livelihood security and patterns;
- Relations between the communities and formal/informal institutions (VDC/DDC, Line department, CBOs, service providers, NGO and others) including strength of institutions, role, scope of control etc. Key issues will include regulation, oversight, protection, resource allocation and service providers;
- Conflict over resources;
- Patterns of migration, their causes and consequences.

◆ Coping mechanisms/strategies, resources, livelihoods, conflicts and outcome—vulnerabilities and risks—How they cope with these? How family members cope with it in groups? How women, children and elderly persons cope with these? (e.g. migrate, eat less, borrow more, sell assets, cut trees etc.) Livelihood and asset-specific coping strategies, vulnerabilities and outcome—what strategies most people adopt?

◆ Comparative historical profiles on poverty, livelihoods and coping strategies—current analysis, past experience and future possibilities—Is the situation a little better now? How do they compare and on what basis? What are the indicators? Comparative historical profile, current profile and future profile, etc. Factors determining poverty and their analysis—how are they inter-linked?

◆ The institutions, structure, processes and policies—inter-relationships—How are they affecting people's lives, levels of living and livelihoods?—Impact on all the 5 capitals—natural, physical, human, financial and social capitals (e.g. what happens to the social capital)—details of each impact and coping strategies—comparison against best time, worst time etc.—What are the long and short run impacts? What were the earlier impacts? Is their any seasonality factor?

◆ Community Based Organisations—How do they affect poverty? What is their current state? Are they still useful? What plans the community has to preserve and protect them?

- Sectors/sub-sectors-programmes, progress and performance—'why?' and 'how'? Agriculture, forestry, off-farm activities, rural artisanship, livestock, food security, consumption patterns, sanitation, education, water, health, income, livelihoods, women's work and wage, men's work and wage, children's well-being etc.
- Policy measures/programmes adopted (direct and indirect)—What measures (social, physical, economic, ecological, technical etc.) adopted, relevant to poverty reduction? What has succeeded and what has failed? What are the lessons learnt? Why? And how? What process was adopted? Will such process/measures be effective in future? If yes, how and how much? What should be done, what changes should be made, how delivery systems can be improved? How can they be made efficient and sustainable?
- Governmental, Non-Governmental, private sector and other (e.g. private) interventions — listing and description of each interventions, their effectiveness—'how much', 'where' and 'why' and their strength and limitations—Suggestions—What is to be done? Plan of Action—What is people's choice? What women and men can do? What the government is doing and can do? How? How effective? What other agencies can do? Can they mutually be complementary and supportive? If so, how?
- Choices and propositions/suggestions/recommendations for poverty reduction and support for livelihoods strengthening and development.

The following aspects are included in the above checklist:

(i) Analysis of poor/disadvantaged groups and criteria of poverty,
(ii) Analysis of resources,
(iii) Poverty over time/years,
(iv) Seasonal poverty,
(v) Analysis of institutions and policies and vulnerabilities,
(vi) Analysis of gender,
(vii) Factors affecting poverty and pathways out of poverty, and
(viii) Preferences, priorities and choices of the poor and the disadvantaged.

Annex B

Integrated Participatory Poverty Assessment (IPPA): A Technical Note

Table of Contents

In Annex "B", selected technical basis of data collation, indexing, syntheses, integration and other related aspects have been discussed. This Annex draws upon a wide variety of ways for up-scaling participatory data. The following are some of the ways adopted for up-scaling participatory data, especially for IPPA, in addition to the ones discussed in different chapters of this book. The type of information/data generation in participatory approaches is often different from conventional questionnaire surveys and hence need to be treated appropriately.

B.1 Types of Data Generated (Including Baseline Data)

Based on open questions, semi-structured discussions, process-orientated sessions and facilitation, the types of information/data generated for IPPA tend to have a wide variety. It could be both qualitative and quantitative and the former, for instance, could be a mental map indicating spatial/temporal data, preferences, a characteristic feature, a relationship, an assessment, a view, a visual data etc. So the participatory data, which would constitute the very basis of IPPA mechanism, need not be neat or easily manageable or easy to up-scale. So it is important to identify ways to synthesize and collate data and integrate such data in a meaningful manner for IPPA which helps maintain a working relationship with the conventional system to the extent possible.

B.2 Data Imperfections, Information Loss and Cross-checking

One issue is how to reduce imperfections in the data generated and what to accept or reject. How to reduce errors in order to increase the trustworthiness of IPPA-related data? Conventional data (which is mostly quantitative 'average picture' based on close-ended questionnaires canvassed to individuals) uses 4 criteria for evaluating data—internal validity, external validity, reliability and objectivity. Internal validity is about causal relationship between two variables; external validity is about causal relationship when applied to other similar context; reliability is the extent to which repetition of the same instruments will yield similar results and objectivity is the extent to which multiple observers could agree on a phenomenon. With regard to qualitative and inclusive data, Katzer *et al*. (1982) mentions that 2 criteria could be applied—one internal and the other external. In simple terms, internal criteria is all about the adequacy of the process and tools followed for IPPA-related data generation, while the external criteria would reflect what the data has to say and how well it compares with data already known and existing. The evaluation of IPPA data could be cross-checked and triangulated in more than one way by changing PRA tools, changing groups of participants, emphasizing process, changing locations, changing time and period of interactive sessions and changing facilitators.

B.3 Prioritized Problem Indices of Poor (PPIP)

In the course of IPPA, problems are generally listed, prioritized and analyzed by local groups and communities, whether rural or urban. The problems that emerge in different areas tend to have many generic similarities but also differ due to local factors. Thus the main problem domain may be similar but some of the sub-criteria may emphasize local features. For example, lack of drinking water could mean the following:

(a) The public tube-well is broken and hence water is not available and the poor are forced to bring water from other's homes and/or distant places,
(b) It could mean that the existing tube-well does not work since there are stones/rocky layer underground, or

(c) It could also imply that the ground water level has fallen and/or gets depleted, especially during the summer months.

The local character of each problem domain is important to be tackled at the local level. Two things which need to be probed in such cases are:

(i) The relative importance of the problem amongst a basket of problems, and
(ii) The local character of the problem. In terms of data collation, each table of prioritized problems can have a box attached to it where the local dimension of each problem domain is explained.

In IPPA, while discussing problems—opportunities with local communities, the local participants could be facilitated to apply scoring/ranking methods to prioritize their list of problems. The results of the discussions on the problems from different sessions could then be collated for inter-community comparisons. An elementary statistical tool of indexing can be used as explained below.

Different communities/groups feel comfortable using different ways to explain and prioritize their problems. Some use fixed scoring (*i.e.* apportioning a fixed score to their set of problems and then a fixed number of stones/seeds to each problem), others use free scoring (*i.e.* using any number of scores with stones/seeds thus reflecting weight of each problem), while others would prefer to only rank their problems without scoring. Some others can merely list their problems and neither score nor rank them. This leads to considerable heterogeneity in participatory outputs and data generation thereby. For comparison across communities and in order to retain diversity and maximum information, the scores, ranks and frequencies of problem listing are indexed to arrive at a set of Prioritised Problem Indices of Poor Communities (PPIPs) similar to PPIP (*see* UNDP: 1996).

This index could be constructed for different locations/groups/communities/gender in the study areas. Not all information can be disaggregated gender-wise since in certain areas people prefer to work only in mixed groups. Such disaggregated information could be shown through bar charts and the poor people's explanation of their problem domains could be provided in accompanying boxes. Some of the explanations to describe the problems need not appear in the prioritized set of problems. The top prioritized problems, which are across study locations of IPPA study can be taken up for further analysis, whether gender-wise/group-wise/community-wise.

B.4 Computing the Prioritized Problem Index of Poor Communities (PPIP)

During field inquiry, listing, scoring and ranking method applied by village participants during participatory sessions help reveal their problem priorities and preferences, which can be further expressed as specifically as possible. So a prioritized problem/priority index could be devised in order to allow inter and intra-community comparisons. It is important to remember that such PPIP or indexing of problems and priorities resulting from listing, scoring and ranking exercises done by participant groups have their own limitations in terms of simplistic portrayal of the complex realities of the poor communities as well as risks associated with aggregating village level location-specific data to convey a general picture. However, such PPIP indices offer a reasonably effective way of comparing the prioritized problems of poor communities and also help to strengthen the qualitative comparisons. Such indices also serve as basis for arriving at illustrative macro and meso pictures of poor communities whether at regional or national level (UNDP: 1996).

As explained above, the participant groups could apply the methods of ranking and scoring for prioritizing their problems and also for showing preferences. Ranking and scoring would involve participant groups in placing their problems/preferences in order of importance. The prioritized problem/priority index seeks to retain the diversity of information as revealed in different localities. Changing problem/priority scoring/ranking to percentage figures help to arrive at further results. For each criterion, the percentage score or percentage rank of different villages could be estimated to arrive at indices with the help of the following formula.

Index = (Actual Xi value—Maximum Xi values) / (Maximum Xi—Minimum Xi values)

For computation of the above index, a fixed minimum value of 0 per cent and a maximum value of 100 per cent are generally taken for each problem/preference criteria. A simple average could be taken of the indices to arrive at a synthesis index of problem prioritization or preference ranking for income generating activities. Based on the value of PPIPs, problem criteria could be prioritized for each of the communities/groups as required. Different areas/sites covered for the IPPA exercise can be given equal weights despite their differences in population size and the proportion of poor people and the proportion of women and men. This could be a conscious decision so as to indicate that the problem expressed by each group is equally important and should not be ignored. Professionals tend to prefer weighted information in order to compare relative or proportional figures. However, this tends to distort information, for example, larger villages could gain more prominence over smaller villages etc. In fact, in participatory approaches, problems expressed by each group are important and can hardly be ignored. Each problem has a place either at the local, the meso or the national level. This helps in maintaining the diversity, which participatory principles tend to favour and help include minority views.

B.5 Cumulative Prioritized Problem Index (CPPI)

It is important to sort out problems and their levels. Some problems are by nature local and would be best addressed at the local level. Some problems relate to the meso or the macro level and accordingly need to be placed in that domain. Problems could be clustered for 3 levels—local, meso and macro. Both at the meso and the macro levels, there is likely to be some problem congruence of a few common and shared problems of the poor communities, which need to be closely examined. Once such shared problems are identified at the meso or the macro domain, the Cumulative Prioritized Problem Index of Poor Communities (CPPIP) can be estimated. The CPPIP at the meso or the macro level could indicate a district picture/national picture of the prioritized problems, which could be gender-specific and/or area/resource-specific/group-specific depending on the way the data has been generated and organized. In both PPIP and CPPIPs, one needs to maintain "a basket of perspectives to coexist" without letting proportions and size dominate. In this case, though the loss is in terms of forgoing an average or representative picture, the gain is in terms of giving both majority and minority perspectives equal importance. This is in line with the essence of PRA/PRRA/PPA which tends to give importance to minority views.

B.6 Poverty Assessment Matrices

The poverty assessment matrices are set up in a manner so as to arrive at comparative pictures on different dimensions of IPPA. It provides a snapshot of different dimensions of poverty assessment. The snapshots could be constructed at a local level, district level, province level and national level. There are at least 7 components of IPPA, whose overviews could be flagged in such Poverty Assessment Matrices. They are short overviews with selected components as follows. Both levels of analysis and sub-components could be selected for preparing overviews for poverty assessment matrices.

(a) Social Group (Well-Being) Assessment
(b) Asset/Resource Assessment
(c) Vulnerability Assessment
(d) Livelihoods Assessment
(e) Problem-Opportunity Assessment
(f) Gender Assessment
(g) Institutional Assessment
(h) Social Opportunity Assessment

B.7 Selected Participatory Methods/Tools

IPPAs are based on PRA methodology and participatory principles. The principles are listening and learning through participatory interactions and learning progressively; and 'offsetting biases', which generally accompany a 'rushed' appraisal by professionals for quick results. Such biases relate to 'roadside' bias, 'seasonal' bias, 'influential people's' bias, 'professional' bias and 'gender' bias. (for details *see* Chapter 2 of this book). PRA involves learning from diverse conditions and different actors. The process of cross-checking is also important as a principle for minimising errors and omissions. In order to minimize cost and time, the principle of 'optimal ignorance' comes is a handy principle. Some selected participatory methods for PPA are described below along with illustrations.

Participatory mapping involves spatial drawing of any area, drawn on ground, paper or on other medium by local people to show and explain their locality and other related areas, such as residential areas, forests, fields, etc. Participatory mapping can include a range of items like households, school, office, infrastructure, crops, livestock, farm size, water bodies, field, forest, trees, road, facilities, common property resources, literacy, disease, etc. depending on the theme/themes under discussion.

Semi-structured interview is a participatory method, mainly based more on open-ended and probing questions and, hence, has a great deal of flexibility. In semi-structured interviews, open-ended questions lead to different kinds of responses based on which further questions are designed and asked. A sequence of open-ended questions help in conducting in-depth probing of issues and their cause-effect relationship (Mukherjee: 1995).

Problem prioritisation and solutions based on ranking and scoring reveal priorities and preferences. They provide opportunities to local people to physically rank and re-rank selected items or preferences or benefits/costs and explain their reasons for a set of given ranking.

Joint walk is based on 'seeing-is-believing' relates to learning from local communities through undertaking joint walks with them. Such walking with communities helps in observing different aspects of a selected area/s in a locality, which require on-site observation and detailed discussions with community members.

Poverty grouping is a method of grouping of households on the basis of local indicators of poverty such as ownership of land, assets, food availability, size of family and other local measures. Different criteria can be used for poverty grouping based on local people's perceptions.

Institutional diagramming is a visual method to represent the role of individuals/institutions and the degree of their importance in decision-making. In such diagrams, circle/s of different size represent individual/s and/or institution/s, whose size shows its degree of importance in local decision-making and the overlapping of circles indicate over-lapping in decision making.

Time line is a participatory method for tracing local changes in different variables over time such as food patterns, wages, days of work, kind of work, survival strategies, changes in vegetation, farming practices, livelihoods, quality of life, etc.

In *seasonal diagramming*, the local people prepare seasonal calendars using local materials either on the ground or on paper, of various socio-economic and physical phenomena such as seasonal wages received, food consumed, prices, crops grown, rainfall patterns, sickness and others.

REFERENCES

Chambers, Robert, (1997), *Whose Reality Counts? Putting the First Last*, IT Publications, London.

Development Tracks,. RTC (2002), *Livelihoods Scoping Study*, West Bengal, Draft Report submitted to DFID, India, November.

Development Tracks, RTC (2005), *Participatory Poverty Assessment,* West Bengal, Interim Draft Report submitted to Asian Development Bank, Manila, June.

ITAD (2004), PPA Manual, PRCD Project Guangxi, ITAD/DFID/The World Bank, Guangxi Province, China.

Meyers, James (2001), "Power Tools", www.iied.org

Mukherjee, Neela, (1995), *Participatory Rural Appraisal and Questionnaire Survey: Comparative field experience and methodological innovations*, Concept Publishing Co., New Delhi.

Mukherjee, Neela (1996), Review of Doon Valley Watershed (Government of Uttar Pradesh, India, European Union & W.S. Atkins), Dehradun.

Mukherjee, Neela (2002), *Participatory Learning and Action with 100 Field Methods*, Concept Publishing Co., New Delhi.

Mukherjee, Neela & Mukherjee, Amitava (2002), *Evaluation Report of Project on Reproductive Health*, State Institute of Family Welfare, Rajasthan, supported by Population Concern UK and DFID, UK.

Mukherjee, Neela (1993), *Participatory Rural Appraisal, Methodology & Applications*, Concept Publishing Co., New Delhi.

UNDP: *UNDP's 1996 Report on Human Development in Bangladesh—A Pro-Poor Agenda*, United Nations Development Programme, Dhaka.

Bibliography

Abraham, C. M., (1999). *Environmental Jurisprudence in India*, p. 331, Martinus Nijhoff Publishers.

Adikeshavalu, Ravindra (2004). An Assessment of the Impact of Bangalore Citizen Report Card on the Performance of Public Agencies, ECD Working Paper Series 12, The World Bank Evaluation Department, The World Bank Washington D.C. June.

Amnesty International (2001). National Human Rights Institutions: Amnesty International's Recommendations for Effective Protection and Promotion of Human Rights, Amnesty International, October.

Anecdote (2007). "Putting stories to work, Most Significant Change – A Primer", September, www.anecdote.com.au/archives/most_significant_change/-28k.

Barahona, Carlos, (2007). "Navigating the trade-offs in the use of participatory approaches for research" in Brock, Karen and Jethro Pettit (ed.) (2007). Springs of Participation: Creating and Evolving Methods for Participatory Development, Practical Action Publishing, Institute of Development Studies at Sussex, Intermediate Technology Limited., Warwickshire.

Blakey, Heather, (2008). "Participatory budgeting in the UK: a challenge to the system", in IIED's (2008). Participatory Learning and Action, 58, towards empowered participation: stories and reflections, International Institute for Environment and Development, June.

Bond, Richard and Neela Mukherjee (2001). *Livelihood Asset Status Tracking (LAST): A Case From Rajasthan*, Impact Assessment for Sustainable Development Unit, Working Paper Series, Institute for Development Policy and Management, University of Manchester, March.

Bradley, Christine (1994). Why Male Violence against Women is a Development Issue: Reflections from Papua New Guinea in Miranda Davies (ed.) *Women and Violence: Realities and Responses*, Worldwide, London, Zed Books.

Brock, Karen and Jethro Pettit (ed.) (2007). *Springs of Participation: Creating and Evolving Methods for Participatory Development*, Practical Action Publishing, Institute of Development Studies at Sussex, Intermediate Technology Limited, Warwickshire.

Brown L, (2001) *Social Auditing and Community Cohesion: The Cooperative Way (A Report to the Cooperative Secretariat and Canadian Heritage)*. February http://www.agr.gc.ca/rcs-src/coop/index_e.php?page=brown&s1=pub.

Bryant, Peter (2008). "Mali's Farmers' Jury: an attempt to democratize policy-making on bio-technology", in IIED's (2008). *Participatory Learning and Action*, 58, Towards empowered participation: stories and reflections, International Institute for Environment and Development, June.

Buhl, Solveig, Qian Wei and Wang Xuixeong (2004a). Report Card – Satisfaction Survey, An initial Observation from China, *Technical Report* 2, GTZ, July.

Buhl, Solveig, Qian Wei and Wang Xuixeong (2004b). *Towards Comprehensive and Participatory Poverty Monitoring and Impact Evaluation in Jiangxi Province*, China.

Burgess, Heidi and Cate Malek. "Public Participation." *Beyond Intractability*. Eds. Guy Burgess and Heidi Burgess. *Conflict Research Consortium*, University of Colorado, Boulder. Posted: September 2005 <http://www.beyondintractability.org/essay/public_participation/.

Cabannes, Yves "Participatory Budgeting: Conceptual Framework and Analysis of its Contribution to Urban Governance and the Millenium Development Goal" Concept Paper", see www.googles.com

Caddy, J. (2002). *Information, Consultation & Public Participation in Policy-making,: Mapping the experience of OECD countries*, OECD, June, E-governance: Agenda-setting workshop Council of Europe, 10-11th June.

Carney Diana with Michael Drinkwater, Tamara Rusinow, Koos Neefjes, Samir Wanmali and Naresh Singh (1999). *Livelihoods Approaches Compared*, DFID, November; www.livelihoods.org.

Central Bureau of Statistics (2002). *Nepal Living Standards Survey II 2002/03: Household Questionnaire*, CBS, Thapathali, Kathmandu.

Cernea, M. M. (1991). *Putting People First*, (Second Edition) Oxford University Press.

Chambers R., and G. Conway, (1992). *Sustainable rural livelihoods: Practical concepts for the 21st century*, IDS Discussion Paper 296. Brighton: IDS (pp.7-8).

Chambers, Robert, (1991). 'Shortcut and Participatory Methods for Gaining Social Information for Projects', in Cernea, Michael M. (ed.). *Putting People First, Sociological Variables in Rural Development*, published for the World Bank, Oxford University Press.

Chambers, R. (2008). *Revolutions in Development Inquiry*, Earthscan, London.

Chambers, Robert (1989) Editorial Introduction: Vulnerability, Coping, and Policy, *IDS Bulletin*, 20(2): 1-7.

Chambers, Robert (1993). *Challenging the Professions Frontiers for rural Development*, Intermediate Technology Publications, London.

Chambers, Robert, (1994). 'Participatory Rural Appraisal (PRA): Analysis of Experience', *World Development*, Vol.22, No.9, pp.1253-1268.

Chambers, Robert, (1997). *Whose Reality Counts? Putting the first last*, IT Publications,

Chambers, Robert, (2004). *Ideas for Development: Reflecting Forwards*, IDS Working Paper 238, Institute of Development Studies, November, Brighton.

Chambers, Robert, (2005). *Ideas for Development*, Earthscan Publications, London.

Chavez, Daniel (2008). "The watering down of participatory budgeting and people power in Porto Alegre, Brazil", in IIED's (2008). *Participatory Learning and Action, 58, Towards empowered participation: stories and reflections*, International Institute for Environment and Development, June.

Clark, Cindy, (2001). "Making Change Happen: Advocacy and Citizen Participation," Institute for Development Studies-Participation Group, http://www.justassociates.org/MakingChangeReport.pdf.

Clay, David (2008). "The changing face of community participation: The Liverpool black experience", in IIED's (2008). *Participatory Learning and Action, 58, Towards empowered participation: stories and reflections*, International Institute for Environment and Development, June.

Clear Horizon, *Most Significant Change Technique Overview*, www.clearhorizon.com.au/page.php?pid=24 - 13k

Commonwealth Secretariat (2001). *National Human Rights Institutions, Best Practice*, Commonwealth Secretariat, London.

Davies, R (1996). "An Evolutionary Approach to Facilitating Organizational Learning: An Experiment by the Christian Commission for Development in Bangladesh", htpp://www.mande.co.uk/docs/ccdb.htm.deptswashington.edu/.../Adult%20and%20Famil%20Consumer%20Surveys/Consumer%20Satisfaction%20Survey%202003%20Final.pdf Consumer *Satisfaction Survey* 2003 Final.doc View as HTML.

Davies, R. and J. Dart (2005). The 'Most Significant Change' (MSC) Technique—A Guide to Its Use, April, www.mande.co.uk/docs/MSCGuide.pdf.

De Haan, Arjan (1999). *Social Exclusion: towards an Holistic Understanding of Deprivation.*

Desai, A.H. and S. Murlidhar, S. (2000). "Public Interest Litigation: Potential and Problems", published in B.N. Kirpal et. Al (Ed.). (2000) *Supreme but not Infallible – Essays in Honour of Supreme Court of India*, International Environmental Law Research Centre, Oxford University Press, New Delhi, www.ielrc.org/content/a0003.pdf

Development Tracks (2000, 2004-5). Typescript, Field Notes on Street Children of Delhi, Development Tracks in *Research, Training & Consultancy*, New Delhi.

Development Tracks, RTC (2002). *Livelihoods Scoping Study*, West Bengal, Draft Report submitted to DFID, India, November.

Development Tracks, RTC (2005). *Participatory Poverty Assessment*, West Bengal, Interim Draft Report submitted to Asian Development Bank, Manila, June.

Development Vision (2004). Process Monitoring of Targeted Programmes, Free Textbook Distribution and National Scholarship Programmes – Doti and Banke Districts, *Final Report*, Submitted to the National Planning Commission by Development Vision, Nepal Pvt.Ltd, Kathmandu.

Development Vision (2005). Community Groundwater Irrigation Sector Project (CGISP): Socio Economic Impact Study, *Development Vision*, Nepal Pvt. Ltd.

Devine, Pat (2003) *Industrial Policy, Ecological Economics and Deliberative Democracy.* European Society for Ecological

Economics. FRONTIERS2: European Application of Ecological Economics, Tenerife, Canary Islands, February 11-16.

DFID UK website.

Donelly, Jack (1989). *Universal Human Rights in Theory and Practice*, Cornell University Press, Ithaca, N.Y.

Dreze Jean and Amartya Sen (1995). *India, Economic Development and Social Opportunity*, Delhi, Oxford University Press.

Dryzek, John S. (1996). Strategies of Ecological Democratization. In *Democracy and the Environment*. (Ed.) William M. Lafferty and James Meadowcraft. Cheltenham, UK: Edward Elgar, pp. 108-123.

Eady, Nigel, Jasber Singh, Alice Taylore-Gee and Tom Wakeford, (2008). "Community x-change: connecting citizens and scientists to policy makers", in IIED's (2008). *Participatory Learning and Action, 58, Towards empowered participation: stories and reflections*, International Institute for Environment and Development, June.

Exchange (2005). Most Significant Change: "An Evolutionary Approach to Monitoring that Facilitates Organizational Learning", February, www.healthcomms.org/comms/eval/le02.html - 20k.

Fitzduff, Niall, Peter Byrant, Gwen Lanigan and Catherine Purvis (2008). "Hearing the real voices: exploring the experiences of the European Citizens' Panel", in IIED's (2008). *Participatory Learning and Action, 58, Towards empowered participation: stories and reflections*, International Institute for Environment and Development, June.

Freire, Paulo (1970). *Pedagogy of the Oppressed*, The Seabury Press, New York.

Garvin, David A., A.C. Edmondson and Francesca Gino (2008). "Is Yours a Learning Organization?", *Harvard Business Review South Asia*, March, hbrasia.org.

Gaventa, John (2005). Reflections on the Users of the 'Power Cube' Approach for Analyzing the Spaces, Places and Dynamics of Civil Society Participation and Engagement, *CFP Evaluation Series 2003-2006*: no.4, Institute of Development Studies, University of Sussex, UK., October.

Gloppen, Siri L. Rakner, A. Tostensen (2003). "Responsiveness to the Concerns of the Poor and Accountability to the Commitment to Poverty Reduction" (WP 2003:9, Chr. Michelsen Institute, Development Studies and Human Rights, Bergen, Norway).

Goulden, Jay and Sarah Glyde, *Development of a Rights – Based Monitoring Tool for CARE Malawi*, www.careinternational.org.uk/resource_centre/human rights/.

Government of South Australia (2008). *The Most Significant Change, Department of Education and Children's Services*, 10th September www.learningtolearn.sa.edu.au/learning_workroom/a8_publish/modules/publish/content.asp?id=13795&navgrp=441 - 14k.

Guijt, Irene and Meera Kaul Shah (Eds.) 1998. *The Myth of Community: Gender Issues in Participatory Development.* Intermediate Technology Publications, London.

Halsbury's Law. Monthly (2001). Sponsored by LexisNexis, August Judicial Activism in Public Interest Litigation, t www.halsburys.in/judicial-activism.html - 14k.

Haq, Jackie (2008). Community participation: 'activists' or 'citizens', in IIED's (2008). *Participatory Learning and Action, 58, Towards empowered participation: stories and reflections*, International Institute for Environment and Development, June.

HealthLink Worldwide, *Networking and Learning, How Stories Help us to Learn*, www.healthlink.org.uk/we-do/network_msc.html - 19k.

IFAD, *Strategic Framework*, www.ifad.org.

IIED (2008). *Participatory Learning and Action, 58, towards empowered participation: stories and reflections*, International Institute for Environment and Development, June.

International Council on Human Rights Policy & UN High Commissioner for Human Rights (2005). *Assessing the Effectiveness of National Human Rights Institutions*, Versoix.

ITAD (2004). *PPA Manual*, PRCD Project Guangxi, ITAD/DFID/The World Bank, Guangxi Province, China.

Jain, S.P. and Wim Polman (2003). *A handbook for trainers on participatory local development: The Panchayati Raj model in India*, Food and Agriculture Organization of the United Nations Regional Office for Asia and the Pacific, Bangkok, 2nd Edition.

Just Associate, *Tools for Analyzing Power, Inclusion and Exclusion.*

Kabeer, Naila, (2000). Social Exclusion, Poverty and Discrimination, Towards an Analytical Framework, *IDS Bulletin*, Volume 31, No.4.

Kanbur, Ravi (ed). (2005) Q-Squared—Qualitative and Quantitative Poverty Appraisal: Complementarities, Tensions and the Way Forward, Q-Squared Working Paper No. 1, October

Kaplan, Allan, (1996). *The Development Practitioners' Handbook*. Pluto Press, London.

Kapoor, Ilan. 2001. Towards participatory environmental management? *Journal of Environmental Management* 63: 269-279.

Kashefi, Elham and Chris Keene, (2008). "Citizen juries in Burnley, UK: from deliberation to intervention" in IIED's (2008). *Participatory Learning and Action, 58, Towards empowered participation: stories and reflections*, International Institute for Environment and Development, June.

Kothari, Uma. 2001. Power, Knowledge and Social Control in Participatory Development. In: Cooke, Bill and Uma Kothari. *Participation: The New Tyranny?* Zed Books, London.

Krishna, Anirudh, and Norman Uphoff (1999): Mapping and Measuring Social Capital: A Conceptual and Empirical Study of Collective Action for Conserving and Developing Watersheds in Rajasthan, India, *Social Capital Initiative Working Paper No. 13*. Washington: World Bank.

Kuruganti, Kavitha, Michel Pimbert and Tom Wakeford, (2008). "The people's vision – UK and Indian reflections on Prajateerpu" in IIED's (2008). *Participatory Learning and Action, 58, Towards empowered participation: stories and reflections*, International Institute for Environment and Development, June.

Lederach, John Paul (2005). *The Moral Imagination: The Art and Soul of Building Peace*, Oxford University Press, New York.

Levy, Sarah, (2007). "Using numerical data from participatory research to support the Millennium Development Goals: the case for locally owned information systems" in Brock, Karen and Jethro Pettit (ed.) (2007). *Springs of Participation: Creating and Evolving Methods for Participatory Development*, Practical Action Publishing, Institute of Development Studies at Sussex, Intermediate Technology Limited., Warwickshire.

Ljungman, Cecilia M., (2004). *Applying a Rights – Based Approach to Development: Concepts and Principles*, Conference Paper: The Winners and Losers from Rights-Based Approaches to Development, COWI, November, based on a chapter in Britha Mikkelsen's *Methods for Development Work and Research – A New Guide for Practitioners* (2005). 2e, Sage Publications, New Delhi, February.

Lydia Fehring, Jenny Pettenon, Ann Fagan, Kathryn Goyen, and Jessica Connor, *Evaluation: LandLearn's most significant change*, www.regional.org.au/au/apen/2006/refereed/5/3083_fehringlr.htm - 37k.

Maiese, Michelle (2005). Source: http://www.beyondintractability.org/essay/voice/, June.

Max-Neef, A. Manfred, Antonio, Elizalde and Martin, Hopenhayn, (1991). *Human Scale Development, Conception, Application and Further Reflections*, The Apex Press, New York.

Meyers, James (2001). "Power Tools", www.iied.org.

Mitchell, Laura Remson (2002) on "Public Policy Making and the Grssroots" http://www.geocities.com/dhcpolwnk/grassroots.html.

Moser, C., and A. Norton: (2001). *To claim our rights: livelihood security, human rights and sustainable development*, ODI, London.

MRDP (1999). "Lao Cai Province: A Participatory Poverty Assessment", Hanoi, Vietnam-Sweden Mountain Rural Development Programme and the Vietnam-Sweden Health Cooperation Programme.

Mukherjee, Amitava, (ed.) (2004a). *Participatory Rural Appraisal, Methods & Applications in Rural Planning*, Concept Publishing Company, Delhi.

Mukherjee, Amitava, (ed.) (2004b). *Participatory Monitoring*, Concept Publishing Company, Delhi.

Mukherjee, Neela & Mukherjee Amitava (2002a). *Evaluation Report of Project on Reproductive Health*, State Institute of Family Welfare, Rajasthan, supported by Population Concern UK and DFID, UK.

Mukherjee, Neela, (1993). *Participatory Rural Appraisal, Methodology & Applications*, Concept Publishing Co., Delhi.

Mukherjee, Neela, (1995). *Participatory Rural Appraisal & Questionnaire Survey: Comparative field experience and methodological innovations*, Concept Publishing Co., Delhi.

Mukherjee, Neela (1996). *Review of Doon Valley Watershed* (Government of Uttar Pradesh, India, European Union & W.S. Atkins): Dehradun.

Mukherjee, Neela (1997). *Participatory Appraisal of Natural Resources*, Concept Publishing Co., Delhi.

Mukherjee, Neela (2002). *Forest Protection Committees of West Bengal*: Measuring Social Capital in Joint Forest Management, (also see www.livelihoods.org)

Mukherjee, Neela (2002). *Participatory Learning and Action with 100 Field Methods*, Concept Publishing Co.. Delhi.

Naponen, Helzi, (2007). "it's not just about the picture, it's also about principles, process and power tensions in the development of the internal learning system", in Brock, Karen and Jethro Pettit (ed.) (2007). *Springs of Participation: Creating and Evolving Methods for Participatory Development*, Practical Action Publishing, Institute of Development Studies at Sussex, Intermediate Technology Limited, Warwickshire.

Narayan, Deepa (1999). *Bonds and Bridges: Social Capital and Poverty*, Poverty Research Working Paper No. 2167, The World Bank D.C. July.

Narayan, Deepa with Raj Patel, Kai Schafft, Anne Rademacher and Sarah Koch-Schulte (2000) *Voice of the Poor, Can Anyone Hear Us?* Published by Oxford University Press for the World Bank, Washington D.C.

Nayak, B., http://orissarti.com/socialaudit/social_audit.htm.

Nicholson, L. (2005). *The Research Shop*, March, www.scotland.gov.uk/Publications/2005/09/16120247 - 15k.

O'Neill, T., Foresti, M. and Hudson, A. (2007). *Evaluation of Citizens' Voice and Accountability: Review of the Literature and Donor Approaches*. London: DFID.

OECD (2007). "Inclusive Civic Engagement: citizens' voice in policy making", 7th Global Forum Building Trust in Government, Workshop V, Civic Engagement, 28th June 2007, Tanja Timmermans, OECD.

Oxal, Zoe with Sally Baden (1997). Gender and Empowerment Definitions, Approaches and Implications for Policy, *Report No. 40*, www.ids.ac.uk/bridge/Reports

Oxfam, GB (1999). *Tra Vinh Province: A Participatory Poverty Assessment*, Hanoi.

Ozanne, Julie.L. and Saatcioglu, Bige (2007). "Understanding Subsistence Marketplaces: Exploring the Contributions of Participatory Action Research" in Rosa, Jose Antonio and Madhubala Viswanathan (ed.) *Product and Market Development for Subsistence Marketplaces, Advances in International Management*, Volume 20, Elsevier, Oxford.

Pennyslvania Department of Public Welfare Office of Medical Assistance program www.dpw.state.pa.us/Omap/rfp/SEStndsReq/

omapSESRappL. asp - 30k, (Appendix L) Guidelines For Consumer/ Family Satisfaction Teams and Member Satisfaction Surveys), also see for details *Advancing Excellence in America's Nursing Homes*, www.nhqualitycampaign.org/files/im/6_Satisfaction_TAW_Guide.pdf.

Perkins, Patricia E. (2005) Public Participation and Ecological Valuation: Inclusive = Radical, Presented at the Capitalism Nature Socialism conference, July 22-24, Faculty of Environmental Studies, York University. "Policy-Making Introduction, MRSC", September 2000" http://www.ci.hunts-point.wa.us/Subjects/Governance/legislative/intro.aspx

Poverty Working Group (1999). "Vietnam: Attacking Poverty" Joint Report of the Government of Vietnam-Donor-NGO Poverty Working Group, Hanoi.

Pretty, J. (1995) "Participatory learning for sustainable agriculture", *World Development*, 23(8). 1247-1263.

Pretty, Jules and Hugh Ward (2001): "Social Capital and the Environment", *World Development*, Vol. 29, No.2, pp.209-227.

Putnam, Robert D, Leonardi, R., & Nanetti. R.Y. (1993). *Making Democracy Work: Civic Tradition in Modern Italy*, Princeton University Press, Princeton N.J.

Remenyi, Joe, (2007). "Participatory village poverty reduction planning and index-based poverty mapping in China" in Brock, Karen and Jethro Pettit (ed.) (2007). *Springs of Participation: Creating and Evolving Methods for Participatory Development*, Practical Action Publishing, Institute of Development Studies at Sussex, Intermediate Technology Limited., Warwickshire.

Right 2B heard Collective and Swingbridge Video (2008). If we have time, motivation and resources to Participate, does that mean we gain authority and power?, in IIED's (2008). *Participatory Learning and Action, 58, Towards empowered participation: stories and reflections*, International Institute for Environment and Development, June.

Robredo J.M. (2007). "Engaging People in Local Development: The Experience of Naga City, Philippines", Paper presented at Conference on Active Citizenship and Social Accountability sponsored by Australian Council for International Development (Mayor of Naga city, Monash University, Victoria, Australia, July 3rd.

Sainath, P. (1996). *Everybody Loves a Good Drought, Stories from India's Poorest Districts*, Penguin Books, New Delhi.

Save the Children UK (1999). "Ho Chi Minh City: A Participatory Poverty Assessment", Hanoi.

Schwandt, Thomas R. (1990). 'Paths to Inquiry in the Social Disciplines—Scientific, Constructivist and Critical Theory Methodologies', in Guba Egon G. (ed.) *The Paradigm Dialog*, Sage, California.

Sen, Amartya (1997). *Social Exclusion: A Critical Assessment of the Concept and Its Relevance* (mimeo). Asian Development Bank, September.

Sen, A.K. (1999). *Development as Freedom*, New York: Knopf Press.

Sen, A.K. (1981). *Poverty and Famine: An Essay on Entitlement and Deprivation*, Oxford: Clarendon.

Serra, Renata (2001). "Social Capital: Meaningful and Measurable at the State Level?" *Economic and Political Weekly*, February 24, 2001.

Singh, Jasber (2008). "The UK Nanojury as 'upsteam' public engagement" in IIED's (2008). *Participatory Learning and Action, 58, Towards empowered participation: stories and reflections*, International Institute for Environment and Development, June.

Social Audit New Zealand 159 Palmerston Streets, PO Box 145, Westport, New Zealand.

Stipak, B. (2008). Towards more thoughtful and responsible use of public opinion data by local administrators, *Journal of Urban Affairs*, published online, vol.5, issue 3, 14th February.

Sudirman, D.W. and S. McGrath (2005). "Public Participation in Local Forestry Policy-Making after Decentralization: Uncertainties, challenges and expectations in Tanjung Jabung, *Barat District, Jambi Province, Forest and Governance Programme, No. 3*, January.

The Participatory Video Revolution, Combining Participatory Videos with the Most Significant Change Approach, www.insightshare.org/case_study_msc.html - 25k

The World Bank (2000-1). *World Development Report 2000*.

The World Bank (2001). Philippines Filipino Report Card on Pro-Poor Services, Environment and Social Development Sector Unit, East Asia and Pacific Region, *Report No. 22181 – PH*, May 30.

The World Bank (2002). "Empowerment: A Framework for Policy and Practice" http://poverty.worldbank.org/library/topic/10143/).

The World Bank (2004). Citizen Report Card Surveys – A Note on the Concept and Methodology, Social Development Notes, Participation & Civic Engagement, *Note No. 91*, February.

The World Bank (2004). Making Services Work for Poor People, *World Development Report*, The World Bank, Washington D.C.

The World Bank, http://www.worldbank.org/poverty/voice/reports/canany/ch1.pdf.

The World Bank, *Voices of the Poor:* http://www.worldbank.org/poverty/voice/reports.

Turk, Carrier (2000). *Linking Participatory Poverty Assessments to Policy and Policy Making: Experience from Vietnam*, The World Bank, Vietnam.

UNDP (1995, 1997 and 2000). *Human Development Reports*, United Nations Development Programme, New York.

UNDP: UNDP's 1996 Report on Human Development in Bangladesh – A Pro-Poor Agenda, United Nations Development Programme, Dhaka.

Uphoff, N. (1992). *Learning from Gal Oya: Possibilities for participatory development and post-Newtonian Science*, Cornell University Press, Ithaca.

Uphoff, N. (2000). "Understanding Social Capital: Learning from the Analysis and Experience of Participation." In Partha Dasgupta and Ismail Serageldin, (eds.), *Social Capital: A Multifaceted Perspective*, 215-249, World Bank, Washington, D.C.

Vadivel, V.S., *Public Interest Litigation: A Boon or Bane*, Legal Services India.com, www.legalserviceindia.com/articles/pil.htm - 30k.

Veneklasen, Lisa and Valerie Miller, (2002). *A New Wave of Power, People and Politics, The Action Guide for Advocacy and Citizen Participation*, Co-Editors, Debbie Budlender and Cindy Clark, published by World Neighbours, Oklahoma, USA, The Asia Foundation, San Francisco and Lisa Veneklasen, Washington D.C.

VICTO Social Audit Project, Social Audit Manual, Canadian Cooperative Association and CIDA, www.coopdevelopmentcenter.coop/Good%20Practices/SocialAuditManual.pdf.

Wakeford, Tom, Bano Murtuia and Peter Byrant (2008). Ignoring and suppressing grassroots participation in a northern English town, in IIED's (2008). *Participatory Learning and Action, 58, Towards empowered participation: stories and reflections*, International Institute for Environment and Development, June.

Walter, Tom. 1995. Knowledge, Power, and Environmental Policy: Expertise, the Lay Public, and Water Management in the Western United States. *The Environmental Professional*, Vol. 17: 153-166.

Wampler, Brian (2000). *A Guide to Participatory Budgeting*, October, www.internationalbudget.orf/resources/library/GPB.pdf.

Warfield, Wallace P., (1993). "Public-Policy Conflict Resolution: The nexus between culture and process ." In *Conflict Resolution Theory and Practice*. Edited by Sandole, Dennis J.D. and Hugo van der Merwe, (1993) Manchester, U.K.: Manchester University Press.

Williams, Suzanne, Seed, Janet and Mwau Adelina (1994). *Oxfam Gender Training Manual*, Oxfam, Oxford. www.coopdevelopmentcenter.coop/Good%20Practices/SocialAuditManual.pdf
www.dcf.state.fl.us/publications/docs/staterpt1.pdf
Family Service, Toronto, People for change, 14 May 2008 Development of the Client *Satisfaction Survey*,
www.familyservicetoronto.org/whatsnew/survey.html
www.epa.gov/publicinvolvement/: U.S. Environmental Protection Agency: Public Involvement.

www.idea.gov.uk/idk/aio/1118552, Innovations in Public Services, Literature Review.

www.ids.ac.uk/ids/particip/research/socpol.html: Citizen Participation in Social Policy.

www.infrastructure.gc.ca/research-recherche/results-resultats/rn-nr/rn-nr-2007-08-eng.html.

www.interpraxis.com/social_audit_resources.htm.

www.law.indiana.edu/ilj/oldsite/volumes/v73/no3/applegate.html, "Beyond the Usual Suspects: The Use of Citizens Advisory Boards in Environmental Decision making" by John S. Applegate.

www.legalservicesindia.com : Jha, G. Problems facing Public interest Litigation in India, www.legalservicesindia.com/articles/pil_ind.htm - 37k -.

www.livelihoods.org.

www.mass.gov/dcr/waterSupply/watershed/documents/quabbinaccessch3.pdf .

www.pc.gov.au/gsp/reports/consultancy/disabsvc - 17k Review of Approaches to Satisfaction Surveys of Clients of Disability Services, Consultancy Report, 1998, *Agency-wide Client Satisfaction Survey Report.*

www.scotland.gov.uk/Publications/2005/09/16120247 - 15k.

www. unpan1.un.org/intradoc/groups/public/documents/un/unpan 027075.pdf, Public Governance Indicators: A Literature Review.

www.blackwell-synergy.com/doi/abs/10.1111/j.1467-9906.1983. tb00040.x.

www.wikipedia.com.

Index